364

EUROPEAN LITERATURE IN THE NINETEENTH CENTURY

European Literature in the Nineteenth Century

BY

BENEDETTO CROCE

Translated from the Italian with an Introduction by
DOUGLAS AINSLIE

NEW YORK
ALFRED A. KNOPF   MCMXXIV

PRINTED IN GREAT BRITAIN BY
RICHARD CLAY & SONS, LIMITED,
BUNGAY, SUFFOLK.

AUTHOR'S PREFACE

I HAD intended to undertake a further examination of the literary production of the nineteenth century, both with the object of making clear certain conclusions implied but not explained by the writers who had supported them, and also of confuting certain prejudices still current, as well as of suggesting certain new views. But my main object has always been the consideration of the *poetry*, which is what should properly be the task of literary criticism and history, although a good many writers who pretend to be professional critics are too apt to forget this fact.

Other studies have, however, stood, and still stand, in the way of this, rendering it impossible for me to bring to an end what I had begun; so I am now gathering together the notes which I had published here and there upon some of the poets and men of letters of the nineteenth century, without, however, abandoning the hope of some day completing and continuing them, in such a way as to furnish a fairly adequate picture of the poetry of that period. Needless to say that the choice of authors discussed in the present volume has been determined solely by the fact that I chanced to re-read them in that order. It will likewise be unnecessary to remark that my notes have no pretension to being substituted for the many valuable studies already in existence upon the authors in question, but would rather serve as a link in further development, while offering

v

here and there some corrections where such are needful. They also do not pretend to exhaust all the subjects discussed, but only to solve certain problems, to fix definitely the true meaning of certain doubtful points, and to suggest a line for the direction of other studies. Such is, indeed, the character of every truly scientific treatise, and this should be clearly understood and practised in literary criticism, which should become truly scientific, abandoning certain habits of individual caprice, of artistic caprice and of false brilliance which it still retains.

To me it matters not at all if those who do not understand me declare that, instead of providing a criticism of poetry, I am providing a criticism of criticism, since those who do understand are well aware that criticism of poetry cannot fail to form one whole with the criticism of the criticism of poetry.

B. C.

Naples,
   March, 1922.

INTRODUCTION

THIS translation, which in Italian bears the title of *Poetry and Non-Poetry*, is, so far as I know, the first attempt to regard European literature of the nineteenth century as a whole, to blend its various qualities, whether expressed technically in verse or prose, as the result of the one eternal beauty-making gift of " expression." For Croce resolutely refuses to accept any technical distinction between verse and prose, but only between what is not poetry, namely, the practical or logical—and the result of the poetic gift. Where the latter is wanting, one or both of the others is present.

Most people have heard of Croce now and many have read parts of his numerous writings, either in the originals or in the translations. This volume, which consists rather of notes made in the course of reading than elaborate studies, such as the *Ariosto-Shakespeare* and the *Dante*, cannot fail to stimulate many readers, for none of the brief Essays contained in it is without reference to the powerful main currents of Croce's thought, as contained in the four volumes of the *Philosophy of the Spirit*, all of them now translated. New light is flashed upon several writers, such as Stendhal, Maupassant and Georges Sand, whose real literary personalities had refused to reveal themselves to previous criticism, inducing wrong views as to their respective places in the hierarchy. The Essay on Walter Scott is likely to attract attention, for the whole problem of literary style is contained in it. The wizard of the north may prove to have qualities of resistance superior to those of some of our contemporaries and like a star he may return again. If, as I believe, the present volume excite as much interest as the *Ariosto-Shakespeare* volume, it will probably give birth to several monographs, seeing that besides voluminous criticism in the Press, a whole volume was recently published attacking Croce's view of Shakespeare's poetry and even falling foul of the translator for heading a phrase of the introduction with the words : *Evviva l'Italia !* The numerous errors contained in the volume in question have been refuted already in the *Critica*, and as regards the phrase *Evviva l'Italia*, I am sure that no one will object if the writer begin every sentence of his next work on Croce with *Rule Britannia !*

DOUGLAS AINSLIE

THE ATHENÆUM, PALL MALL : 1924.

CONTENTS

artificial liberty of Venice" and the "sixty idiot wigs" of Geneva). He sees no other state of being in his own life, nor any other ideal in his art, than that of "the free man," able to move about, to talk, to act, to realize his own thought and his own vocation, neither oppressed and suffocated by any external force, nor opposed or hindered by any obstacle. His passions are extremely violent, like those of the other conscious or unconscious followers of Rousseau, on their way to attack moral Bastilles. He loves solitude, as though to give these passions some repose, abandoning himself with pleasure to melancholy, and to the charm of such natural beauties as mountains, waters, and the shores of the sea. Cold intellectualism and its representative, Voltaire, displease him, and he cannot bear the "pleasant style," that light and facile prose of the "enlightenment," so well adapted for purposes of vulgarization, but for that very reason seeming to him to be a prostitution of "our virile art." And if he is not altogether Shakespearean, like his German affinities, if he soon abandoned the reading of that poet, which he had begun, that is not because Shakespeare fails to please him, but because he pleases him too much. "The more that author went to my head," he writes, "the more I made up my mind to avoid him," the reason being that he does not wish to run the risk of imitating him and wants to remain spontaneously Shakespearean. There is even to be found in Alfieri an occasional thought about Catholicism, although he was not a Catholic, which anticipates Chateaubriand (no one has ever been able to make out whether the latter were or were not really a Catholic). I allude to that singular sonnet which begins, "Lofty, devout, ingenious mysticism, Pleasant to the view, suave to the ear, Ours is the harmonious worship of celestial hymns : Amiable in its seriousness," and further on occurs the verse : " Rome alone understands fully all the secrets of man."

Alfieri should therefore, in my opinion, be looked upon as a proto-romantic. This does not exactly mean that he was a romantic, as it has become the fashion to call him, thereby confusing two very distinct spiritual periods. Traits essential to romanticism were wanting in him, such as religious self-searchings as to the end and value of life, an interest in history, and enjoyment of the particular and realistic aspects of things. Even his autobiography runs on lines similar to Rousseau's Confessions, in its strong, passionate element and lack of historical sense, both in respect of his own time as of his life itself. He was conscious of this limitation and of his incapacity to depict what he called " our poor sad nature," social and individual pathology. " I wrote poems and prose in various styles, I do not say that I was gifted, but I was certainly courageous; History I never wrote." The epic, orations, tragedy, philosophy in the form of moral and political reflections, that was his field : " All alike divine arts, in which the portrait of man as he might be raises in an instant to heaven both him who writes and him who reads."

Such is about the place occupied by Alfieri in modern mental and moral history. But in order to understand and to judge his art, to succeed in the study of his æsthetic development, which is also a historical study, we must have clearly in mind the conformation of his soul. For Alfieri, before being a poet or while he was a poet, was a man of such ardent passions ("fury" is the commonest word in his writings) as to plunge straight into action, guided thereto by an inflexible firmness of intention. Certainly this action did not realize itself elsewhere than on paper and in words, but action it certainly was, if oratory is essentially action. Craving for liberty and abhorrence of tyranny had caused a fearful phantom to arise in his imagination, in the shape of the Tyrant, who is by no means a poetical fancy, but a kind of passionate incubus, a sort of condensation of blackest human iniquity, which assumes the form of a definite individual, one does not know why, unless it were owing to the invincible power of attraction and agglomeration. Are his tyrants guilty? One would not dare to say so, or at any rate they are not more guilty than anyone who is unfortunate enough to be infected with hydrophobia or with tetanus. "Ah! maybe ye speak truth!" exclaims the tyrant Timophanes, addressing his allies and friends, who are trying to recall him to a sense of his duties as a citizen,— "but no words, however strong, can any longer turn me from my purpose. I cannot become a good citizen again. One unchangeable mode of life alone must be mine: I must reign. Brother, I told you this before: you can only correct me with the sword: any other means are vain." Another of Alfieri's tyrants, Poliphontes, in the *Merope*,—he too is neither son, husband, nor father, but "altogether a tyrant," and lives for "nothing but the joy of ruling,"—sighs at the end of the first act, oppressed with the weight of his own ineluctable wickedness: "Oh, what an undertaking it is, to maintain thee, O throne!"

Alfieri constructed his tragedy in the form we have it, without confidants, without episodes, without love scenes, a skeleton, as precise and as rapid of movement as a machine, cutting his way in his well-known style. He does this that he may have the pleasure of massacring the said Tyrant with an iron mace, for the latter has rendered himself if possible yet more odious in the poet's eyes, because Alfieri has represented him to himself in such a way as to be quite incomprehensible. Alfieri's style has also in it something of the fixed idea, of the plan to be carried out at all costs, of inveterate obstinacy. He could not bear, as we have seen, the pleasant lightness of the prose style of the enlightenment, and the other popular style of the period in Italy was equally detestable in his eyes—I refer to the sing-song manner of Metastasio, which was not confined to Italy. For this reason his style and his dramatic writing are the reverse of the metastasian melodrama (as I believe Madame de Staël and William Schlegel were the first to remark); and the songs and airs by which his personages make their presence known come hissing through their teeth in harsh, broken sounds. And when his wrath happens to become sarcasm and mockery, as in the satires and in the *Misogallo*, the frown of tragedy becomes comic, but yet still remains a frown; hence his coining of grotesque words and expressions concocted in some odd manner, or strange diminutives, and verses as hard as the iron verses of the tragedies.

This, however, does not amount to saying that Alfieri failed to construct his tragedies with vigour and knowledge; but what he constructs is not poetry in itself, but rather passionate oratory. His grandiose exhortations and invectives, such as that of Virginius in *Virginia*, will be remembered :

> " O gregge infame di malnati schiavi ;
> tanto il terror può in voi ? l'onore, i figli,
> tutto obbliate per amor di vita ?—
> Odo, ben odo un mormorar sommesso ;
> ma niun si muove. Oh doppiamente vili !
> Sorte pari alla mia, deh ! toccar possa
> a ognun di voi ; peggior, se v'ha : spogliati
> d'aver, d'onor, di libertà, di figli,
> di spose, d'armi, e d'intelletto, torvi
> possa il tiranno un di fra strazio lungo
> la non ben vostra orrida vita infame,
> ch'or voi serbate a cosi infame costo. . . ." [1]

Here the oratory is highly charged with feeling, yet the personage in question is not poetic. Two of his tragedies are perfect, in the opinion of all the most esteemed critics : these are *Brutus I* and *Brutus II*. They are two sound instruments of steel, well tempered and burnished, two of such shining executioner's swords as one sees in museums. But poetry is not a steel instrument. The endless, wearisome disputes of the critics on the method followed by Alfieri in his tragedies and as to whether it were suited or not suited to its purpose, its differences from Greek or English and its likeness to French methods, are fallacious and superfluous. The defect, as always in such cases, does not inhere in the technique of the tragedy or in any other like

[1] " O infamous flock of ill-born slaves : can terror work so much in you ? Honour, sons, and all else forgotten for love of life ?—Yea, I hear, clearly I hear that murmur of submissive obedience to my commands, yet none moves to obey. Oh ! doubly vile ! Would that such fate as is mine might one day befall every one of you ; and a worser yet, if might be : stripped of your possessions, of honour, of liberty, of sons, of wives, of intellect, may the tyrant one day after long slaughter take from ye your infamous, ignoble lives, which now ye preserve at so infamous a cost."

imaginary element, but in the poetical substance of the work.

And that is the " practical " Alfieri, the Alfieri who supplied amateurs of liberty with words and just the right intonation, towards the end of the eighteenth century. Alas ! those were the same Italian Jacobins, friends, followers, and imitators of the French, upon whom he afterwards bestowed such a copious dose of virulent contempt. His tragedies, however, were for a short time, during the ephemeral Republic of 1799, really represented on the public stage and the *Timoleon* was produced at Naples as " a spectacle of Republican virtue." The truly Italian patriots of later times needed other words with a different accent, or were not satisfied with Alfieri's alone ; Pellico and Niccolini were equal to this task, although they were poets of second-rate order, just as Alfieri in his oratory was a second-rate poet. Those, however, who say that Alfieri is henceforth dead as a poet, have their eyes fixed upon what in him is non-poetry, and his poetry escapes them. Neither are we speaking here of the usual " lovers of kinds," who judge poetry as an aspect of " the theatre," or of " the national theatre " or of " Italian tragedy," for they too allow the poetry to escape them.

Among other things, that happens to the poetry of Alfieri which he would never have believed possible, but which seems altogether natural to me, when I take into consideration his temperament, as I have described it, and the spiritual movement of the period to which he belonged, and which belonged to him : he ends by admiring and sympathizing with his tyrants, who remained incomprehensible to him when blinded with hatred, but now become comprehensible both to him and to ourselves, when observed in the light of this new sympathy. He is not only astonished at and admirative of such wide-minded tyrants as Cæsar, whom yet he strikes down inexorably with the axe; but of the most malicious, the most atrocious, the blackest of all. Lorenzo dei Medici is speaking, and a conspirator among the Pazzi cannot escape from being impressed, murmuring in his emotion :

> " D'alti sensi è costui, non degno quasi
> d'esser tiranno. Ei regnerà, se ai nostri
> colpi non cade : ei regnerà. . . ." [1]

(This is like an anticipation or an echo of the line which concludes the sonnet on the death of Frederick II of Prussia : " But perhaps he was worthy of not being born a king.") Eteocles has Prometheutic or Capaneian capacity :

> " Un re, dal trono
> cader non debbe, che col trono istesso ;
> sotto l'alte rovine, ivi sol, trova
> morte onorata ed onorata tomba." [2]

And while this terrible fratricide is in the throes of death, supported by his mother, he asks of her anxiously, " Tell me : do I die a king ? "   Philip is so full of his sovereign majesty that he does not feel the goad of such mean, small human passions as love and jealousy, and throws in the face of the spouse

---

[1] " This man has lofty senses ; he is not made of tyrants' stuff. He will reign, if he does not fall before our blows ; he will reign."

[2] " A king should not fall from the throne, but with that throne itself ; only beneath such high-piled ruin, there alone, does he find an honoured death and an honoured tomb."

who has betrayed him and whom he has punished
with severity and contempt the following :

> " Mai non mi calse
> del tuo amor ; ma albergare in te si immenso
> dovea il tremor del signor tuo, che tolto
> d'ogni altro amor ti fosse anco il pensiero." [1]

And is not Alfieri's Saul also a tyrant, a king?
He has made him most sublime and venerable in the
delirium of his deluded greatness. I remarked above
that this proceeding was perfectly natural, for a poet
who belonged to the *Sturm und Drang* could not fail
to instal the personage of the *Uebermensch* at the
summit of his soul. Both the notion and term
descriptive of the *Uebermensch* appeared at this time.
Alfieri's dominating tyrants must have seemed super-
men to him and have attracted him as such far
more than his honest advocates of liberty, who
are all of them rather doctrinaire and generally
mediocre.

The superman does not only assert himself in the
immoderate dream of domination, but also in the
uprush of untameable and conflicting passions, in the
struggle between the great and the small, the lofty
and the base, between intransigent duty and envelop-
ing cupidity. Alfieri was always sensible of this
internal struggle, this tragedy, in which strength is
sometimes conquered by weakness or cowardice.
When he discovered his wounds, he described himself as " now Achilles, now Thersites," and he also
discovered in himself, whenever it was a question of

---

[1] " I was never jealous of thy love ; but so immense should have been
thine awe of thy lord that it should have removed from thee even
the thought of any other love."

"lofty senses," "the dwarf beside the giant." In addition to his marvellous *Saul* ("my favourite personage," he writes in his Autobiography, "because there is something of everything in him, of absolutely everything"), his greatest tragedies seem to me to be the *Agamemnon* and, even greater, the *Orestes*, which continues it. The *Saul* is a tragedy of old age, of suspicion, of jealousy, and of the greatness which underlies the feeling of the mysterious and divine. It is also the most complex work of Alfieri, and I do not dwell upon it, because it shines in the memory of all. Let us in the *Agamemnon* and the *Orestes* pass over their evident defects, which are inherent in his style, such as the intellectual reflection which often precedes the artistic vision and confers upon it something of the analytic and calculated. This defect is apparent in the celebrated scene, where Ægisthus insinuates to Clytemnestra the thought of slaying the husband. But what a living, palpitating, sorrowful thing is this Clytemnestra, slave to her terrible love! She cannot be better portrayed than in the words of Electra, who condemns but pities her, trying to arouse pity on her behalf in the breast of the avenging brother, who sees only the fact that she has slain his father and espoused her lover:

> "Ah! tu non sai qual vita ella pur tragge!
> Fuor che d'Atride i figli, ognun pietade
> ne avria. . . . L'avremmo anche pur troppo noi.—
> Di terror piena e di sospetto sempre;
> a vil tenuta dal suo Egisto istesso;
> d'Egisto amante, ancor che iniquo il sappia;
> pentita, eppur di rinnovare di fallo
> capace forse, ove la indegna fiamma,
> di cui si adira ed arrossisce, il voglia:
> or madre, or moglie; e non mai moglie o madre:
> aspri rimorsi a mille a mille il core

squarcianle il di ; notturne orride larve
tolgonle i sonni.—Ecco qual vive. . . ." [1]

And when Orestes, who has presented himself before
her disguised and exclaims astonished at seeing her
lament at the false announcement of his death : " Did
you then still love him much ? " returning in her turn
from her fit of grief, replies in gentle sorrow : " O
youth, hadst not thou a mother ? " And Electra,
the pious and austere, who watches with vigilant eye
the course of the criminal passion towards the infernal
abyss into which it will fall, how she bursts forth
when at last she assists at the outbreak of the hostility
which has long been hatching between the two
accomplices :

" Oh nuova gioia ! oh sola gioia, ond'io
il cor beassi, or ben due lustri ! Entrambi
vi veggio all'ira ed ai rimorsi in preda.
Di sanguinoso amore alfin pur odo,
quali esser denno, le dolcezze ; alfine
ogni prestigio è tolto ; appien l'un l'altro
conosce omai. Possa lo sprezzo trarvi
all'odio ; e l'odio a nuovo sangue. . . ." [2]

She who hopes without hope for the redemption
of the disgraced mother, represents thus the waiting

[1] " Ah ! you know not what a life she lived ! All but the sons of
Atreus would have pity on her. We have indeed too much of it
ourselves. She was always full of terror and suspicion and thought
ill of by her own Ægisthus, by her lover Ægisthus, although she knew
him to be wicked ; she has repented her deed, yet were she perhaps
capable of renewing it, if the unworthy love which angers and shames
her were again to will it : now mother, now wife, yet never mother
or wife : bitter remorse with its thousand fangs rends her heart by day,
while at night terrible phantoms deprive her of sleep—thus she lives."
[2] " Oh ! joy renewed ! Oh only joy, in which my heart rejoiced
ten good years ago ! I see both of you prey to anger and remorse.
At last I hear what must be the result of blood-stained love ; at
last are all barriers broken down ; they hardly know one another
now. May mutual contempt lead to hate and hate to new spilling
of blood."

upon the future, upon a future of justice, a future of purity :

> " Involontario è un moto in me, qualora
> straniero approda a questi liti, il core
> sentirmi incerto in fra timore e brama
> agitato ondeggiare. . . ." [1]

Ægisthus has certainly in him something of Iago, and is also a less satanically superb force than he, but in contradistinction from Iago, he feels himself to be the depository of a tradition, the executor of a decree of fate. " I knew thee," he says to Orestes, whom he saw first in disguise and finally revealed in his own person :

> " Io te conobbi
> al desir che d'ucciderti sentia ! " [2]

And Agamemnon had had the same feeling towards Ægisthus :

> " Il crederesti, Elettra ? al sol suo aspetto
> un non so qual terrore in me sentiva,
> non mai sentito pria. . . ." [3]

Alfieri is poetically successful in his rendering of these presentiments, this hatred, realized without words in a gesture, a look, an intonation of the voice, reflected in the environment. Agamemnon returning triumphant and full of tenderness for the family from which he had been separated for so many years, and whose presence he had always felt " amid the blood, the glory and the death," becomes

---

[1] " There is in me an involuntary emotion, whenever a stranger approaches these shores, I feel my heart agitated in uncertainty between fear and desire. . . ."
[2] " I knew thee by the desire I felt to slay thee ! "
[3] " Wilt thou believe it, Elektra ? The mere sight of him aroused in me an extraordinary emotion, which I had not felt ever before."

aware that something has changed profoundly in his house :

> " Son io tra' miei tornato ? ovver mi aggiro
> fra novelli nemici ?   Elettra, ah togli
> d'orrido dubbio il padre.   Entro mia reggia
> nuova accoglienza io trovo : alla consorte
> quasi stranier son fatto ; eppur tornata,
> parmi, or essere appieno in sé potrebbe.
> Ogni suo detto, ogni suo sguardo, ogni atto
> scolpito porta e il diffidare e l'arte. . . ." [1]

I have given but a slight specimen of the many beauties to be found in these two tragedies and I must not dwell upon those others that are scattered elsewhere, as in the *Mirra,* which is also too analytical and calculated, but in which the figure of the protagonist, seized hold of guiltless by a guilty love, against which she struggles, is conquered and dies, is surrounded with a halo of pity and of reverence of a poor gentle creature, an unfortunate little maiden, touched by the wing of death.   The moment in which Mirra allows herself to caress the flattering hope, that by marrying Pereus and fleeing the scene of her folly she will be able to flee from herself and create for herself a new soul, is like a ray of sunlight, shining for an instant on the surface of the dark tragedy. As we read, we also follow her dream with throbbing hearts, and try with her to give reality to her illusion :

> " Sì, dolce sposo, ch'io già tal ti appello ;
> se cosa io mai ferventemente al mondo

---

[1] " Am I returned and among my own family ?   Or am I straying among new enemies ?   Ah, Elektra, relieve thy father from miserable doubt.   I find a new kind of greeting in my palace : I am almost become a stranger to my consort ; yet it seems to me that she might by now have become as she used to be.   She speaks, looks, acts as though she were a statue carving her own being ; she is distrustful now and full of art."

bramai, di partir teco al nuovo sole
tutta ardo, e il voglio. Il ritrovarmi io tosto
sola con te; non piú vedermi intorno
nullo dei tanti oggetti a lungo stati
testimon del mio pianto e cagion forse;
il solcar nuovi mari, e a nuovi regni
irne approdando; aura novella e pura
respirare, e tuttor trovarmi al fianco
pien di gioia e d'amore un tanto sposo;
tutto, in breve, son certa, appien mi debbe
quella di pria tornare. Allor sarotti
meno increscevol, spero. Aver t'è d'uopo
pietade intanto alcuna del mio stato;
ma non fia lunga; accértati. Il mio duolo,
se tu non mai me 'n parli, in breve svelto
fia da radice. Deh! non la paterna
lasciata reggia, e non gli orbati e mesti
miei genitor; né cosa, in somma, alcuna
delle già mie, tu mai, né rimembrarmi
déi, né pur mai nomarmela. Fia questo
rimedio, il sol, che asciugherà per sempre
il mio finor perenne orribil pianto." [1]

Eternal lines are to be found also in the weakest of
the tragedies, such as the words of Ottavia, who
returns to the palace of Nero and says to Seneca:

" Nel rientrare in queste
soglie, ho deposto ogni pensier di vita.

---

[1] "Yea, sweet husband of mine, for so I call thee already; if ever
I earnestly longed for aught in the world, I burn with longing now to
depart with thee towards the rising of a new day. I long to find
myself again alone with thee; not to see around me any more any of
the many things which so long have witnessed and perhaps been the
cause of my lamentations. I long to furrow new seas, to disembark
in new kingdoms, to breathe a pure fresh air, and immediately to
find such a husband as thee at my side full of joy and of love; in
one word, I am sure that all will be restored to me as it was before
my misfortune. Yet must thou have some pity for me, reduced to
such a state; but be sure, O my love, that I shall not be long in
recovering my happiness. My sorrow will speedily be torn up at
the roots, so be thou speakest never of it to me. Ah! remember
never to speak of my father's palace deserted, nor of my unhappy
childless parents, nor in a word of anything that once was mine.
That is the only remedy for my terrible grief, which has persisted
through the years."

Non ch'io morir non tema; in me tal forza
donde trarrei ? La morte, è vero, io temo :
eppur la bramo ; e sospiroso il guardo
a te, maestro del morire, io volgo." [1]

There is a whole tragedy in these few lines. But
one should read the tragedies of Alfieri as one reads
lyrics, that is to say, poetry, setting aside all pre-
conceptions and preoccupations with dramatic or
theatrical writing. Yet it is wonderful how well
the better of them still hold their own on the
stage, when actors can be found capable of inter-
preting them, a condition which they share with the
plays of Shakespeare and Sophocles; and one should
also read Alfieri's occasional verse, which I see with
pleasure is coming again into some favour. His
vigorous sonneteering gives expression to love, to
hate, to the tedium of life, to the meditative scrutative
return upon oneself, to the expectation of death, the
sigh for fame. I shall mention the following sonnets
among many : " Alone with my sad thoughts upon
the shore . . ."; " There where silent, solitary, severe
. . ."; " Sweetest melancholy, which ever . . .";
" At all hours, no, but at many in the day . . .";
" Now late I suffer when I know the longing . . .";
" Things seen and seen again to satiety . . .";
" Behold there rises from my tenth lustre. . . ."
And I shall record the prophetic sonnets of the
Misogallo, and also certain touches which give the
spirit of the French Revolution, such as the scene of
Marie Antoinette's execution, in which judges, jailers,
executioners, are all alike aware of the crime they

[1] " Crossing this threshold, I have laid down all thought of life.
Not that I do not fear death ; for where should I find strength to do
that in myself ? Yea, truly I do fear death : yet I long for it ; and
I turn my gaze on thee, thou master of dying, with a sigh."

are committing and tremble as they act (" I beheld there the pallid jailers tremble, tremble the headsmen, who are awaiting the sign from the trembling Herods ").—He began his lyrical writing with descriptive passionate sonnets, which belonged to the old Marini-Arcadia tradition, relinquishing this to place himself under the guidance of " the profound master of gentle love," Petrarch.   But taking his lyrical and dramatic work as a whole, it is Alfieri himself that we find in it, or, if you like, he may be described as Dantean, but he is not Dantean in the sense of being a merely external and decorative imitator, like Monti; Alfieri is Dantean, because his genius and his nature are so constructed.

We observe this in the *Satires*, which are also Dantean, although anthologists and essayists are accustomed to connect and compare them with the other so-called satires to be found in Italian literature, but the latter are either something totally different, or they are nothing at all.   The *Satires* contain his views upon politics, manners, morals, religion, the social classes of his time, expressed in an epigrammatic form, and let us call this his " sociology." They are certainly prosaic in essence, but their prose is strong and original, with an outlet here and there upon true poetry, especially in the *Journeys*, so full of traits which are sometimes austere, like this memory of Sweden :

> " Svezia ferrigna ed animosa e parca,
> coi monti e selve e laghi mi diletta ;
> gente, men ch'altra, di catene carca ; " [1]

---

[1] " Sweden, so hardy, so courageous, so parsimonious, you delight me with your mountains, woods, and lanes, and your folk too are less charged with claims than those of other lands."

sometimes contemptuously kind as in the general impression upon him of the Germans :

"Piú m'attalentan quelle oneste zucche. . . ."[1]

Or, again, they tremble with sarcasm and weariness of self, as in that *terzina* upon Naples, and upon the company he expected to meet with there, the aristocratic society of the time, devoted to horses, play, theatre and ballet girls :

"Ignoranti miei pari assai piú d'uno
la neghittosa Napoli me 'n presta,
con cui l'ozio mio stupido accomuno."[2]

It is strange that at one time Italian critics with romantic tendencies, accustomed to exalt foreign above national literature, used to set up Schiller, as more modern, more liberal and spontaneous, than Alfieri, whom they regarded as abstract, antiquated, and tyrannized over by pedantic rules. Schiller, however, is nothing but an Alfieri grown cold, composed, temperate, cultured, and reflective, in his admired dramas such as *Wallenstein, Maria Stuart, William Tell;* he is no longer a poet. He is also closely related to the poetic Alfieri in his juvenile drama, such as the *Robbers, Love and Stratagem*, and *Fiesco.* Uncouth, obscure, incorrect and often puerile, they were despised by the severe Italian, and some of them belonged to that middle-class tragedy which Alfieri described as " the frog's epic "; but the same blood circulates in them as in Alfieri's tragedies and lyrics, the tumultuous blood of those who at the end of the eighteenth century felt what was called in Germany the *Sturm und Drang*.

[1] " Their honest noddles please me more."
[2] " Idle Naples which knows nothing of men such as I really am, yet lends me other associates, mingling with whose stupid sloth I too become commonplace."

C

II

MONTI

WHEN recording the history of Italian poetry at the beginning of the nineteenth century, it is difficult to resist the temptation of opposing Vincenzo Monti to Foscolo, Leopardi, and Manzoni, describing his poetry as old and on the decline, theirs as the dawn. One cannot, in truth, write a general history of a literature without having recourse to such expedients of passages from ·one group of poetic works to another : they are links, sometimes with a foundation in fact, sometimes merely verbal. That described above is not one of the worst, and merits some indulgence. But it does not, on the other hand, obviate the reflection : but why do you call it old-fashioned poetry ? Old Italian poetry might also, let us say, be described as that half sensuous, half clever writing peculiar to Marino and to his followers ; or as that which followed it of Metastasio and his imitators, which is half sentimental, half intellectualistic. But Monti has very little in common with any of them. If we examine the emotional content of his work, we find there the influences of Ossian and of Goethe's *Werther*, which were paramount at the beginning of the romantic period. If we turn to its political content, we shall find there all the ideals that rose, fell and rose again during his long life; the imprecations of Catholic monarchy hurled against revolutionary France, Jacobin enthusiasm, Napoleonic exaltation, greetings to the Restoration, all of them new things at the time, and indeed excessive in number. If, again, we turn to the literary forms, we find the cult for Dante returned, blank verse and pre-romantic polymetric, imperial neo-classicism, and so forth. No, it will not do : Monti can certainly provide a contrast with Foscolo and Leopardi and Manzoni, but on other grounds than these of the historical distinction between old and new poetry.

The youthful Leopardi gave us the true explanation of this when he remarked in his note-book (II, 131–2) : " Monti is really a poet whose appeal is to the ear and to the imagination, by no means to the heart " ; for what in him is of the highest value and may be called original are the ease, the harmony, the softness, the yieldingness, the elegance, the graceful dignity and the dignified grace of his verse. All of these qualities are equally to be found in his images, to which may be added happy choice, applicability, clarity of outline, etc. On the other hand, he lacks altogether " everything of soul quality, fire, emotion, truly deep and profound inspiration, both of the sublime and chiefly tender sorts." Further on he remarks more crudely (II, 155) : that " he is not a poet but an exquisite translator, when he is plundering Latins and Greeks, and when it is Italians such as Dante, he appears as a most alert and dexterous modernizer of the old style and of the old language."

The same thing is to be read or rather extracted from the summing-up with which Zumbini concludes his studies of Monti's poetry : ". . . an exquisite art in all his work, and in all its particulars, indeed in every word, every accent of his. No thought or image ever entered his imagination but it came out a butterfly with golden shining wings. Even in the greatest poets is to be found here and there a passage in which the art languishes and the material remains colourless, and this is especially due to the use of scientific thought or of scientific proofs, which they have sometimes believed will better assist them in obtaining the end in view. But with Monti the image is at least never wanting, even where a personal original idea is to seek. Everything is verdant and scented in his fields; and when we traverse them from end to end, we never find ourselves even in an unpleasing, much less in a deserted spot. Vaster horizons there are than Monti's, but in his heavens is never a cloud; there is not a scrap of his sky which does not shine and smile upon us." From this we gather that Zumbini intended to suggest first the same conclusion as Leopardi, namely, that an intellect of this sort is not genuinely poetic, and that the very absence in him of the sense of labour, of obscurities and of harshnesses, so common in true poets, is evidence to that effect.

This conclusion is, on the contrary, quite clearly drawn by Steiner in his recent and very well-balanced study of Monti, which contains the following passage (we see that Monti's imagination is contagious to such an extent as to infect even Zumbini, who generally expresses himself drily): "We stand before his magnificent literary poetry as before a great stage scene, all arches and columns with a suite of superb loggias opening upon gardens adorned with statues and fountains amid the verdure, upon which the eye wanders certainly with pleasure, yet without being by any means deceived by the artful arrangement. The reader becomes aware on reading Monti's poetry of the simple play of imagination, and objects to allowing himself to be dominated by it. While he admires the artist, he does not admire the man, for he feels that he is really different from what is presented, and remains rather uncertain than conquered when brought face to face with all the prodigies which a perfect technique displays to his imagination and with the waves of harmony which are ringing in his ears. He is, in fact, rather desirous of allowing himself to be carried away than carried away in reality, because he feels the artifice that underlies that art and his heart rebels, for the poet has never been able once to make it burn or to make it really drunken with poetry."

Monti, then, was a poet of the ear and of the imagination in respect of the poets with whom he is usually contrasted; he is not at all the representative of one period opposed to another : the difference is mental, not historical.

And so little does he end an epoch or belong to a closed epoch, that we find him, on the contrary, forming a school. This school certainly has little or no value, but that is only because all poetical schools have little or no value. In extent and diffusion, Monti's school was not inferior, indeed it was, if anything, superior, to the schools of Foscolo and of Leopardi, and perhaps it is not altogether extinguished in our own times, for in the death of Rapisardi we have seen the disappearance of one of its most valiant champions. The poetical type, of which Monti was the splendid representative, is to be found at all times : in the early Renaissance, for instance, among the many humanistic poets; in the sixteenth century among some of the elegant followers of Petrarch, and in his own century in certain parts of the works of Prati, Carducci, Pascoli and D'Annunzio.   If, in these matters, flying quotations and rapid mention did not run the risk of conveying little conviction or perspicuity to the reader, the same mental outlook might be found in writers who differ from Monti—who rarely or never has realistic curiosity and is altogether literary—in being free from literary images and very rich in realistic images and in those of direct observation, and nevertheless work with the fancy and not with that imagination which derives from feeling.

If we re-read the *Prometheus*, we shall be astonished to find the use to which Monti turns that antique mythological figure, which Goethe had lately fashioned anew and bestowed upon it that sublime pride of the man who knows that he has made himself, with his own labour and anguish, with tears and blood, and feels that he has the right of not reverencing Jove, who idles yonder in the sky.   Read *Basvilliana* again, and think of the iambics of André Chénier, or, indeed, of the prose of Edmund Burke.   Read the *Feroniade* again and listen with astonishment to Monti's poem, which is altogether indifferent to such profound considerations as these, satisfied with something altogether different, although Foscolo in Italy itself, Goethe, Hölderlin and others in Germany had shown how the antique images can be transformed into modern words and symbols :

> " Ma di Giove non seppe un'amoròsa
> frode fuggir.   La vide ; e da' begli occhi
> trafitto, il nume la sembianza assunse
> d'un imberbe fanciullo, e si deluse
> 'incauta ninfa e la si strinse al seno
> con divino imeneo.   L'ombra d'un elce
> del Dio protesse il dolce furto ; e lieta
> sotto i lor fianchi germogliò la terra

la violetta, il croco ed il giacinto,
ed abbondanti tenerelle erbette
che il talamo fornîro ; e le segrete
opre d'amore una profonda e sacra
caligine coprio ; ma di baleni
arse il ciel consapevole, ed i lunghi
ululati iterâr su la suprema
vetta del monte le presaghe ninfe. . . ." [1]

It is not surprising that Monti was deeply grieved
at the ban against the mythology which the romantics
attempted to establish, nor less so that he lamented
the ancient fables in a way so different from contemporary poets or those who succeeded him. They
lamented the loss of a treasure-house of feeling,
Monti the menaced disappearance of a treasure-house
of literary forms. The inclination to blame him
vanishes when we see him passing from one political
party to another, while always carefully preserving
his decorous literary style, because it is clear that,
for him, this was the serious matter, not the political
party, which represented at most a certain amount
of worry and trouble in life, of which it was necessary
somehow to get the better, and after all, in politics,
compromise is the best solution. A man who can
write, as Monti did, the well-known letter to Salfi,
in which he excuses himself for having indited in
the *Basvilliana*, not only an invective against the

[1] " But she was not able to escape an amorous subterfuge of Jove.
He saw her and transfixed with a beauteous look, the god assumed the
appearance of a beardless youth, deluded the uncautious nymph,
and clasped her to his bosom in divine nuptials. The shadow of an
oak tree protected the sweet theft of the god, and the earth gladly
saw blossoming in her sides the violet, the crocus, and the hyacinth,
and the abundant tender grasses which provided the couch ; a profound and sacred darkness covered the secret works of love ; but
the sky was aware of it and burned with lightning flashes, and the
nymphs who read the future uttered again and again their long-
drawn cries upon the very summit of the mountain. . . ."

French Revolution, but an " extremely eloquent "
invective, and who goes on to say that being " obliged
to sacrifice his *personal* opinion, he had decided to
preserve at any rate his literary fame as a writer of
good Italian," and that " the love of poetical glory
had got the better in him of the blushes of bad reasoning," is surely a child. Monti was, as it were, confounded at the consequences and inferences which
were drawn by others from that which is merely an
accident and a pretext in his poetical work, and in
his confusion he excuses himself by accusing himself
of talking and acting against his conscience, adding
as a plea in his own favour the duty of preserving,
in any case, the honour of good literature ! I do
not think that he did act or speak against his conscience, but believe that the various events and
conflicting doctrines of his time kindled each in turn
the fire of his imagination, and that he remained always
faithful to the same party, namely, that of fine
literature.

Notwithstanding this, how can one fail to take
pleasure in his verse ? Personally, I find pleasure in
all of it, including even the extract quoted above,
which is described by Leopardi as a " centone " ; and
when memory brings to my lips the *terzine* of the
Bellezza dell' universo, with the apostrophe to God :

> " Di tante faci alla silente e bruna
> notte trapunse la tua mano il lembo,
> e un don le festi della bianca luna ;
>   e di rose all'Aurora empiesti il grembo,
> che poi sovra i sopiti egri mortali
> piovon di perle rugiadose un nembo. . . ." [1]

---

[1] " Thy hand stitched the skirt of dark and silent night with so
many torches, and thou gavest to it as a gift the white moon ; and
thou filledst the bosom of dawn with roses, so that a cloud of dewy
pearls fell upon drowsy ailing mortals. . . ."

I am quite well aware that here we have neither
religious emotion nor a clear impression of nature,
but that " stitched skirt " of night, and that " gift "
of the " white moon," and those " roses " thrown
into the bosom of Aurora procure for me a particular
kind of pleasure. The same thing happens when
Monti describes in the *Prosopopea di Pericle* the active
fervour of Hellenic art at the nod of that master of
the arts :

> " Per me nitenti e morbidi
> sotto la man de' fabri
> volto e vigor prendevano
> i massi informi e scabri :
>   ubbidiente e docile
> il bronzo ricevea
> i capei crespi e tremoli
> di qualche ninfa o dea. . . ." [1]

I am perfectly well aware that this prosopopœia is
a scholarly exercise, yet I enjoy every syllable, and
become fascinated as I contemplate those " curled
and waving locks " that blossom in the bronze.
Exquisitely delightful to me is also that vision of
distant stars which reveal their countenances to the
telescope, in the praise of astronomic science which
occurs in the *Ode al Montgolfier* :

> " Svelâro il volto incognito
> le piú remote stelle,
> ed appressar le timide
> lor vergini fiammelle. . . ." [2]

although I speedily become aware that there is nothing
behind all this and that it is merely a question of a

[1] " For me shapeless rough metallic masses assumed form and vigour,
becoming exquisite and brilliant beneath the hand of the artificers ;
docile and obedient the bronze took the shape of the curled and
waving locks that adorned the head of nymph or goddess. . . ."

[2] " The remotest of the stars revealed their unknown faces, and
their timid virginal flamelets drew near. . . ."

graceful diversion. Certainly the Muses who surround the dead Mascheroni, weeping and lamenting as they kiss his hand, lack the ingenuousness of the Franciscan monks, who in like manner surround the body of Saint Francis in Giotto's picture, weeping, gesticulating and kissing the body; resembling rather an academic group of allegorical marble figures. But this group is wonderfully done in its own way:

> " Ecco il cor,—dicea l'una,—in che si santo
> si fervido giusto arse il desiro :—
> e la man pose al core, e ruppe in pianto.
>   —Ecco la dotta fronte onde s'aprîro
> si profondi pensieri,—un'altra disse :
> e la fronte toccò con un sospiro.
>   —Ecco la destra, ohimè !, che li descrisse,—
> venia sclamando un'altra : e baci ardenti
> su la man fredda singhiozzando affisse." [1]

To describe Monti as a non-poet, as a lettered rhetorician, endowed with fancy, but lacking feeling and imagination, does not seem to be adequate, in view of these impressions, which every reader of Monti shares with me. Simple literature, simple eloquence, and technique are odious or tiresome, and in any case incapable of inspiring pleasure, or that kind of pleasure afforded by the verse of Monti. For this reason, the characterization given above should be regarded as negative and provisional, stating rather what Monti is not than what he is. Was he really altogether without feeling or imagina-

---

[1] " Here is the heart—said one of them—the heart in which love of justice burned with so holy and fervent a fire :—She placed a hand upon the heart, and broke into lamentations.—Here is the learned forehead, whence came thoughts so profound, said another. She touched his forehead with a sigh.—Here is the hand, alas ! that wrote them down, exclaimed another, as she covered the cold hand with ardent kisses."

tion? Was he entirely a non-poet? We are aware
of uncertainty as to this point, even in Leopardi,
for whom Monti is sometimes " a poet of the ear
and the fancy," sometimes a " non-poet."

We must consequently add to our statement by
way of elucidation that Monti lacked that kind of
" feeling," which is generally understood as feeling
for real things, moral, political or religious, etc.;
he was not a poet as a poet is understood in ordinary
language, one whose imagination consumes in its
flame and idealizes the passions of the real world.
But there is a corner of the world, which is called
" literature " and has a reality of its own, inspiring
emotions which also have their reality and which for
that reason is capable of giving rise to a particular
kind of ideation, a particular kind of imagination and
poetry, the poetry of the literary man. In this sphere
Monti was sincere and really moved, and hence comes
the attraction which nevertheless cannot be denied to
his verse. But we must also hasten to note that this
sort of feeling, which is properly literary and artistic
feeling, is among the most modest and the poorest,
because it is limited to love of external forms, images,
movements, cadences, vocables, and tunes of phrase,
void of the life which they once synthesized and
contained, like jars and phials which have held perfumes and still retain something of their odorous
traces. A feeling for literature easily becomes gradually more and more attached to the external and
particular in themselves, and is thus turned into
pedantry; indeed, there is always a touch of the
pedantic in lovers of literary forms, as there is something of the lover in the pedant. This confers upon
them sometimes a sympathetic aspect, an aspect of

saintly simplicity, of saintly stupidity and pious devotion, as Bruno would have said. When a comparison is set up between this poor, thin emotion and the poetry it inspires and the far richer ethical, religious, political, and such-like emotions and their lofty poetry, the inclination is to describe the pure man of letters and his work as " non-poetry," as did Leopardi in the case of Monti. But this view is excessive, unless it be taken as merely relative to those other poetical works. A more equitable formula would seem to be, that Monti was a " poet of the ear and the imagination," because this formula asserts that he was nevertheless " a poet," and determines his characteristics, which it places among those of " fancy " and " ear," which is precisely the circle where literary forms take refuge and persist, when they have been separated from their emotional context.

Summing up, what is agreeable in the verses of Monti is the light breath of poetry which inspires and moves within them, though it be literary poetry, poetry upon poetry. And our love for him is in direct relation and proportion with the love which burned in his breast; it is directed towards the things which he really loved, and not towards those which he pretended to have, or made himself believe that he had at heart, those outlines, attitudes, gestures, looks, smiles, motions, which had already been felt by Homer, Virgil, and Dante; it is not directed to political thoughts and works, which had been those of popes, tribunes, kings, and emperors. In his last days, on one occasion, and perhaps the only one, when he contemplated his own self and not another person, he only evinced affection and pride in the fair literary form which he had once bestowed upon the *terzine* of the *Basvilliana* and the blank verse of the *Iliad.* I refer to that poem of 1826 dedicated to his wife, in which, anticipating his own early end and surprising the confirmation of this in the silent and preoccupied looks and the furtive tears of the woman he loved, he uttered the following words of consolation, little elegant, indeed, in comparison with those which he was formerly wont to employ in former days, but sincere :

> " . . . datti pace, e il core
> ad un pensier solleva
> di me piú degno e della forte insieme
> anima tua.   La stella
> dell viver mio s'appressa
> al suo tramonto ; ma sperar ti giovi
> che tutto io non morrò : pensa che un nome
> non oscuro ti lascio, e tal che un giorno
> fra le italiche donne
> ti fia bel vanto il dire :—Io fui l'amore
> del cantor di Bassville,
> del cantor che di care itale note
> vesti l'ira d'Achille. . . ." [1]

Those " dear Italian notes " had been his true ideal, the cult to which he had devoted his whole life.

[1] " . . . be tranquil, and raise thy heart to a thought more worthy of me and also of thy strong soul. The star of my life draws near its setting, but may it comfort thee to hope that not all of me will die and think that it is no obscure name that I am leaving to thee, a name which one day you may be proud to utter among Italian women, saying : I was the beloved of the singer of Bassville, who clothed the wrath of Achilles in dear Italian notes."

III

SCHILLER

FREDERICK SCHILLER is a great name, which has
filled a great place and will continue to fill a great
place in the history of poetry. Yet how does he
come by that name and that position unless it be due
entirely to the hybrid method usual in the writing of
poetical history? Indeed, his case can be quoted as
a clear instance of the errors in perspective due to
such hybrid treatment. For it is only owing to the
confusion of history of poetry with that of culture
that it has been possible to create the couple Goethe-
Schiller, *par nobile fratrum, lucida sidera* of poetry in
general and of German poetry in particular. This
equivalence or juxtaposition is due to motives really
external to art, and to some extent dissimilar from
those which led to the coupling of Dante and Petrarch,
Ariosto and Tasso, Corneille and Racine. It was
suggested and imposed, from the fact that the two
men had been friends and collaborators for some
years, that both had received the applause and the
confidence of their compatriots at the moment of
their first appearance in the literary world, from their
common lot of being selected as standard bearers in
Germanic literary and political conflicts. And, on
the other hand, it is only owing to the confusion of
the history of poetry with that of literary classes and
institutions that we hear Schiller exalted as the poet

who " created the German national theatre," the poet whose plays (as a recent historian of literature has declared), " whatever may be their deficiencies, and were they even greater than they are, belong always to the classical drama of Germany."

If we regard the matter, on the other hand, from the exclusive standpoint of poetry, and if we argue with the simplicity of heart which is not unsuitable to that form of history, we should come to the natural conclusion that Schiller belongs to it only as a poet of the second rank. In saying this, we go against the opinion of Horace, for whom poetry of the second rank is unacceptable to gods, men, and booksellers. From our point of view, poets of the second rank would be those ingenious and expert men of letters who avail themselves of artistic forms already discovered, employ them with judgment, and enrich them with psychological, social, and natural observations, in order to compose instructive, elevating or agreeable works. Such men are sensible and decorous writers, yet they are not poets : a fact which does not imply that their works are not sometimes most acceptable, and in their way more " useful," than those of the true poets. That Schiller was a poet of this secondary sort is a conviction which has now penetrated, although not always very clearly stated as having done so, not only the consciousness of other peoples, but also of the Germans themselves. The former, for a brief period, read, translated, and imitated Schiller, looking upon him as a sort of modernized Shakespeare, but now he is neglected, and with the change of political conditions, the recurrence of the first centenary since his death was celebrated in a very different fashion from that of the famous centenary of his birth, in 1859. German artists and critics, on being asked for their opinions, have confirmed the fall of the poetical reputation of Schiller, though expressing themselves in pious euphemisms. A certain British writer, too, who must be set down as a crank, on being also invited to express a judgment on the matter, candidly confessed that he had never read a line of Schiller, but declared, at the same time, that since he had been endowed with the gift of deducing from the sound of an author's name the quality and value of his work, this gift enabled him to infer that " Schiller " was one of those authors highly recommended in schools, who extract vast yawns from the breast. The gentleman in question was not altogether wrong in his theory of the sound of the name, because the name of a celebrated man becomes impregnated with all the impressions aroused by his work, with the judgments of admiration or of disapproval which it has received, and with the greater or lesser degree of warmth of the said judgments. For this reason, it is very often possible that one who knows nothing but the sound of a name may yet be able to gather from that, whether it be a question of a great, a little or a mediocre writer, of a genius or a pedant, of an author mysterious and profound in thought and feeling, or easy and accessible to the delight of everyone. It is true that, in reducing the glory of Schiller to modest dimensions, an attempt has also been made to change the value of its various components and by belittling the merit of his mature plays, those which used to be considered perfect, to extol that of his early plays, which are imperfect and chaotic. But I have strong reasons for suspecting that this inversion of values has been brought about by a criterion active in Germany (and also outside Germany properly so-called). This criterion came into fashion with the great value attached to the *echtdeutsch*, the *ur-Germanisch*, whereby a realism over-excited and convulsed has been taken as the mark of genuine, sublime poetry. This realism, save for its crudity, seems to me to be quite other than purely and primitively Germanic, derived from the forest of Arminius; indeed it is nothing but an indigestion of Shakespeare, blended with the generous vintage of Rousseau, which first appeared in Germany at the end of the eighteenth century and several times renewed itself, with other vinous admixtures, among which must not be forgotten powerful but perfidious draughts drawn from the Catholic—sacrilegious—incestuous *cantines* of the Vicomte de Chateaubriand.

Shakespeare is a moment of the spirit's history, and he cannot be repeated at pleasure; so that when we see his Lears, his Edmunds, his Cordelias in the costumes of the old Moor, or of Franz Moor, or of Amalia in the *Raüber*, we seem to be passing from myth and fable to a brutal realism, which violates the lofty and delicate creations of great poetry. Giannettino Doria too, in the *Fiesco*, is an evil-minded, tyrannous bully compared with Richard III, and the Moorish assassin of the same play, instead of attending to his ignoble business, engages in fool's talk like certain of the Elizabethan clowns, thereby transporting something foreign into the society where it is introduced. The imitation is strident. I am quite well aware of the effect that must have been produced in those days by the furious tirades of Charles Moor against social laws and tyrannies:

D

" No, I cannot think of it.—I am to constrict my body in stays and let my will be snared by the laws. The law has reduced what should have been the flight of an eagle to the crawling of a snail. The law has never yet formed a great man, but liberty breeds Colossi and extraordinary beings. . . ."

And the frantic resolution which follows :

" Behold, it falls like a cataract from my eyes : how mad was I to wish to return to the cage !—My spirit thirsts for action, my every breath is liberty's.— Assassins ! Robbers !—With these words was law rolled beneath my feet. Men have concealed humanity from me, when I appealed to humanity. Away from me, sympathy and pity ! . . ."

But this Moor, who selects the trade of brigand, yet is seized with indignation when the brigands proceed to act according to the logic of their trade, is a brigand who looks round him and wishes to retain the sympathy of the pit :

" Shame ! Slaughter of children ! Slaying of women ! Slaying of sick people ! How this deed overcomes me ! It has poisoned my most beautiful works ! "

The structure of the play shows itself to be intellectualistic and calculated in the midst of all this din and violent action : nothing ever happens un-expectedly. Charles Moor's relinquishment of society and his repugnance for the deeds of the brigands, his sadness and return to the paternal abode that he may salute it and again depart, the death of Amalia— all this has been calculated. The composition of

Kabale und Liebe is also intellectualistic, and this play is for the rest a literary reminiscence of middle-class French and English drama and fiction and of Lessing's dramatic work. There is little to admire in it, save here and there a trait in the personage of the old musician Müller.

Schiller was a moralist and a polemist in these dramas of which he had borrowed the literary forms, and for this reason I am unable to join recent critics in regretting his abandonment of his early style and in noting the decadence of the later work, beginning with *Don Carlos*, that is to say, *Don Carlos* in verse, which alone survives. To me it seems to be altogether natural and most praiseworthy that with the refinement of his taste and the heightening of his conception of art, he should have separated himself from his juvenile manner, which although quite suitable to a medical student, was no longer in place with the refined and thoughtful man of letters he had become. Nor do I discern any loss of his natural gifts in the course of this transition. He did not lose the gift of imaginative spontaneity, which he had never possessed, nor the moral enthusiasm and the polemical energy, which he had possessed and retained, adding to it a better knowledge of history, of philosophy and of art itself. These gifts of an apostle of morality and of a sententious psychological playwright were what acquired for him the favour of democracies, both in his own country and elsewhere, in our Italy, for instance, where Mazzini, among others, admired and preferred him to Goethe and also to Shakespeare. The reason for this is to be found in the fact that it is proper to democracies to prefer declining values in art to genuine values, which are aristocratic and anti-utilitarian. The Marquis of Posa has been defined as a " personified categoric imperative "; but such a personage as he was already present in the juvenile plays, as the old Republican conspirator who slays his friend Fiesco because he suspects him of ambitious plans for the domination of others, and the change is only in the wider ideal circle in which moves that champion of religious tolerance and of the freedom of peoples, and in the greater experience acquired by the artist. Nor has the possibly changed political attitude of Schiller, inclining him rather towards interior freedom than towards politics, as a possible result of the revolutionary events in France, any importance as regards his poetry. It may be true and it may be false that he changed his point of view, but poetry might equally well appear in either or neither of these cases.

What becomes clear, on the contrary, in the period of Schiller's maturity after the *Don Carlos* is that, when the effervescence of youth, which he himself and others mistook for poetical genius and inspiration, had calmed down, Schiller entered into that spiritual condition which is almost equally as painful for him who suffers from it as for him who contemplates the suffering. He was not carried away or guided by an interior necessity to solve a problem, developing within him as though it were an objective process, with its necessary stages and a natural passage from one to another of these, shaping itself in a natural way or determining with ever increasing accuracy its own form, but, on the contrary, he remained puzzled, uncertain which way to go, and began to argue and distinguish minutely what themes he should treat and what forms were to be considered the best adapted and the most beautiful. This is a condition (we must speak the unkind word) of impotence which is frequently to be observed. No remedy can be applied, for it is possible to correct a force which has strayed from its correct line owing to accidental circumstances, but not to inspire force when it is absent. Then the artist becomes clever and begins to conceive thoughts which seem to him and to others to be astonishingly poetical, but which have precisely the defect of being thoughts very like those deduced by critics from works already composed. These thoughts, due to an intellect seeking a possible expression in art, will never have vigour enough to generate it. Hence the lamentation, so apt to fall from the lips, when contemplating the splendour of such thoughts : " What a pity ! "—just as though they were residues and remainders of magnificent works lost or destroyed. To mention one of them, let us take Mary Stewart, the beautiful yet sinful lady, who, although rendered austere by misfortune, yet arouses frantic desires and disseminates death. Or again, that *Jungfräu von Orleans*, Joan, who, no sooner does she brandish the spear and is seized with a feeling of human affection, than she is abandoned by the prodigious strength which God had conferred upon her for an ideal Cause, superior to any individual affection or inclination. Or take the sketch of that unfinished play *Die Maltheser*, where a group of Cavaliers, who should defend to the last a certain position, yet are not equal to the task, although renowned for their prowess and heroism, owing to these being of a mundane nature mingled with other motives, such as love, riches, ambition, national pride, and therefore no longer that pure ecclesiastical heroism,

such as is required for the carrying out of the enterprise : they have become void " of the pure spirit of
the Order." In such conceptions as these, the artist
feels that, like Peter Schlemihl, he has lost his shadow,
his natural form, and goes looking about him in search
of an artificial one or one that he can appropriate.
Thus he plans to combine Greek tragedy with Shakespearean drama, or to introduce the chorus of the
ancients, or to revive the idea of fate, or to employ an
altogether objective style, in which the true inclinations of the author shall be altogether impossible to
divine events and personages moving of themselves;
and so on. In all these attempts, Schiller traversed
a field identical with the fruitless efforts of the most
modern literature; he was even a precursor of that
ideal, which is the most characteristic sign of artistic
impotence for everyone who understands the question
—the ideal, that is to say, of drama as " pure condensed poetry," free from all traces of imitation of
nature, obtaining light and air by means of the introduction of " symbolical concepts taking the place of
the object in all respects where such object does not
form part of the true artistic environment of poets
and cannot be represented, but must be merely mentioned," thus approaching the nature of music and
opera.[1]

The plays of Schiller's maturity, constructed on such
models as these, are, *kalt und gemacht*, cold and artificial,
as his ballads seemed to Schopenhauer. The unexpected is even more to seek in them than in the early
plays; everything is exactly as was to be expected,
because everything answers to a conception, which
becomes immediately known to us the moment it is

[1] See the letter to Goethe of the 29th December, 1797.

uttered, with its facile inferences. In true poetry, on
the other hand, there is discovery, penetration by the
imagination of a world previously unknown; here
the simplest expressions fill us with surprise and with
joy, because they reveal to us ourselves. But the
schematic William Tell of Schiller would not be
Tell if he did not save the fugitive about to perish
in the waters of the tempestuous lake, and if he
did not reject with disdain the parricide John, who
knocks at his door certain of finding a warm greeting
from a colleague in political assassination. The
knightly Max Piccolomini must hurl himself upon the
foreign regiment which comes to the assistance of
Wallenstein, and allow himself to be slain, between
his love for Wallenstein's daughter and his loyalty to
the Emperor. The sense of manufacture is present
too in the masterly picture of Wallenstein's camp;
and the Switzerland of William Tell, with its mountains and lakes, its shepherds and its fishermen, its
flocks and their bells, has the appearance of a *crèche*.
Instead of the poetically unexpected, we find sickly
romanticism and melodrama in those plays. We read
such scenes as the reconciliation of the Duke of
Burgundy with King Charles I in the *Jungfräu von
Orleans* with a feeling of nausea, when, for instance,
the Duke says carelessly, referring to Agnes Sorel:
" Why did you not send her to me ? I would not have
resisted her tears," or, even worse, when the King
proceeds to make fatherly suggestions of matrimony
to the Maid : " Now the voice of the Spirit speaks in
thee, and love is silent in thy breast filled with God.
But, believe me, it will not always be silent. Arms
will be still, victory will bring peace. . . ."
These frequent sweetenings, whether they occur in

the action or in the dialogue, and the allocutions, and they are to be found even in the melodramatic passing from recitative to the rhymed and vocal portions, are tinsel, *clinquant*, substituted for the gold of poetry.

It demands some effort, but the effort is due, to prevent the lack of sympathy aroused by this quality of art from leaving that sphere of art and attaching itself to the person of Schiller, who was a man of noble and gentle character, both as thinker and author, imbued with that austere moral feeling, that *sittliche Ernst*, which his compatriots praise in him. He was not merely the poet to please the fancy of young ladies and cause old maids to shed tears, but the educator of several generations of Germans, both in the family and in the school. And if his work must be excluded almost altogether from the history of poetry, properly so-called, I believe that a more important place should be granted to him in the history of philosophy than is usually done, even if this resolve itself into receiving there those souls who were moved to make their contribution by genuine impulse, and to restore to the history of academies and universities the greater part of those arid and tiresome makers of systems and followers of schools, who continue to encumber it to-day. What happened to Schiller was that on having recourse to philosophy, in order to strengthen the fibre of his talent as a poet instead of employing it capriciously and turning it to his own uses, as a poet of vigorous temperament would have done, he considered it attentively and became to such an extent its devotee that he was obliged to confess to its having rather injured than aided his artistic end, as a distraction

leading him off the right road by splitting up his
spiritual strength and depriving him of the ingenuousness required. He turned his mind chiefly to the consideration of two problems, to that of the nature of
art, being dissatisfied with Kant's definitions, which
seemed to him both vague and negative, and to the
ethical problem of the conciliation of freedom of the
will and necessity. He was dissatisfied here with
the rigid abstractness of the Kantian imperative of
duty, and, indeed, attempted to solve both problems
by blending them together. His *Letters on Æsthetic
Education* contain this attempt, but the two problems
were essentially different, and his theory of art as
mediating between the scientific world and that of
moral freedom, between nature and spirit, runs the
risk of presenting art as an exercise or a game. Notwithstanding this, Schiller elaborated a theory of art
in the course of his studies far more lively and homo-
geneous than that of Kant, which contained dualism
and mechanism in its union and co-operation of
intellect and imagination. As regards the ethical
problem mentioned above, he did well in noting the
asceticism and lack of humanity contained in Kant's
morality, which always faces natural inclinations with
arms in its hands. One would be disposed to say
in the light of it that the loftiest moral being was one
who, constantly goaded by his naturally evil tendencies,
yet drives them from him and makes them his slaves,
thus achieving his duty with soul robust. Such a
person as this inspires a sort of dread : it would be
disagreeable to have such a being about one in real
life, since one would be apt to wonder what would
happen if the moral brake were not to act for a
moment ? Schiller set in relief the opposite personage

of the man who is naturally good, the elect of soul, the "beautiful soul" (*schöne Seele*), who acts nobly and worthily, realizing himself in joy, as one who is thus satisfying the desire of his heart. Spontaneous moral tendencies are certainly nature, in the language of Kant, but a nature which has been created by the spirit in the course of its history, which the will tends to preserve and increase, and duty is certainly a moment, but is not the whole of the dialectic of morality. In addition to the merit of having discussed these problems, to Schiller belongs also that of being among those who tried to throw a bridge across between nature and spirit and to realize the Kantian critique of the teleological judgment in a philosophy of nature, and to have tried to treat the history of literature in a philosophical manner, organizing it as the two recurrent moments of ingenuous and sentimental poetry (classical and romantic) and their subforms. He cannot, however, be praised for having brought to a successful end these problems, but it was necessary to deal with them on the way to a correct solution, and he was followed on the same path by philosophers called Schelling and Hegel. Schiller gathered some fruits of truth on this voyage in a wrong direction. I am unable to understand how recent critics arrive at the decision to deprive Schiller of these philosophical merits, alleging that he was limited to the pre-Kantian philosophical positions of Shaftesbury and Leibnitz, because, so far as I know, to make use of old philosophical motives for developing and enriching new philosophy is precisely the path followed by Schiller and leads to an advance in science. Schelling also makes use of the philosophy of Spinoza, Hegel of those of Spinoza, Bruno,

Aristotle, and Heraclitus, directing them against the positions of Kant, and no one will accuse these philosophers of being reactionary and retrogade.

Schiller the philosopher liked to render his thoughts in verse, whether in the plays (the chorus of the *Braut von Messina* on war and peace : *Schön ist der Friede*, etc., will be recalled), or in the lyrical poems, of which the best are the philosophical, because the absent poetical vein is there compensated by the importance of the thoughts expounded, and the lack of the personal note in their form by their clarity of design and limpid eloquence. This didactic poetry is, of course, not really poetry, but no one would wish that it had never existed, for it has rendered and will render services in its own way and within its limitations. His epigrams have been even more useful and continue to be so, for they come to the tip of the tongue with apt conciseness in æsthetic, ethical and metaphysical discussions. For example, we still quote Schiller when we wish to make clear the contradiction and unity of the two ethics, that of spontaneity and that of effort : " If you cannot *feel beautifully*, you can still *will rationally*, and do as *spirit* what you have not the strength to do as man." And we gladly repeat the following lines, when we wish to criticize those who believe that the classifications of physics and of the natural sciences are the reality of nature :—

" Since you read in her what you have yourself written there, since you arrange her manifestations in groups to meet the eye, and stretch your little cords in her infinite field, you illude yourself with the belief that your spirit grasps and understands Nature in her vastness."

And in order to signify what the philosophy of

nature proposes to carry out, we are ready to avail ourselves of his distinction between the " three ages of nature " :—

" Fable gave it life; school has deprived it of soul; reason restores to it creative life."

Such verses as these are for modern philosophers like the texts of Port Royal; but they have the advantage over those of being more than little grammatical rules and of being expressed in noble artistic form.

IV

THE plays of Werner, together with those of Schiller's youth, find an ever-increasing number of admirers among those who collect with ardour proofs of the realism and marked sensationalism which, in their belief, are proper to pure Germanic drama; but here too may be noted the vanity of applying to works of art considerations and deductions other than æsthetic.

Zacharias Werner, the man, is well known from his biography, and very easy to understand. He was vicious and dissolute, rolling himself furiously in the mud, like Ciacco, but at the same time exercised with anxiety for religious salvation. When he went to Rome for the latter purpose, he used to pass the morning on his knees in the churches, and the evening in altogether different localities. This trait represents him accurately. *Parallèlement*, something of the same kind is to be found in the case of the French poet Verlaine, save that one of the two parallels, the religious, was in the French poet fictitious, the result of careful search for literary *blague* and *réclame*, not uncommon in France, whereas in Werner's case both parallels were equally solid. For many years he wavered and vibrated from one to the other, until finally he broke through the parallelism and gave himself over entirely to the Church, becoming a penitent, a preacher of penitence, and a priest. What

was always lacking in him was the feeling for human
nobility, fineness, internal delicacy; and here we do
not refer to his ethical knowledge and sense of moral
distinctions, of which he possessed a good supply,
both as a German and as living at a period of great
ethical and philosophical culture and also as a Catholic
and a priest. He was eventually able to discover
clearly the error into which he had fallen in attempting
to place the ideal of salvation in Love—he had first
sought salvation in a sect of reformed Freemasonry,
then in Love, finally and resolutely in the Catholic
Church. . He proceeded to criticize the mistake he
had made in confounding sensual love with *caritas*,
to which it is diametrically opposed. He suggested
bestowing the name *Liebe* upon *Caritas*, and upon
sensual love the old German word *Minne*. But all
this belonged to his intellectual side and did not suffice
to change the real rhythm of his spirit. He was
certainly destined to end in ecclesiastical Catholicism,
for it had been given to him there to confess his sins,
to express his contrition, to mortify and abase himself, and thus to obtain or to believe he had obtained
absolution and salvation; but there it was not indis-
pensable to become noble in spirit, which for him
would probably have been an impossibility. His
Weihe der Unkraft, written in 1814, after his definitive
conversion, and in the midst of the Germanic patriotic
movement, is a work of a very singular kind—a
rough popular song, alternately violent and sarcastic
in tone, or humble, confidential, and meek;—but
confirming by its content that Werner was quite
capable of rolling himself in the dust before people's
eyes and of carrying out the most humiliating acts of
penitence, but not of accomplishing in himself the

truly human redemption which gathers itself together in silence and feels the dignity of its new condition, where a watchful moral being has appeared in place of a blind sinner. One feels embarrassed in listening to his words, as though before a person whom one does not wish to blame, because he already blames himself sufficiently, yet whom there is no way of regarding with sympathy. Werner, dancing like a bear, tells the German people that he had once fought and driven the stranger away from the soil of the Fatherland :

" I well know that I am not worthy of showing myself to the people in your shining dance, as a bold standard-bearer; but however I may have erred and however much evil I may have done, my song has never done an injury to the honour of Germany."

One thinks on reading this that a person who feels unworthy of the nation to which he belongs does not possess the right of addressing it, and that the excuse of not having said anything against the Fatherland is of no avail when social behaviour has shown the individual in question to be unworthy.

" But away with these trifles, be they mine or others'; away with impotent feeling, now is the time to go direct to the point. The best sort of repentance is doing better; we prated as boys, but only if we live it in fact can the way of liberty be restored to us."

Certainly the best repentance is to " do better "; but in order to do better one must " feel better," that is, the delicate moral consciousness must have been aroused in us, and Werner rapidly passed over this, preferring to direct his exhortation and recommendation of humility to men who had not the same reasons as he for limiting themselves to this attitude of resignation.

The artist, too, has evident characteristics and qualities in Werner : the quality of realistic representation, of vivacious dialogue, of a vivid style, which we admire in his plays, especially those preceding his conversion, and eminently so in the historical didactic play upon Luther, *Die Weihe der Kraft*. But the interior is feeble in the midst of so much dazzle, for where, indeed, could he ever have obtained strength? Certainly not in his fragile and insecure intellectual reflections upon reformed Freemasonry or in his erotic idealism. Nor could he obtain it in his sensual enjoyments, which, although numerous, were of a base and trivial sort, and were also limited and chilled by his utopian humanitarianism. Thus he was not even able fully to portray the troubled joys of spiritual sensuality, which sometimes rises to the level of poetry or opens a way for poetry, owing to the anguish which it bears within itself. In this respect, his life is like his art. Monks and mystics arise from sensual men, but only a comedian of the pulpit could come out of the sensuality of a Werner, striving to obliterate in himself sinful acts, themselves almost animal and external, with internal acts of devotion.

The only feeling that dominated in Werner and was capable of animating his dramatic talent was fear of the obscure vengeance suspended above the head of the sinner himself. He was haunted with dread of the punishment which would, in his belief, infallibly follow upon his sin as the work of a mysterious power, God or something else, and by the impossibility of avoiding expiation. Here, too, his life meets and unites with the logic of his art : his conversion arose from terror, from the desire to expiate in order to escape certain and yet more severe punishment. It was upon this, the real foundation of his soul, that was built the famous one act tragedy : *Der vierund-zwanzigste Februar* (24th February).

We shall not enter into disquisitions concerning so-called " dramas of destiny " in discussing this work, which is regarded as the most conspicuous example of the sort, because what is here important is not at all the idea of destiny but the form which the idea assumes with different authors, thus causing the differences in their poetry. There is really nothing that makes either useful or possible an æsthetic comparison between the feeling which animates Schiller's *Braut von Messina* and that of Werner's tragedy and those of Müllner's, Houwald's and others' dramas. In Schiller, the idea of destiny serves the attempt to renovate Greek tragedy; in Müllner and Houwald, it is employed to interest and move the pit, in conformity with the tendency which manifested itself in French popular drama at the beginning of the nineteenth century, and also in the numerous novels of Radcliffe, and is brought about in our day by means of new methods, such as the representations of the Grand Guignol and the cinemas. But in Werner, the crime is committed on the 24th of February and drags in its train at long intervals other crimes always occurring on the same day. A final crime, on a 24th of February, destroys the race of the criminals. This is the imaginative form taken by Werner's guilty apprehensions as a sinner, impotent to free himself from his wickedness, but always awaiting, always dreading, in the near or distant future, a blow from some unknown quarter, an event which shall hurl him

E

to the ground. As he himself says, in the prologue which he added to the tragedy after his conversion, he had sung that song of terrifying poetry (*Schreck-gedicht*), " when a tempest cloud confounded the sad feelings, the inebriated spirit; and as I sang, it whirred like the wings of an owl." Such solicitude as this, the outcome of a troubled soul, gathered around it Werner's best literary qualities, as we have described them. They enabled him to paint a bitter and darkly realistic picture. The sure science of the psychologist is evident in the characters of this work, and their language is highly charged with passionate feeling. We see vividly before us the isolated hut in the mountain gorge, the old couple stricken with adversity, and suffering from cold and hunger, ruin impending, and a black record in the past. The third personage appears late in the evening, and the crime is planned at the prompting of desperate misery and condoned with internal sophistry. Then comes the catastrophe : he who had been cursed by his father slays from motives of robbery, and without knowing him, the son whom he had in his turn cursed and who had returned to his parents bearing with him peace and salvation.

This tragedy remains, nevertheless, an imaginative combination of horrors, capable of making spectators and readers shudder, but it will never produce emotion purely poetic, because the feeling of guilt is only poetical when it has been clarified by the light of conscience, which is the true subject of the poem. Here, on the contrary, the guilt is so little guilt that there is never any moral basis to reveal it, and the criminal act thus fails to be distinguished from the merely accidental. Werner was, indeed, incapable of giving what he did not in any way possess. The last words of the drama are there to prove the obscurity of the author's mind and the emptiness of the work itself. The father speaks as follows, when he is about to hand himself over to the judge and executioner as an assassin :—

"Courage! in the name of God—I shall pay for my crime what I well deserve to pay! I am going to the court to confess the murder!—When the headsman's axe has done with me, God will judge—He sees all!—It was a twenty-fourth of February! That is a day! God's grace is eternal! Amen!"

Here the only proposition that contains a meaning and rings true is that God alone can judge, God alone can unravel this tangled skein, because all is clear to Him, whereas in the mind of the author all remains confused.

V

THERE is some artistic relationship between Werner and Henry of Kleist, who was also a blind soul, although the quality of his blindness was somewhat different from that of the author of the *Twenty-fourth of February*. In practical life, having sought and failed to find his proper path, this blindness ended by slaying him.

What should we call the blindness of a poet? The incapacity of seeing particular passions in the light of human passion, aspirations in the fundamental and total aspiration, partial and discordant ideals in the ideal which shall compose them in harmony : what at one time was called incapacity of "idealizing." For poetic idealization is not a frivolous embellishment, but a profound penetration, in virtue of which we pass from troublous emotion to the serenity of contemplation. He who fails to accomplish this passage, but remains immersed in passionate agitation, never succeeds in bestowing pure poetic joy either upon others or upon himself, whatever may be his efforts.

It is an annoying and repugnant habit of German critics to go morselling out literary works and attaching these morsels to the biographies of authors with the assertion that they have been suggested by this or that real sentiment experienced as the result of not less

real plans and intentions. Goethe has been an illustri-
ous victim of this sort of criticism, living and dead,
and protested against it. When the same method was
introduced into Italy and applied in particular to
Leopardi, it seemed sometimes an unworthy profanation, sometimes ridiculous obtuseness, for people were
sensible of the absurd inappropriateness which lay
in comparing this or that girl of Recanati with the
ideal figures of Silvia and of Nerina. Yet this habit
finds some sort of justification in the crudely realistic
character of a great part of German literature, and
since it is an anti-æsthetic method, suits the interpretation of what has little æsthetic quality. Thus,
although even for Kleist the commentators often
make foolish statements—as, for instance, when they
note, in relation to the *Schroffenstein Family*, that if the
two families inhabit opposite sides of the lake, it is
because the poet dwelt for some time upon a small
island in a Swiss lake, whence but two houses, on
opposite shores of the lake, were discernible !—it is
not altogether without importance to know his
Penthesilea was due to a violent fit of rage at his own
vain flights in the sky of art; that *Käthchen von Heilbronn*
understood how to oppose an ideal of feminine devotion to certain deceptions which the author had
experienced at the hands of some Julia or Juliet, and
that the Cunegonde of the same play was the result
of dislike for some other lady, and that the *Hermannschlacht* was due to Kleist's patriotic revulsion against
the French occupation of Prussia. The critic can
easily reduce these works of art to the level of documents, for they are intrinsically documents rather than
works of genius.

Completely dominated by the emotions of the

moment, Kleist was led to express them sensually in his writing, because an emotion, however noble may have been its origin and tendency (and Kleist certainly had noble ardours and impulses), if it be regarded only on its external side, if it be not entirely dominated and its place assigned on the vast background of reality, appears as nothing but an instinctive movement, animal or mechanical, and with the one-sided revelation of its sensible aspects alone, these aspects are exaggerated and deformed. Hence the horror which his Penthesilea has always aroused. Full to overflowing with the one longing to conquer and bind to herself Achilles whom she loves, seeing that she fails to conquer him, she slays him in a delirium of fury, inflicting blows and bites upon the corpse of the hated loved one. This was not due to any pleasure taken by Kleist in the libidinous, sanguinary, and horrible, as might have been the case with other writers; on the contrary, the original motive lies in the vain longing after a most lofty ideal and in despair at having failed to attain it. But the motive remains symbolical and almost allegorical, beyond the representation which clothes it with a garment of gross sensuality, taking the form of hysterical fury. This becomes yet more evident where the motive appears as essentially ethical, as in the *Hermannschlacht* are love of country and aversion to the conquering stranger. Yet Kleist has only been able to create a treacherous, cruel, and almost criminal Arminius, whose affection for his own people is what Kant would have described as pathological. We find this again in *Käthchen von Heilbronn*, a sort of Griselda, where the argument is the irresistible attraction felt by a simple girl for a great noble, whom she follows, fascinated, like a slave, deaf to paternal appeals, patient of rebuffs, of abuse, and of the blows bestowed upon her by her idol. This argument especially asks the airy lightness of treatment due to a legend, but in the heavy hands of Kleist it becomes contaminated with superstition, hysterics, and somnambulism. Finally, the prevailing tone of the vigorous fragment *Robert Guiscard* is terror of the plague raging in the Norman camp before the walls of Constantinople, and the painful effort of the hero, who, himself attacked by the disease, rises from his couch to address the people and lead them to believe him scathless, strong, and ready to carry on the war. In like manner, Kleist's stories, so swift, precise, and compact in detail, appear to sink and be drowned in the course of the narrative, giving an impression of the strange, the curious, or the terrifying, but not of the moving or tragical. This can be seen in such tales as *The Earthquake in Chile* and the *Betrothal in San Domingo* or in the *Marchioness O———*. In the first of these, a young girl is on her way to the scaffold for a crime of passion, when an earthquake lays the city in ruins; she finds herself free and in the company of her youthful lover. They enter a church together, but are recognized by the supplicants, pointed at with the finger as the cause of the divine wrath which has fallen upon the city, and put to death by the crowd.

This is a well-told anecdote, but is not a page of poetry : the idea of poetry is lacking. A white man, during the revolt of the negroes at San Domingo, stays a night in a house where those belonging to his side are put to death after having been induced to enter. The girl who is the instrument of these assassinations falls in love with him and saves him by pretending to bind and hold him captive. But when his rescuers appear, he believes himself to have been betrayed by the girl and fires at her. " Ah ! you should not have mistrusted me ! " cries the poor thing, dying. These are the only words which indicate the line that the story should have followed, but does not follow, because, like the others, it remains merely a picturesque anecdote.

When Kleist sets to work translating and adapting that light and graceful play of Molière, *Amphitryon*, upon what aspect of the story does he dwell? Upon the irremediably shocked modesty and the desolate and invincible sadness of Alcmena, when she learns that she has been possessed by another than her husband, although that other is neither more nor less than Jove and from their union is to spring a divine son. Critics may, if they like, boast of the " originality " of such an idea and of the " altogether German " figure of the new Alcmena. But this idea is in bad taste, and the figure of Alcmena thus renewed by means of the unconsolable sadness that envelops it is foolish and out of place in this smiling fable. It is also impure, owing to the anguish experienced at the loss of purity, whereas it would have been pure in art if it had remained in the sphere of jest. They boast of Kleist's being able to endow or re-endow the fable with a mystic value, by treating it as a sort of " Annunciation of the Virgin." But religious imagination beats its wings without soiling them in the mud of erotic psychopathology, as may be observed in primitive representations of the Virgin Mother or of Judith.

Kleist, since he remained permanently materialistic, was induced, in order to confer life upon his work, intentionally to exaggerate it, either in the sphere of morality or of politics. Hence the intellectualistic element of which we are sensible in his plays that often closely resemble an *opus oratorium*, attaining sometimes to the level of the edifying tale, such as the *Prinz von Homburg*, where material details are met with less often, but are not, on the other hand, altogether absent— the dozing and waking of the prince, his wandering while the orders for the battle are being given, his physical terror at the idea of death. Here Kleist is more successful in suggesting a sort of calm, the result rather of a moral than of an artistic conception. So intellectualistic is Kleist's method that he is often unable to avoid banality, superficiality and puerility of treatment. The *Prinz von Homburg*, for instance, inclines to melodrama, with its scenes and dialogue, suitable to a play of the " happy ending " sort. Here the Grand Elector, rigid custodian of the laws, who condemns the prince to death, does not seem to be serious in doing so, and seems to seek by means of his actions to represent a moral apology.

In the *Penthesilea*, the amorous Achilles, who deludes Penthesilea into believing that she and not he is victorious, and when the deception has been revealed, challenges Penthesilea, in order to satisfy her, decided to let himself be conquered by her and made prisoner, is an Achilles fit for operetta and below the level even of Metastasio . Certain remarks occurring in the dialogue—as when Achilles is unable to conceal his sad astonishment that Penthesilea the amazon should have mutilated her left breast, one of the " seats of amiable youthful feelings," and when she reassures him that he will find them all transferred to the right breast—are involuntarily facetious. Kleist is intellectualistic also in the comic, because, although *The Broken Pitcher* is celebrated as a most delightful comedy, type of the much-desired light comedy lacking to Germany, it is, as a matter of fact, nothing but a farce pedantically drawn out to an incredible length.

The truth is, that Kleist shows himself to possess little poetic talent, notwithstanding, and indeed just because, he is endowed with limitless ambition towards the great and important in art. This ambition, this search, is proper to those who are naturally feeble in gifts, without that pure impulse which achieves what is great without proposing it as an object, without knowing that it does so, as a simple expansion and manifestation of itself. His gifts were secondary, gifts proper to the orator, such as clarity in dramatic exposition, lively description, energy of tone. There is, perhaps, not a single truly poetical passage in all his work. We can see how high he was capable of rising in the words with which Penthesilea, withdrawing into herself, slays herself by means of her own intense suffering, as though with a dagger :

" Now I descend into myself as into a mine, and extract a feeling of destruction, cold as metal, for myself. I purify this metal in the ardour of sorrow, until it becomes hard as steel ; then I imbue it with the corrosive poison of repentance ; I bear it to the eternal anvil of hope, sharpen and refine it into the shape of a dagger, and to this dagger I now present my breast ; thus ! thus ! thus ! and again !—Now all is well." His reputation grew at the time that verism and naturalism were esteemed in art, because he seemed to be the founder or among the founders of the " psychological drama." This word designates the exact opposite of art, namely, observation and arrangement in sections of life, removed from the influence of the creative imagination. It assumed other forms at a later date, when people started hunting for crude Germanic drama, and Kleist, Werner, and Hebbel seemed to be the Shakespeares of a new age, ranked with Ibsen, a different and far more lofty artistic spirit. Kleist still pleases many, because many delight (and in Germany more than elsewhere) in the colossal, the noisy, the roll of the drum, the sound of the trumpet, that hubbub in which pure poetry is suffocated like Cordelia, whose voice was low and whose words were few. But Goethe (whom Kleist designed to combat and surpass), writing to him about the *Penthesilea*, remarked that " it was of so marvellous a race and moved in so remote a region " that he had to make efforts to understand it. He condemned altogether the final act of the *Amphitryon* as dirty (*klatrig*) and held Kleist to be " a Northern hypochondriac," who for that reason selected themes that a fine mind would have rejected, and was destined for ruin both as man and poet. He compared to their detriment Kleist's tales with the serene tales of Italy, which were nevertheless composed in time of pestilence. Hegel, too, who was a very fine judge of art, opposed the powerful and logically constructed Shakespearean characters to those of Kleist, in whom magnetism and somnambulism were dominant motives.[1] I seem to have read in some biography of Kleist that at one time he intended to challenge Goethe to fight a duel, owing to the severe criticism of his work and the prophecy above-mentioned. Kleist was certainly without any other more effective means of stilling the voice of simple truth, which his own death by suicide tragically confirmed.

[1] See *Vorlesungen über Aesthetik*, II, 182, 198.

VI

CHAMISSO

Peter Schlemihl

Among the spurious forms of fable is that in which the narrative is conducted in such a way as to suggest a definite moral, prudential, or other thought. It may be that, if the thought appears clearly, this method produces an effect of grace and elegance; but this would be a case of successful fable, not of poetry, because the thought and the narrative will always remain two separate things, the second acting as a didactic expedient for communicating and fixing the former in the mind.

Fable employed to illustrate a biography or a biographical episode is a variant of this form, because here, too, persist the dualism of form and content, of literal and hidden meaning, and the fable becomes classed as belonging to " narratives with a key," and as in the previous instance, may be clever, opportune, necessary, but not intrinsically poetical.

A third spurious form oscillates between the fable or key narrative, on the one hand, and the work of free imagination, on the other, being an alternation or mingling of these different attitudes. The celebrated romances of Hölderlin and of Novalis are a case in point. They are again greatly in vogue, but as a matter of fact they never attain to poetic maturity or artistic perfection, owing to that opaque, disconnected,

60

abstract, arbitrary element of which we are aware, although they also contain fragments of delicate and vigorous poetry. The singular attraction which they exercise upon the present writer and others resembles the attractiveness of an illness, an aristocratic illness, which sets in evidence traits of beauty by means of suffering and languor.

But the true fable-poem is that which contains the whole of its meaning in itself, like any romance, story, play, or lyrical poem, because the fabulous or prodigious elements, from which it is woven or which are interlinked within it, make no difference whatever in respect to art.

For this reason, *Peter Schlemihl* is a little masterpiece, and since it is a masterpiece, should be read according to its own unique meaning, its literal meaning, with a mind cleared of all the innumerable hermeneutic researches as to the real nature of the shadow, of the seven-leagued boots, and of Peter Schlemihl, and as to what can possibly be the real signification of this slice of his life which he is introduced for the purpose of narrating. The shadow is nothing but the shadow, a part or a virtue of the person himself, which seems to be of no account and such that it can be dispensed with, yet it cannot be dispensed with, because he who has deprived himself of it is at once regarded with just suspicion and is banned by society as a man with a secret taint. And Schlemihl has, in effect, this taint, because he has not lost his shadow owing to a misfortune, but has sold it owing to greed for money to a mysterious personage who has given no good or valid reason for his desire to purchase it, and Schlemihl has asked for none, although his character had been evidently insidious, maleficient, and wicked. But Schlemihl, if he has made a false step at the promptings of poverty, is, all the same, an honest, pure-souled man. He is quick to realise his fault and to experience shame and remorse for it, eager to redeem it at the cost of any sacrifice. His shadow, which he used to regard as insignificant, becomes the dearest thing that can be lost, a loss lamented and a former possession eagerly desired. The day comes when he again meets the mysterious man, who takes from his pocket Schlemihl's shadow and stretches it out in the sun, " in such a way " (he says) " that he is followed by two shadows as he walks, mine and his own, prompt to obey his commands, for mine too had to obey him, displaying and adapting itself according to his movements." Then a desperate struggle takes place in Schlemihl's breast. " When I again saw my poor shadow after so long an absence, and found it reduced to such abject servitude, at the moment when I was the prey of such incredible anguish on its behalf, I felt my heart break and broke out into the bitterest lamentations." But he resists the new temptation, how great soever his desire, however urgent his need to reacquire his own shadow; and if he has given away his shadow on account of the fatal purse, he does not yield his soul up for the shadow. He goes even further, and although he knows he cannot obtain the shadow, throws the accursed purse into the abyss. " I stood there without purse and without shadow; but my breast had been relieved of a great oppression, and that rendered me serene. If I had not also lost my self-esteem, or if, though losing it, I had felt free from blame, I think that I might have been happy. . . ." And now fortune comes to his assistance, not to give him back what he had irremediably lost (who can ever annul a mistake once made ?—what has been done remains perpetually a part of ourselves), but to allow him to find the marvellous seven-leagued boots, with which the man who has been banned by society, excluded from the joys of love, of the family, of friendship, for he has been obliged to renounce all these good things, can yet find an employment, propose an object to himself, enjoy carrying it out. What is there of allegorical or hidden in all this concrete, vivid and limpid narrative? Certainly, the shadow is not only the physical shadow, but yet it is not a thought. So true is this that it is not definable as a thought, for Chamisso himself was not able to define it, and even if he had been able to state his real intentions, the intentions would have been intentions and the fact fact, that is to say, the work of art which all are able to understand and to enjoy in its literal, or rather, in its only sense. The shadow is not only the physical shadow, because no personage, no action, no event, is in poetry simply that personage, action, or event in its external material- ity, but they are all the ideal forces of the human spirit, which have become poetical motives and plastic forms. And the motive of motives in Peter Schlemihl and his marvellous story is the eternal drama, the eternal combat between dream and reality, purity and impurity, impulse and duty, pleasure and dignity. Whoever seek anything else in it, wishing to determine and reduce that poetical motive to a moral motive, either loses himself in subtleties artistically non-existent, or finds himself in possession of some most general generalization, applicable to any form of art.

The critics have tortured the story of Peter Schlemihl

not only in order to reduce it to the rank of false poetry, according to the first type described, which is the fable, but also, and above all, in order to reduce it to a key-story, and have seen the author's life there transfigured beneath the veil of the prodigious. Chamisso, as is well known, was a French emigrant become German and Germanized so completely as to be the author of *Lieder* and romances, taking an interest later in life in botany, and making several journeys for scientific purposes.   We have no wish to contend that there may be some autobiographical references in Peter Schlemihl; but since German critics, as remarked above, strangely abuse the right of poetical-biographical researches, with no other result than to diminish poetry where poetry exists, it is worth while to repeat once more the only doctrine which avails upon this subject, because it is the only true doctrine.   The work of art, then, like the work of thought, certainly receives its impulse from biographical incidents, but is as impossible to measure by comparison with them as is the law of the pendulum with the famous lamp of Pisa Cathedral, or the law of universal attraction with the apple that fell upon Newton's head, when he was lying under the fine apple-tree. The critics who stress so heavily those incidents, which have been converted into poetical vibrations, reconvert the poetical vibration into practical fact, and then proceed to erect it into the generative poetical motive. The results of this upon taste and judgment can easily be conceived. They become the more pernicious the more beautiful, objective, and classical are the works upon which is effected this labour of extraction and abstraction; the less pernicious the more ugly and material are the works in question, because, in this second case, they are wont to contain more aggregated elements which have not been fused, reproduced but not idealized, and to extract and abstract these merely makes evident the analysis which already exists in the work itself.

VII

ANY writer belonging to the first half of the past century and treating of the then recent literary history of Europe, would not have hesitated to place Walter Scott among the stars of the first magnitude in the firmament of poetry and art, Walter Scott the great Scottish poet and novelist. The admiration which he received was nowhere contested; his work spread itself triumphantly through all countries, and everywhere aroused imitators; rarely has a writer had so many or so eminent pupils. This praise and enthusiasm did not proceed from middle-class readers alone, from the great public : suffice it to recall Goethe, who held Scott to be " a great mind unequalled anywhere, who naturally produces the most extraordinary effects upon the whole world of readers." The comparison of Scott with Shakespeare, with whom alone it seemed possible to compare him for " fertility of invention, for the infinite variety of his original characters, historical scenes, situations, and adventures, for his universal human sympathy and moral purity," was common, especially in his own country.

Then all this glory faded. Here in Italy only a few stray volumes were reprinted in the second half of the century as forming part of the library of agreeable literature, in place of the numerous translations and complete editions of his tales and of some of his poems which had filled the first half of the century. Forgetfulness and estrangement took the place of frequent mention of his characters and their actions in speech and writing. The criticism of the critics showed itself hard, ferocious, and contemptuous, especially after Taine's well-known attack. A similar tone has recently been observable in Cecchi's book entitled *History of English Literature*. It is, indeed, difficult to refrain from impatience in speaking of those tales, after having read them. There are too many of them, and the effort entailed upon the reader of to-day, who is at once sensible of the monotony of Scott's art and of his mechanical method, finds vent in the angry tone with which he proceeds to discuss them. Were there but two or three tales, how much easier would it be to remain calm and indulgent! How eagerly would one seek their positive qualities, carefully noting the minute flashes of art which here and there illuminate them!

Yet we must retain our calm, if we wish to apply to Scott's work also the laws of historical style. Imposing, therefore, upon ourselves the requisite serenity of tone, we observe that in speaking of Scott we must in the first place have an eye to the official function which he performed, namely, that of an industrial producer, intent upon supplying the market with objects for which the demand was as keen as the want was legitimate. Are there or are there not wants of the imagination, which ask to be entertained or diverted? And is not that a healthy form of such wants which demand images of virtue, of prowess, of generous feelings, and wishing also to avoid wasting its time in this imaginative gratification, seeks also to avail itself of the opportunity in order to obtain

instruction as to historical customs and events? Scott
had the genius to carry out the commercial enterprise
which supplied this want. He began by composing
poems, which were a first step towards its satisfaction.
But after some years of this practice, he realized that
this kind of merchandise was beginning to pall, that
the vein he had exploited was exhausted, especially
since the appearance of Byron, who was a dangerous
competitor for popular esteem. He thereupon turned
from verse to prose, surrounded his name with
mystery as " the Author of the Waverley Novels,"
and obtained a most brilliant success, which lasted
throughout his career. The impression left upon
reading Scott's biography is that of having before one
the life of a hero of industry. His biographers illustrate and admire his sagacity of invention, his diligence,
which enabled him to write two or three stories every
year, the castle which he was able to build, to decorate
and to throw open to princely hospitality as the result
of his large earnings. Nothing is said as to his inner
life, his loves, his religion, his ideas; less than nothing
as to his spiritual struggles and development. The
dramatic moment of his biography is that of his
publisher-partner's failure, whereby Scott found himself ruined and several millions of lire in debt. He rises
high above this moment of adversity, does not lose
courage, again takes pen in hand and promises to pay
all his creditors by this means, exhausts himself in
maintaining his promise, and when he is at length
crushed by the weight of this immense labour, the
greater part of his debt is paid and the remainder dis-
charged after his death by a grateful posterity. This
national movement may have been in commemoration
of the great writer or of the great man of business—

one remains doubtful which of the two it was that
English commercial honesty proposed to honour.
The biography is not a literary biography at all, but
to be ranked with Smiles's *Self-Help* or some such
similar production.

The second point to notice in regard to Scott is
also outside the sphere of art and belongs to the
particular way in which the demand of the English
public and the European public in general expressed
itself and the goods with which Scott satisfied it.
They consisted of the new historico-ethical-political
sentiment which had arisen as the result of the
reaction, first against eighteenth-century rationalism,
and secondly against the Jacobinism of the French
Revolution. Other elements in this new attitude
of mind were consciousness and respect for history,
value attributed to traditional customs, awaking of
nationality in the place of a superficial and one-
sided cosmopolitanism. Scott was certainly not the
author of all this. The authors were innumerable,
many of them born prior to himself, in Germany,
France, Great Britain, and also in Italy. He it was,
however, who divulged and successfully exploited
the movement from the commercial point of view.

Nor should the importance and spiritual repercussion of this work be denied. Scott's facile fiction
found its way into minds out of reach of philosophical
or historiographical thought, out of reach of poetry.
Scotland generated many other Scotlands, that is to
say, many other evocations of the past and representations of popular customs in every part of Europe, and
Scott's manner of describing and narrating exercised
its influence also upon professional historians. This
influence was beneficial to the extent that it led them

to abandon the colourless and uniform method of illuministic and humanistic historiography; but, on the other hand, it provided a bias towards conceiving history as historical romance, as a glittering picture of little significance. Such exaggeration was afterwards eliminated while the good effects were retained, and no one can henceforth write the history of historical studies in the nineteenth century without taking Scott into consideration.

The third point also is alien to art, because it belongs to the ability which Scott displayed in the construction of his romances. This ability must not be gauged by later or contemporary standards. Judged by them it would perhaps seem poor and inexpert, and in fact lacking ability, precisely because it is now out of fashion. So true is this that we should not tolerate anyone now resuming Scott's beginnings and modes of developing his stories—we should certainly make them a butt for ridicule. The comparison should, on the contrary, be made with fiction prior to Scott and with the disposition of the public of that period, in order to form an equitable judgment. Goethe had really but little talent for composing stories, as may be seen from the halting and naïve methods which he employed in those masterpieces of poetry, the *Meister* and the *Wahlverwandtschaften*. He admired above all in Scott his ability as a teller of historical tales, and " the altogether new art obeying its own laws " which he discovered there set him " thinking furiously."

Scott started well equipped in antiquarian and *touriste* lore; he described scenery, illustrated manners and customs by the doings of his characters, held the interest of his readers in suspense by means of mysterious personages possessed of extraordinary qualities; he gave the illusion of beholding the history of the Normans, the Saxons, the Puritans, and the Jacobites, just as it had actually taken place in word and deed. He varied epic with comedy, portraying with a benevolent smile personages possessed of a single idea or of a single desire. But the noble and the brave always occupied the first places and won the hearts of his readers.

In the fourth and last place comes the consideration of art or poetry, which cannot be the principal criterion applied to the work of Scott after what has been said, precisely because it was not a principal thing in him. If it be assumed as the principal criterion, then there is nothing for it but to " slate " the work, which, however useful a method of dealing with contemporaries, it is very unpleasing to have to employ in relation to writers of the past. Such a person as Gosse, of course, who declares that the defects of Scott are not even to be referred to and asserts that " England may challenge the literatures of the world to produce a purer talent, or a writer who has with a more brilliant and sustained vivacity combined the novel with the romance, the tale of manners with the tale of wonder," we feel disposed to contradict flatly. But is the gravity of the historian worth losing on account of this? Is it not clear from this excessive emphasis of his statement that Gosse himself feels anything but confident of its truth? This is proved by what follows, to the effect that if Europe has tired of Scott, then his English fatherland will keep him all to itself and find exaltation in him, who while preserving the most perfect style in national literature, never wrote a' morbid, base, or petulant word, and was the perfect type of the English gentleman :—of the *gentleman*, not of the poet.

Scott's poetical vein, always slender, rapidly dried up in his altogether prosaic temperament. It was slender even when he wrote in verse, and one can judge of the quality of these compositions by turning to the most celebrated extracts of the poems, such as the portrait of the last minstrel :—

> " The way was long, the wind was cold,
> The minstrel was infirm and old ;
> His withered cheek, and tresses grey,
> Seemed to have known a better day ;
> The harp, his sole remaining joy,
> Was carried by an orphan boy. . . ."

or the description of Melrose Abbey :—

> " If thou would'st view fair Melrose aright,
> Go visit it by the pale moon-light ;
> For the gay beams of lightsome day
> Gild, but to flout, the ruins grey.
> When the broken arches are blank in night,
> And each shafted oriel glimmers white ;
> When the cold light's uncertain shower
> Streams on the ruined central tower . . .
> Then go—but go alone the while—
> Then view St. David's ruined pile ;
> And, home returning, soothly swear,
> Was never scene so sad and fair ! "

The art of his novels is equally superficial, where we find what are called interesting personages and events displayed before our eyes. *Ivanhoe*, for instance, begins with a journey through a forest, where we meet with mysterious pilgrims and astonishing cavaliers, arriving at nightfall at the castle of a Saxon lord, where the great beauty of the Lady Rowena is very much in evidence. The narrative continues with duelling adventures, with jousting, with the advent of bandits, with sieges, with judgments of God, and presents a variously coloured host of invincible and heroic warriors, such as Ivanhoe and the Black Knight, who eventually reveals himself as Richard the Lion-Hearted, abbots who enjoy life, such as Prior Aymer, templars valiant and corrupt, such as Boys-Gilbert, Jews such as Isaac and his lovely daughter Rebecca, bandits such as Robin Hood and Friar Tuck, clowns such as Wamba, Norman barons such as Front-de-Bœuf, Saxons such as Cedric, and terrific betrayers of the Saxon cause such as Ulrica. But when we have ended the reading, our souls are empty. This narrative is without epic feeling, without passion of love, without religious or any other passion. The characters exist for themselves; they afford a spectacle to the eye, or to the fancy. But a real development is to seek, because the artistic idea is absent, and its place taken by a series of interesting happenings and historical notions. Sometimes an attempt seems to be made to strike a deeper chord, as in the celebrated episode of the Knight Templar's passion for the Jewess Rebecca; but that episode, like all the others, is inspired with the desire for the picturesque; the character of the Knight and his dialogues with the Jewish girl are treated in a conventional and often absurd manner. The outward appearance of a soul's drama is there, but the soul is absent. The most successful passages are those which refer to generous feelings in the breast of the Templar, and especially his death in a duel, not from an enemy's sword, but from his own excess of passion. The personage of Rebecca, too, is not without here and there an elevated and delicate touch, especially in the last scene of her visit to Lady Rowena and of her leave-taking. She is a Jewess who remains Jewish by her fidelity to her ancestors and at the same time attains to pure humanity. Such accents as these are also to be heard in other novels, such as *Old Mortality*, for example, in the personage of the rough and licentious Sergeant Bothwell, who seems ridiculous owing to his frequent references to his own noble Stewart blood. When he dies bravely in battle, Morton finds on his breast a pocket-book containing his Stewart pedigree, a few letters in a beautiful feminine handwriting of twenty years ago, a lock of hair, and a few verses composed by himself. Morton then piously directs his thoughts to the destiny of that singular and unfortunate man, who seemed to have fixed his mind continually upon the lofty rank to which his birth entailed him, although plunged in misery and contempt, and raised his eyes with bitter regret to the days of his youth, when he nourished a virtuous passion. Some hint of poetry is also to be found in that desire for travel and for unexpected meetings expressed in the early chapters of *Rob Roy*, and in traditional semi-barbaric existence as rendered in certain chapters of *Waverley*. Certainly, everything becomes lost again in intrigues and insignificant details. Thus it happens that one begins reading such a tale as *St. Ronan's Well* with pleasure, and yet when one comes to the romantic, that is, to the artificial part, boredom sets in, though at the same time a fine trait here and there will give life to the portrait of the priest Saint Ronan (as I have mentioned that novel), which is executed with a feeling for goodness at once moving and graceful.

This smile of goodness is perhaps Walter Scott's

most purely poetical possession, for it illumines even
his comic personages, who sometimes descend to
the level of the stereotyped, but are often contained
within just limits. For this reason, I am inclined to
look upon *The Heart of Midlothian* as the best of his
novels, because it is compacted of goodness, not only
in certain details, but in the very web of the narrative
itself. Here, too, we find plenty of intrigues, and
the usual brigands, who are not brigands, but high-
souled gentlemen, and other properties of the reper-
tory. But who can resist being carried away by the
story of sweet Effie, imprisoned (on the false accusation that she has put her own child to death), and
by the adamantine veracity and courageous temperament of her sister Jean, who will not lie to save her,
and yet saves her by affronting every peril, and obtains
her pardon? And how can one avoid being delighted
with the lead-like heaviness, yet timidly sentimental
love-making, of the *Laird* Dumb Dikes, or fail to
admire the character of crazy Madge, malign and
generous, clever for all her madness at outwitting
suspicions, and although described in the most
realistic manner, yet enfolded in pity? The author
collects and renders clear what of pedantry, of the
habit of preaching, and of complacent vanity, there is
in good David Deans, the pious father of the two girls,
yet shows how he can remain noble and moving in the
midst of his bitter predications and severe religious
notions. " You " (says to him the minister who is
trying to comfort him), " you have been well known,
my old and revered friend, a true and tried follower
of the Cross; one who, as Saint Jerome hath it,
' *per infamiam et bonam famam grassari ad immortali-
tatem*,' which may be freely rendered, ' who rusheth

on to immortal life through bad report and good report.' . . . This heavy dispensation, as it comes not without divine permission, so it comes not without its special commission and use.

" ' I do receive it as such,' said poor Deans, returning the grasp of Butler's hand, ' and, if I have not been taught to read the Scriptures in any other tongue but my native Scottish ' (even in his distress Butler's Latin quotation had not escaped his notice), ' I have, nevertheless, so learned them, that I trust to bear even this crook in my lot with submission. But, oh ! Reuben Butler, the kirk, of whilk, though unworthy, I have yet been thought a polished shaft, and meet to be a pillar, holding, from my youth upward, the place of ruling elder—what will the lightsome and profane think of the guide that cannot keep his own family from stumbling ? How will they take up their song and their reproach, when they see that the children of professors are liable to as foul backsliding as the offspring of Belial ! But I will bear my cross with the comfort, that whatever showed like goodness in me or mine, was but like the light that shines frae creeping insects, on the brae-side, in a dark night—it kythes bright to the ee, because all is dark around it; but when the morn comes on the mountains, it is but a puir crawling kail-worm after a'. And sae it shows, wi' ony rag of human righteousness, or formal lawwork, that we may pit round us to cover our shame.' "

Gudeman Saddletree too, very vain of his pretended judicial knowledge, is presented as a mixture of sincere interest and personal self-complacency : " Mr. Saddletree would have been very angry had any one told him that he felt pleasure in the disaster of poor Effie Deans, and the disgrace of her family;

and yet there is great question whether the gratification of playing the person of importance, inquiring, investigating, and laying down the law on the whole affair, did not offer, to say the least, full consolation for the pain which pure sympathy gave him on account of his wife's kinswoman."

A little further on is a trait which greatly moved Italian readers when imitated by our novelist Grossi in his *Mario Visconti*, where he describes the cabin of the boatman, father of the young man who was drowned. (This Grossi copied both Scott and Manzoni.)

" The sun set beyond the dusky eminence of the Castle, and the screen of western hills, and the close of evening summoned David Deans and his daughter to the family duty of the night. It came bitterly upon Jeanie's recollection, how often, when the hour of worship approached, she used to watch the lengthening shadows, and look out from the door of the house, to see if she could spy her sister's return homeward. . . . As they sat down to the ' exercise,' as it is called, a chair happened accidentally to stand in the place which Effie usually occupied. David Deans saw his daughter's eyes swim in tears as they were directed towards this object, and pushed it aside, with a gesture of some impatience, as if desirous to destroy every memorial of earthly interest when about to address the Deity. The portion of Scripture was read, the psalm was sung, the prayer was made." The account of the public trial, where all depends upon what the sister will say, upon the word that she will not utter, because she cannot lie, and David Deans knows she cannot utter the word and would never have asked her to utter it or wished that she should utter it.

Yet, when Jeanie is pressed on all sides to say that her sister had confided in her and thus supply the reason for an acquittal, declares to the judge : " Alack ! alack ! she never breathed word to me about it."

" A deep groan passed through the Court. It was echoed by one deeper and more agonized from the unfortunate father. The hope, to which unconsciously, and in spite of himself, he had still secretly clung, had now dissolved, and the venerable old man fell forward senseless on the floor."

Let us seek these little rivulets of human goodness and kindness, which run hither and thither and refresh the romances of Walter Scott. All the rest is either business or erudition ; but in them lies his modest poetry. Thanks to them we are able to take leave with sympathy of a writer who delighted our fathers and grandfathers, and who, if only for this reason, does not deserve ill-treatment from their sons and grandsons.

VIII

FOSCOLO

A RESOLUTE effort is necessary to prevent Alfieri from being looked upon as exclusively and narrowly Italian—either politically as the apostle of the national Risorgimento, or from a literary point of view as having enriched Italian literature with tragedy, sole among literary forms which is supposed to have been lacking to it, and to present him as a European writer and an extreme individualist, which he was really, or, as others are now crudely putting it, as a libertarian and an anarchist. It is an easier matter, to a certain extent anticipated by common consent, to affirm that Ugo Foscolo was a European man and writer; although the European literary world has happened to be ignorant of his personality as a whole and as expressed in his most important works. His youthful *Ortis* was, however, read outside Italy, from his own days onwards, and is still translated and reprinted. This work directly connects him with the pre- and early romantics of despair and suicide. His poem the *Sepulchres* forms one of the series which critics and philologists place with the English, French and German poetry of that time dealing with tombs and cemeteries. During his residence in England, his criticism at once found its place in the chief English reviews. A work recently published by the lamented Joseph Manacorda cites at every step Hölderlin,

Novalis, Tieck and Heinze, Goethe, Rousseau and Chénier, not as authors whom he imitated or knew, but as kindred spirits, belonging to the same period and to the same spiritual environment as he. Certainly we have no intention of denying that Foscolo had an even greater share than Alfieri in powerfully stimulating national sentiment, and that the Italian patriots of the nineteenth century had every right to claim him as their father, as he had claimed Alfieri, whose name, he said, was " sacred " to him " to the point of adoration." Perhaps it may even be said that Foscolo's influence was hardly equalled by that of any other writer, since he had influenced Mazzini, and Mazzini the young men of the new generation. But the use made by a people of its poets and writers does not suffice to determine the character and meaning of these poets and writers, considered in themselves.

Foscolo's view of things was dark : he felt himself oppressed by an unknown violent power, which forces men into the world under the sun and obliges them to live out their life with that " fever " in their veins of which Shakespeare speaks, and then inexorably hurls them into the darkness of death and of oblivion. The thought of death, if it did not predominate in him, at any rate dominated. He liked to be at home with death since a boy, just like a character of Shakespeare, and not only with that form of death which comes upon us as fate, but also with that other form of it, which must be invited and desired, suicide, a way out of life that must always be kept open. This conception and disposition of spirit produces as a general idea the most different practical attitudes in life—asceticism and cynicism, ferocious renunciation and frivolous enjoyment, acting and abstaining from action, quietistic self-abandonment and fervent labour and travail of spirit. This last form alone was possible to Foscolo, with his sensitive, energetic mind, requiring expansion and action, and open to generous impulses of all sorts. And here we find a definite instance of the relation between life and philosophy, to which life offers itself, that is to say, the experience of itself, which thought then restores to it rendered more clear and more strong. His mind and thought enabled Foscolo to detect a light in the darkness of overpowering, unknown and external and therefore materialistic forces, which served as a rallying point from which he was able to regain his spontaneity, autonomy and freedom. What does it matter if he found this freedom in the beat of " pleasure " or of " pain " ? What does it matter if he symbolized the negative yet dialectical and propulsive moment as " *ennui*," *ennui* that obliges to action ? What does it matter that he called the ideals of beauty, virtue, friendship, fatherland, humanity, " illusions " ? By calling them so, he recognized their existence practically and asserted them theoretically, paying them homage and admitting their necessity. Hence his life as a citizen, a soldier, an artist, a learned man, a friend and a lover. He always felt and affirmed with pride the loftiness, the dignity and the profound excellence of this life, a view shared by all the youth of Italy at the period of the Risorgimento, and to-day held to be such by those who are able to judge of human value, even when it is mingled with human vices. This holds true of Foscolo's life in the face of those malignant, petty and envious minds who have often exercised their spurious

G

morality, their lack of understanding, in speaking ill of him. May they receive their deserts !

This is not the place to narrate or even to illustrate briefly the life of Foscolo as soldier and citizen, or to recall once more the epigram of Cattaneo, so full of truth, to the effect that Foscolo, whatever he may have failed to do for Italy, at any rate provided her by his own example with a new institution to be of the utmost utility in the future : exile. I shall also not dwell at length upon his work as a thinker and critic, although it would provide me with the occasion to repeat a favourite thought of mine, that the habit of seeking the history of philosophy exclusively among philosophers by profession should be corrected, because many of these scholars, writers of treatises and compilers of systems, have far less value than certain thinkers who are not professionals, but speak of things, while the professionals utter words. Very well : Foscolo held to a speculative position that was agnostic and materialistic and of great import- ance to him both practically and politically, but is of little importance and of little originality in the history of thought; this was his boundary in philosophy, the hemispheres of darkness which sur- rounded him. But Socrates also renounced philo- sophizing as to nature and the Cosmos, yet he produced, as is well known, something extremely philosophical, which has been fruitful in the course of centuries. I mean by this that Foscolo, although he limited his researches to the sphere of the human mind and declared that he did not wish to ascend to the origin of things, was yet the author of lively and fecund thoughts upon man, art, politics, morality, history and religion.

Here too he belonged to the highest level of European culture of his time, and here too the names representative of that spiritual period rise to the lips. Foscolo was among the profound renewers, among the very first of those who profited by the doctrines which Vico had enunciated a century before on the theory of poetry and criticism. He was fully conscious of the close connection between life and poetry, denying the possibility of producing or of judging poetry to those who were learned in rules and models of art, but had never known human passions in their own hearts, nor fought the fights of the will, who had never quivered or suffered, loved or hated. Polemic, against academical writers, against desk writers and " cloister men," against the schools of old Italy, runs all through his pages. His remedy for all this is the historical interpretation of poetry, of true poetry, which, since it nourishes itself with the passions and affections of man at various times, can only be understood in that way. He was romantic in this respect and romantic in the best sense, culminating in admiration of the " primitive poet "; but he was also classical, because he did not like " the sentimental tinge " so " often artificial " of modern writers, preferring the naturalness of the ancients " who described things as they saw them, without desiring to magnify them before the eyes of satiated readers " and placing " harmony " at the summit of art. He always preferred the energetic, sober and condensed style of the Greek writers to the easy, flowing style of the modern French, which " dissolves one thought into ten periods." He met the romantic theories of " national drama " and of " historical drama " with the remark that poetry is by no means bound to " national subjects " and does not know what to do with historical exactitude. He possessed the most powerful possible sense of poetic form, which is not external form agreeing with rules and models, and the sense of great poetry. This enabled him to judge of Dante's poetry and of that of other poets in a new manner; he perceived that much of what men of letters of his day were still calling poetry was not poetry at all, and that Italy was almost without poetry during the two centuries, so rich in verse, which elapsed between Tasso and Alfieri. He assigned to poetry and the arts the end of potentializing life and making man sensible of it, effecting what might be described as an internal " catharsis " or " æsthetic education." Imperfections, hesitations and omissions can be noted in his theories and critical studies, but main lines, as we have indicated them, remain clear.

The same holds good of his other doctrines, and particularly of his view of movement, agitation, passion, action, as the sole reality, which he did not flee from or depreciate, but accepted. We see him altogether possessed of the spirit of the new times, which places salvation in action, happiness in creation, between pain and pain. For this reason, agnostic, pessimist and almost materialist as he was, he yet maintained the value of history, thus contradicting himself in a significant manner. His ideal of history was objective and substantial history, not erudition, anecdote or historical instances. He recalled Italians to the study of history, and wished that these studies, together with poetry and the judgment of poetry, should be removed from the hands of monks and academicians and should be infused with humanity and a serious understanding of the subjects treated, himself setting the example. In politics he disdained to lend an ear to the babble of the crowd, ever ready to accept what may feed it with easy hopes, repeating in this connection the bitter truths of Machiavelli and of Hobbes, confirmed for him both by perusal of their histories and his own daily experience. He advised military training to the Italians, " the sole hope for our country," shaming them of those wordy invectives with which they adorned their ease and inertia. Bonaparte's rule he did not oppose, just because he held that he shook them out of their secular inertia and forced them into agitation and action. Austrian rule, on the contrary, was repugnant to him and aimed at soothing and lulling Italy to sleep. He held it to be a duty to take part in affairs of State and of his country, in opposition to the Epicureans and to other philosophical sects. Literature, too, was politics for him, inasmuch as he could not conceive of health in one part of social life without health in every other part of the organism. The theoretical justification of these practical and political views cannot, however, be regarded as strictly utilitarian, as might appear from certain philosophical conceptions which he had accepted, because he felt " compassion " welling up from the depths of the human soul, a compassion which in Vico's sense would be called " shame." He was not an " atheist," receiving, as he writes, support both from his own " conscience " and from " God " during the course of a life by no means exempt from error and from severe hardships.

If all Foscolo were to be found here in his practical life and in his critical and political writings, he would nevertheless be a great man, an educator of manly generations to come, a renovator of the criteria both of ethical and of artistic life, and founder of Italy's new literary criticism. But he was a poet, a very pure poet, author of few but perfect and eternal lines. We are sensible of his poetic soul in his prose also, especially his early prose, where the impetus of the poet is such as not to permit the deliberate balance of prose, although endowing it with force and colour. Sometimes, too, it will impede the logical disposition and proportioning of his theses, as, for instance, in the inaugural discourse on the function of literature. On one occasion he surprises himself in the midst of this shock of internal treasures, remarking in a letter : " I think this mode of writing prose comes from my having for so many weeks accustomed myself to think and to form images of my thoughts, singing them in my mind as though they were verses expressed in language quite different from prose." He added that " the Greeks and Latins were wiser when they devoted themselves entirely to verse or to prose and made no attempt as we do to embrace all trades." In this respect, Europe came to know, or knows Foscolo, in the very book which suffers most from this hybrid style, the juvenile *Ortis*. This very noteworthy book is not a simple literary imitation, but conveys, beneath the aspect of a literary imitation, important knowledge both of the author and of his times. It is a collocation of Foscolo's own thoughts and feelings during his first struggles in life. Its fault lies in an over-close realism of presentment of this world of thought and feeling, in its loudness of tone and hence in its rhetorical and emphatic form. Italian criticism has been in agreement on this point ever since the time when the book

first saw the light and the old man of letters Bettinelli
noted its extreme tension of feeling and of style
and its effort to interest and to move. It is well
to give an example or so in order to note clearly the
relation between *Ortis* and the later works. Foscolo's
various poetical motives are already all present here,
as, for instance, his longing for memory beyond and
upon the tomb. " Yet the hope that I may be
regretted," he writes, " comforts me . . . my grave
will be washed by thy tears, tears of that celestial
maiden. Who would ever yield this dear troublous
life of ours to eternal oblivion ? Who would ever
look upon the light of the sun for the last time, take
leave for ever of nature, who would abandon his
enjoyments, his hopes, his deceptions, his very sorrows
themselves, without leaving behind him a longing,
a sigh, a look ? Our dear ones whom we leave
behind are a part of us. Our dying eyes ask of others
a few drops of tearful sympathy, and our heart loves
that the body from which the latest breath has just
fled should be sustained in loving arms, and seeks a
breast on which to draw its last breath. Nature
laments ` even in the tomb, and the lamentation
conquers the silence and obscurity of death."

There is no doubt that Foscolo really moved in
such a circle of feelings as this, and that he was what
is called sincere. But he was only sincere here in the
general sense of the term, because he had not yet
found a spontaneous and beautiful form of expression,
and his sincerity thus remained in a way compromised,
because form and content should become identified.
In the instance here recalled to mind, he has recourse
to rhetorical argumentation reinforced with a couple
of interrogatives, instead of directly expressing the

emotion of the moment, and all this to demonstrate something that does not require demonstrating, thus giving proof of exaggerated sentiment both of phrase and of vocabulary (" some distillation of lament," " celestial maiden," etc.). This exaggeration cannot maintain itself, and the prosaic here and there becomes apparent, as in such expressions as " the recent corpse." But in the *Sepolcri*, where the same thought reappears, word and rhythm become spiritualized, and there " the correspondence of amorous senses " is effected and we scent on the breeze " the friendly tree odorous with flowers," which consoles the dust with " soft shadows," and the love-lorn woman prays, and the solitary passer-by hears the sigh, " which nature sends to us from the tomb." " Oh, Lorenzo "—he writes a few pages further on—" oh, Lorenzo, I often lie stretched out on the bank of the lake of the five springs : I feel my face and hair caressed by the little winds that move the grass in their passage, delighting the flowers and rippling the limpid waters of the lake. Can you believe it ? Delightfully delirious, I see before me the nude nymphs, leaping, crowned with roses, and I invoke Love and the Muses in their train, and I see the Naiads, lovable guardians of fountains issuing from them up to the breasts, their locks dripping upon dewy shoulders and with laughing eyes." That " can you believe it ? " clearly shows that the author himself knew he had not experienced the hallucination, and was merely trying to give emphatic narrative form to a longing which, poetic in its origin, yet required finer and more perfectly poetic form, such as are realized in some of the many pictures of similar subjects which Foscolo realized in the *Graces* and which we admire to-day. To cite the first verses that come to the memory, I mention those " amorous Nereids of ocean," who rise " with half the breast revealed," crowding around the Goddess Venus " shining on the surface of the vast waters."

We have said that Foscolo's poems are small in bulk, because we must certainly exclude the two tragedies, which he composed owing to that sort of attraction which the actual boards of the theatre with the crowd of spectators seem to exercise even upon great poets, as though it were a symbol of the other and greater theatre which they have in the hearts of the generations of mankind and which sometimes leads them astray towards what is external and does not correspond with their true inspiration. We must also exclude the bundle of juvenile verse, which the author himself had rejected, yet which the editors have had bad taste enough to unite in the volume of *Poems*, with the addition of some later utterances and partly unfinished and unfelicitous burlesque epistles.

For this reason, the true and proper poetry of Foscolo is reduced to fourteen sonnets, of which only a few are of first-rate quality, to two odes, to a pair of brief compositions in unrhymed hendecasyllabics, to the poem of the *Sepulchres*, and to the fragments of the *Graces*. As regards the *Sepulchres* and the *Graces*, we must further bear in mind the didactic presupposition which was accepted by Foscolo, and which perhaps had its origin in him from Vico's idea of the " primitive poet," a master of civil and religious life. To this was due the didacticism which insinuates itself into the lofty lyrical poetry of the *Sepulchres* and prevents the *Graces* from becoming more than sketches and fragments. Contemporary Italian literary criticism has given an excellent account of itself as regards these few poems, which can be verified by mentioning the recent studies of Donadoni, of Manacorda, and to Citanna's extremely subtle book. Certainly the spirit of Foscolo rejoices in these studies, finding in them that ultimate and mature form of criticism, both historical and artistic, vaunted by him and towards the attainment of which he was the first in Italy to show the way.

It would be useless to undertake here the analysis that has already been done excellently well, and the discussion of some details that are still open to discussion does not enter into the scope of these notes, which are rather directed to indicate the general characteristics of Foscolo's poetry. His poetry contains the most intense manifestations of his soul : from it (as he once remarked when speaking of certain particular poems) " flows without any exterior aid that ethereal liquid which dwells in every man," of which " nature and heaven " had accorded him his share.

Four fundamental themes are to be discerned in this poetry : Death, in commemorating which is summed up all melancholy; Heroism in which the value of the human will is asserted; Beauty, in which voluptuousness is present; Art and Imagination, which rescue human affections from death, making them immortal by pouring out upon them their balsam of eternity. These four themes are sometimes united and sometimes each one seems to rise above the others in turn, though they, too, are active or one feels them to be near at hand. These four themes are indeed inseparable, because they form the sole

motive of life in its direct reality, not weakened
by any thought of another world : they are life as
fully expressed in Love, Sorrow, Death, Immortality.
All that is one-sided and simply particular is here
abolished.   Is there perhaps in Foscolo that spasmodic
horror of death which is to be met with in so many
romantics and pre-romantics and amounts to desperate
rebellion ?   Death is reflected and takes form in the
image dear to him of the evening, of nocturnal
shadow wherein his war-like, trembling heart finds
assuagement and becomes softer, and everywhere
throughout the *Sepulchres* is present the severe accept-
ation of death.   But on the other hand, the feeling
for death as that which destroys colour and extin-
guishes vigour, common in other writers, is not to be
found there.   The words and accents in which he
sings the heroes of thought and action, voices his
joy in beauty and pleasure, paints modes and aspects
of feminine charm, or landscapes and scenes of
nature, and celebrates the virtue of Poetry, are those
of one who receives into his bosom all human passions,
fully abandons himself to them and uses them as a
means of self-expression.   His verse is beautiful with
that dolorous passionateness that is also joyous and
amorous, and flows together there so as to form a sweet
living being, soft and flexible, harmoniously resonant,
seductive in every movement.   The union of opposites is not with Foscolo a wise counsel of calm
philosophic serenity, but the complexity of a soul
richly endowed, which realizes all its riches.   Those
images that are the chilled material of thought
operative in its own sphere, or memory of past
conflicts, are not to be found in him : they are here
active, living drama, which adapts itself to its own

development.   The final impression is not separation
from life, but increased love of life : to think, to act,
to enjoy, to know how to die, trusting oneself to the
affection of the dear ones that remain and to the
hearts of the poets.

The classic quality of Foscolo does not reside in
his exquisite Græco-Latin culture nor in his love of
antique mythology, but in this whole-hearted feeling,
which ranks him among the great poets of the nineteenth century.   In order to make clear this essential
quality of his poetry, it will perhaps suffice to examine
the two extremes of his poetical production, the ode
to Pallavicini and the fragments of the *Graces*, the
former written in 1799, at the age of twenty-one,
the latter the posthumously published work of his
full maturity.   In the ode has been suspected a certain
tone of eighteenth-century gallantry and frivolity,
and in the *Graces* a presentiment of that sensuous
dilettantism which later became manifest in the poets
of the end of the nineteenth century, Italian and non-
Italian. In neither case is this true, despite appearances.
The ode to Pallavicini is also a hymn to Beauty, to the
graceful, amiable, voluptuous beauty which appealed
to his senses and to his imagination.   The lovely
woman reigns there, that queen of hearts, whom
he remembered as he used to meet her in Society,
shedding, as it were, an unwonted fragrance upon the
air, as she danced with a loose lock of her rebellious
hair falling upon her rosy arm, a gentle hindrance to
her progress, which she shook off with a graceful gesture.   We can still catch the sound of her harmonious
speech and feel the smiles, the acts and the gestures
which formed a conversation that breathed of love
and invited to love.   The poet, whose imagination

is full of antique images of beauty, irradiated with the effulgent figures of Hellenic goddesses and remembering clearly their schemes and adventures, conceives of the lovely Ligurian lady in the same manner, for no reason of frivolous gallantry, but because the women he meets and admires in the earthly round of existence revive and set in motion those images of divine beauty, and of such dreams and idolizations and exaltations is formed his love.

But the much admired beauty is in danger of being lost or is already lost : the fair lady has been thrown and dragged over stones by a runaway horse and now lies pale and exhausted in bed, anxiously scanning the faces of the doctors that she may read therein " the flattering hope of regaining her former beauty." This almost childish trepidation of the perpetual child that is woman here touches us as it does the poet, who realizes the fear and the hope of those glances and addresses words of caress and consolation to the anxious spirit, making pass before her gaze a splendid sequence of mythological pictures, which delight her with their lofty comparisons or lead her to hope with their tales of health renewed and of beauty triumphant. He interposes among these pictures a formal imprecation against the evil-minded one who made it the fashion for women to ride horses and thus provided " a new danger to beauty." A smile seems to float over the whole of this consolatory eloquence, but it is a smile of deeper origin than would appear at first sight, because, says the poet, beauty is destined to perish by misfortune, age and death; but lo ! I make it eternal, I who " paint and breathe an eternal soul into my visions " (as he will say later in the *Graces*), and the fair lady, whatever be her fate, is already smiling on the paper of the same ode that describes the catastrophe to her beauty and pretends to obtain its material restitution. And so she will smile in her eternally youthful freshness upon the generations to come. Far from being connected with the art of the gallant eighteenth century, this ode is closely linked with that which follows, entitled the *Friend Healed*, which presents the same emotional disposition in a new way, and repeats the magical–poetic process of creating life not destined to perish.

The like may be said of those landscapes of Zacinthus in the *Graces*, all redolent of orange blossom and flowering cypress, or of the hill of Bellosguardo, whence Galileo gazed upon the stars (" and the distant water flowed with a murmur in the night, passing beneath the poplars of Arno's banks furtive and silvery "). The magic process is repeated again for those visions of Venus caressing the Graces, while the Nereids sighingly regard them, and of Pallas, whose azure eyes rule over her virgin heart; of Psyche, who tells over again in her heart the story of her passion as she weaves with closed lips; of the harpist, who sheds harmony through the valleys, and when she ceases, " the hills still hear her "; or, again, of the dancer, from whose fair body and smile flows all harmony of sound as " she inspires with unexpected beauty a movement, a gesture, a caress "; or of the swan " who sails with wings of pure snow," and so on among many varied and marvellous evocations. Never, in any of these extracts that are truly fragments, is there anything of the fragmentariness of dilettantism, which, while it spreads itself out in breadth and enjoys its own virtuosity and appears very rich to the eye, is poor

in soul. Not only do human suffering and human
pity gaze forth from the midst of the smiles of the
Graces (hence even on the sail worked by them is
figured the dream of dawn that shows to the warrior
the faces of his father and mother in their anguish,
and as he arises, he "looks upon his prisoners and
sighs "); but one feels the whole of humanity at every
point, even where the charm of beauty and voluptuousness seems to dominate : " love promising joy
and sending sorrow ! " Classical line is steadily
maintained in the *Graces* also, where the affections
have that " modesty " which Foscolo deemed to be
inseparable from Love, as indeed it is inseparable
from true Poetry.

IX

1 BELIEVE that Sainte-Beuve, usually so measured in his utterances, was altogether in the wrong when he placed Stendhal's defect as a writer of fiction " in his having approached this style of composition through criticism and through following certain earlier presuppositions." Hence, in Sainte-Beuve's view, his characters are not " living beings, but ingeniously constructed automata, in which we notice almost at every moment the hinges that the mechanic has arranged and manipulates from without."

To begin with the latter assertion. Were it true, how are we to explain the fascination that emanates from the romances of Stendhal, the fact that once read, it is impossible to get the characters, actions and words of his personages out of one's mind, for they constantly insist upon returning and set the imagination and the mind to work ? Such a thing never occurs in the case of personages constructed by critical processes, for these at once disappear from the mind, or if they remain there, are cold and rigid, suggestive of nothing whatever. But Julien Sorel, Fabrice del Dongo, Madame de Rênal, Mathilde de la Môle, the Duchess Sanseverino, Count Mosca, Julien's seduction first of one and then of the other of his lady-loves, his life as tutor in the Rênals' house, his retreat to the seminary, the nocturnal visit that tears

Madame de Rênal away from her repentance and
religious fervour, and Fabrice at Waterloo, in love
with Marietta, prisoner in the castle of Parma, and
many other characters, scenes and episodes, have
about them that something of the unexpected, which
is life. Nor have I here to make appeal to those who
feel as I do and to unprejudiced readers or to fall
back upon my own personal taste, for all now see
the growing attraction of Stendhal's books, and the
great influence he has exercised upon the literature
of the latter years of the nineteenth century and of
our own days, the curiosity aroused by every page of
his which sees the light for the first time, and every
new anecdote about his life. As regards the last
statement, if it is to be attributed to the fashion of the
moment, we must not forget that the fashion does not
yield its favours, however capricious, without some
definite reason.

Passing now to Sainte-Beuve's other statement,
where indeed are the " ideas " upon which Stendhal
is supposed to have founded his romances ? Sainte-
Beuve speaks of " two or three ideas, which Stendhal
believes to be true and above all stimulating, and is
bent upon recalling at every step." Does he mean
the " energy," the " passion," the " utility," of which
so much is said in these works ? But one sees at
once on reading any one of the stories, and even from
Sainte-Beuve's own mention above quoted, that these
are not thoughts but feelings of Stendhal, his loves,
his fanaticisms. I shall not tire of repeating that the
" ideas," that is to say the philosophical strength, of
an author are commensurable with his critical and
systematic spirit. By critical I mean the extent to
which he takes count of difficulties and objections,

H

and by systematic, the extent to which he links together the various propositions and reduces them to unity. What is neither critical nor systematic may apparently resemble an idea, while it is in reality a feeling. To me, indeed, this great labour devoted to the practical philosophy and to the politics of Stendhal, or to his judgments and characterizations of famous individuals and peoples, and above all of Italy, seems to be labour lost. The substance of his critical writing, of his place descriptions, of his histories of painting and literature, is the same as that of his fiction. The Italy which he depicts as a writer of fiction and a historian is always the Italy of his dream, or rather his dream in garment of Italy. (Needless to say the inevitable " professors " who like to talk about art have condemned the *Chartreuse de Parme*, because it portrays an Italy that has never existed, and less than ever in 1830). That Stendhal noted real facts and observed true aspects here and there or to a great extent is quite beside the point, because such facts and aspects belong to a whole which is not critical but imaginative.

Stendhal, then, was not a theorist of energy and passion and expediency, but a lover of those things; in other words, he was obsessed by them and for this reason, far from being unpoetical of soul, he was in the highest degree poetical, by which I mean that he was naturally adapted for artistic creation. To understand the true nature of his art, we must therefore have a clear conception as to the conformation of this love of his, a conformation already in a way expressed in the words we have employed. Stendhal's soul was not energetic, utilitarian and passionate, but, in his own words, enamoured of these attitudes and dispositions; and since attitudes and dispositions taken in themselves are generic, he was enamoured of empty forms lacking determination and concreteness.

For what is the content of the passion, of the utilitarian spirit and of the energy, towards which he turned with so keen a desire ? Stendhal had no political ideals nor any desire for political activity or reform of any sort. Even the Napoleon whom he idealized was empty of all Napoleonic idea, purely and simply a " professor of energy." Nor must we believe that if great human ends failed to make his heart beat, he therefore felt the shock and the burning breath of personal desire for such narrowly utilitarian ends as wealth and power as means to self-enjoyment. It is altogether a mistake to compare his ideal with that of Casanova (whose *Memoirs* were for a time attributed to Stendhal). Casanova aimed at something solid and definite and was logical in his own way, which lay in the direction of deceiving the credulous and of gathering flowers and fruit in the gardens of Cythera. This it was that pleased him and this he described with perfect coherence and in the most vivid colours in his autobiography. All this was wanting to Stendhal, who was unable to experience a profound passion for anything, owing to this lack of true utilitarian as of ethical motives. Passions begin for him as though they were a game, an experiment, a means of killing time; they serve as a mere distraction to one in whom it would appear that they should altogether dominate. Stendhal, although he discourses of love and cherishes so keen an admiration for calm resolve in its practice and for the extreme measures adopted by Italians, yet is never really dominated by it at heart; love does not colour his thought and feelings as in the case of true lovers.

Whether we describe it as formal or generic, Stendhal's ideal remains most contradictory and confused, because, while it appears that he does not conceive of any other mode of energy and passion save that belonging to individual self-gratification, he yet attributes to this self-gratification a degree of greatness, an heroic quality, due only to the loftier modes of moral energy. Again, while he seems sometimes to be aware of the difference between energy and passion and makes Fabrice remark that " a being who is half stupid but attentive and always on his guard very often has the satisfaction of getting the better of men of imagination," yet he generally makes them identical and concordant. Here, of course, he is wrong, for they are intrinsically opposed, because true energy is not different from passion reduced to will, the will dominating passion, and when energy throws itself open to passion, it becomes weak to a proportionate extent, ending in ceasing to be energy but its contrary, lack of energy or weakness.

Stendhal was thus the first, or one of the first, to formulate the false notion so often repeated since his day, to the effect that truly energetic characters are to be found among criminals, galley-slaves and convicts (he refers to the penal institution at Civita Vecchia when he was Consul in that town). He draws the characters of his fiction after two fundamental types, that of the cold, calculating, tenacious and dissembling priest, who never allows himself to be diverted from his end, and of the man of inflammable imagination, who becomes blind with anger and is carried away in the whirlwind of passion, and has recourse to sword and pistol, losing in an instant all he had won at the price of prolonged efforts. He unites these types in a single individual in both his principal personages, Julien Sorel and Fabrice del Dongo, both alike destined for the priesthood, both violent and homicidal in the most untimely and maddest way.

If Stendhal's ideal or fount of inspiration be held clearly in mind—heroism that is not really heroism but mere empty energy and passion is in a position to render prompt justice to the censures usually directed to his method of constructing his romances. Faguet, for instance, holds that the beginning and mode of development in *Le Rouge et le Noir* are altogether sound, but that the solution arrived at is accidental and therefore false and insignificant. He thinks that the author should have decided upon one of two possible logical solutions : " either Julien should marry Mathilde with her father's consent and become little by little an aristocrat, hard and cruel to his inferiors ; or he should marry Mathilde against her father's wishes and drag her down with him into the depths and they should become an unclassed, envious, bitter and rebellious couple." Now either one of these suggested solutions would imply in Stendhal an ethico-social sentiment which he altogether lacked, and for this reason he would only have been able either to make of Julien a sort of anticipatory Rabagas, or describe the perversion and corruption of an energy without moral character, and, in fact, write quite a different story from that which he did write, because the new solution would have required new premisses, a new mode of development and a new style.

With greater semblance of truth it might be maintained that Stendhal's ideal, since it was abstract and contradictory, should have given rise, not to a positive and serious representation, but to one of a negative and satirical nature, to a sort of Don Quixote of mere energy. Such a contention would find support in many passages of Stendhal's fiction, where irony seems to be making way. For instance, the notion of taking this or that historical or literary character as a model, which we find in the case of Stendhal's personages, is ironical and quixotic. For Don Quixote it was Amadis of Gaul or the Knight Esplandian, for Julien and Fabrice it is Napoleon. Thus Julien compares himself at every step with the portrait of Napoleon and consults the *Memorial of Saint Helena;* and when he accomplishes successfully a small stage in his career of seducer, " à force de songer aux victoires de Napoléon," he finds something new in his own victory. " Oui, j'ai gagné une bataille—se dit-il,—mais il faut en profiter, il faut écraser l'orgueil de ce fin gentilhomme pendant qu'il est en retraite. C'est là Napoléon tout pur." And on another occasion of a like sort :   " Il faut—se dit-il—que je tienne un journal de siège : autrement j'oublierais mes attaques." Fabrice invokes and promises in a similar strain : " O roi d'Italie, cette fidélité que tant d'autres t'ont jurée, je te la garderai après ta mort !" And Mathilde de la Môle has her own model in the person and life of her ancestor, Olivier de la Môle, who is for her the type of amorous energy of the age of the Renaissance, presenting the other aspect of Stendhal's two historical admirations, Napoleon and the erotic, blood-stained Italian or Italianate Cinquecento. Her love for Julien is an imitation of the latter, culminating in her obtaining the head of her lover Julien, dissevered from the body, and carrying it about with her, just as Marguerite de Valois, " la Reine Margot," had done in former days. " This idea," says Stendhal himself, " transported her to the best days of Charles IX and of Henri III." The insistence upon his *grands exploits*, the rigid feeling for duty of Julien, when engaged upon his very mean operations as a seducer, might also be described as ironical. Ironical, too, that continual self-questioning of Fabrice in search of love as to whether what he has experienced be really love, and even the magnificent episode of Waterloo could be described as ironical, when all the details and incidents seem to be directed to contrast dream and everyday life, ideal and reality, poetry and prose, for here, too, Fabrice asks himself : Have I truly taken part in a battle ? In the battle of Waterloo ?

We might therefore conclude that the inner and outer sense of Stendhal's romances is irony. Their fault in this case would be, not, where Sainte-Beuve sought it, in the critical construction, but, on the contrary, in the lack of critical construction, namely, that this irony is not made sufficiently clear and is capriciously repressed or contradicted by the author, who should have allowed free motion to the events narrated and have arranged for them to develop their own dramatic elements.

But this interpretation also would be wrong in supposing Stendhal to be something different from what he was and could be in his own day : it would be the substitution of a counter-Stendhal, such as we are now able to conceive, after a century of Stendhalism or Beylism and of the gospel of energy. The citations ticketed as ironical are not so save in our logical and ethical judgment; taken in themselves, or in the complex whole to which they belong, they are perfectly serious. Stendhal is at the most a Don Quixote, who "undertakes to tell of himself," and does not find the sublime or the extraordinary, but is always seeking it, and in doing so falls into the grotesque, but takes no notice of it.

It is impossible to correct the romances of Stendhal, as Faguet maintained, by altering this or that part of them, nor can we change their tone without imparting to them an altogether different quality of thought, which further implies their present form, as the parody implies the thing parodied. Disproportionate, accidental, intermittent as they appear to be in their texture, they yet show themselves upon close inspection as necessary and natural forms of Stendhal's ideal.

This ideal was not ironical, but on the contrary serious, though lacking ethical or passionate seriousness and consisting rather of a troublous and disunited desire for great things, for the display of energy and passion. Stendhal objectified himself in all his books, but more intensely in his two greatest works of fiction, and portrayed nothing other than that boundless desire in the characters of Fabrice del Dongo and of Julien Sorel, who are indeed one and the same person twice presented and in two different environments, or rather in two different decorative backgrounds. But seeing that this desire was unbounded and what is called egoistic or egotistic, lacking passion with a definite object and swaying and rebounding from one extreme to another, from reflective energy to savage impulse, from the figure of the Machiavellian prelate to that of the romantic knifer and shooter, it was altogether impossible for Stendhal to place it in an action of definite outline, meaning or logic. He found it necessary to leave it free to create the suitable representation in a kind of romance which is more full of adventures than romances of adventure, where things change but the character of the protagonist remains constant. Here, on the contrary, the protagonist himself proceeds in zigzags and abounds in sudden and unexpected movements. And since, on the other hand, Stendhal's state of mind was a real state of mind and not a cold conceit or construction of the intellect, we come to understand how it is that in these strange stories his personages attain to and preserve the vivacity proper to creations of the passionate imagination.

The true hero is Stendhal himself, with his impetus, at once sublime and ridiculous, toward passion and energy, with his instantaneous rising to fever heat and his no less sudden chilling off. For Stendhal possessed a sort of double soul, one part watching the other at work and registering results, one imagining and thinking, the other criticising the thinking and imagining. This condition would to-day be looked upon as a form of nervous affection, and there can be no doubt that it is unharmonious and implies division of personality.

Behold him in the vestments of Julien, when at last he clasps Madame Rênal in his arms : " Instead of being attentive to the transports of which he was the cause, or to the remorse which increased their poignancy, the idea of duty never ceased to be present to his eyes. He feared terrible remorse and eternal ridicule, if he were to swerve from the ideal model of action which he had decided to carry out In one word, what made of Julien a superior being was precisely what prevented his enjoying the beauty which lay there before him."

And here we see him again in the scene where he wins back Mathilde by means of showing coldness :

" His arms grew stiff, so painful was the effort which his policy imposed upon him.—' I must not allow myself to press this supple and charming body against my heart, for if I do, she will despise and ill-treat me. . . .' "

And again :

" ' Ah ! if she love me eight days, only eight days,' said Julien to himself in a low voice, ' I shall die of bliss. What does the future matter to me, what does life matter ? And this divine bliss can begin at this moment, if I wish, it depends only upon me ! ' "

Mathilde saw him pensive :

" ' So I am quite unworthy of you,' she said, as she took his hand.

" Julien embraced her, but at the same instant, duty's iron hand gripped his heart.—' If she sees how I adore her, I shall lose her. . . .' "

We cannot be sure if there be passion here or no, in this constant watching and measuring of every action. Elsewhere, speaking of his love affair with Mathilde, he says :

" These transports were indeed rather forced. Passionate love was still rather a model to be imitated than a reality."

And Fabrice never succeeds in discovering whether he is really in love or not, as we have already remarked :

" ' But is it not really most amusing,' he used sometimes to say to himself, ' that I am not susceptible to
that exclusive passionate preoccupation which they
call love? Among all the affairs that chance set in
my way at Novara and Naples, have I ever met a
woman whose presence, even in the first days of
acquaintance, was more agreeable than a first ride
upon a good horse? Is what they call love also a
lie?' he added. 'I love, no doubt, in the same
way that I am hungry at six o'clock! Can it be this
rather vulgar inclination that those liars have turned
into Othello's or Tancred's love? Or must I look
upon myself as built differently from most other men?
Does my soul lack one of the passions, and if so,
why? It would be a singular thing!' "

This doubt, joined to the pleasure, the *amusement*
of defying her lover's wrath, her lover, " whose
aspect was more alarming than that of an ex-drill-
sergeant," is the only motive for his courtship and
for his wish to possess the beautiful singer Fausta.
" Is this love at last? " he asks himself; and the girl
herself has a sort of instinctive fear of him, intuitively
aware of his peculiar feelings. Meanwhile Fabrice
" was retained only by a lingering hope of arriving
at experiencing what is known as love; but he often
bored himself."

Boredom, subtle boredom, circulates in the veins
of Stendhal's hero. And for this reason, the more
he wishes his acts to be calculated, the more accidental they become. Fabrice fights with his unworthy
antagonist Giletta, who has assaulted him : but why
does he proceed to kill him?

" The combat seemed to have relaxed a little its

intensity : the blows did not follow one another with the same rapidity, when Fabrice said to himself : ' I feel a pain in my face, he must have disfigured me.'—Enraged at the thought of this, he sprang upon his enemy with the point of his hunting-knife directed at him. . . ."

Fabrice is sent for by the Archbishop in the midst of his experiments in love and politics, profane and ecclesiastical. The Archbishop opens the way to preferment in the church by nominating him his vicar substitute. Is this a thing which he truly had much at heart ?

" Fabrice hastened to the palace of the Archbishop. He was simple and modest, a tone he adopted with too much facility ; he needed on the contrary to make efforts in order to play the part of a young aristocrat. As he listened to the rather lengthy disquisitions of Monseigneur Landriani, he said to himself : ' Ought I to have fired a pistol at the valet who held the thin horse by the bridle ? ' His reason told him yes, but his heart could not accustom itself to the picture of the handsome young man falling from his horse bleeding and disfigured.

" ' Is the prison into which I should have fallen if the horse had moved the same prison with which I am menaced by so many signs ? '

" This question was of the utmost importance for Fabrice, and the Archbishop was pleased with his air of profound attention."

During his imprisonment, the announcement is made to him of his father's death and he bursts into uncontrollable tears :

" When the judges had retired, Fabrice wept a great deal more, then he said to himself : ' Am I a hypocrite ? It seemed to me that I did not love him.' "

He takes a certain interest in the new love affair which he begins with the youthful Clelia, as Julien had done with Madame de Rênal. But the woman is again this time more passionate than her lover. Most subtle observations abound here :

" She had great reason for shame on the eighth day of Fabrice's imprisonment : she watched the blind which covered the prisoner's window with fixity, absorbed in her sad thought; he had shown no sign of his presence that day. All of a sudden a small bit of the blind not bigger than the hand was drawn aside by Julien, who looked at her smiling and she saw his eyes were greeting her. She could not withstand this unexpected trial, and turned quickly to attend to her birds; but she trembled to the extent of upsetting the water she was giving them and Fabrice was perfectly well able to observe her emotion; she could not endure the situation and took the course of running away out of sight."

And Fabrice, who had for so many years been under the charm of his most beautiful, majestic and intelligent aunt, the Duchesse de Sanseverino, suddenly feels the charm growing less, after the image of the girl had got possession of his imagination. But would it always remain thus lessened ?

" One night Fabrice began thinking rather seriously about his aunt; he was astonished to find himself hardly able to recognize her portrait, so completely had his memory of her changed; she was fifty for him now."

Here lie the force and beauty of Stendhal's art, in this rendering of his own self with his empty aspirations and the involuntary ironies arising from them, with his illusions and delusions, his coherences and his incoherences. He thus succeeds in not claiming to be more than he is, a sufferer from his nerves, a sufferer who cured himself by telling about himself, because his narrative is always most limpid. If he had also been diseased in his art, he would have needed what has since been several times observed, a refined style, "artistic writing," and other such things. But the style of everyday conversation, simple and unadorned, sufficed him, and it is well known that he claimed to have used the prose of the *Code Civile* as his model.

X

LEOPARDI

THE dolorous spirit of the Italian poet Giacomo Leopardi was very soon placed in the pleiad of those other tortured and disconsolate spirits who had appeared everywhere since the end of the eighteenth century and had sung the funereal song of despair to the human race bound to wander henceforth in a universe without a God. It seems impossible to avoid taking count of this furrow of sorrow and of nobility which he wore upon his forehead as a sign whereby kindred souls should know him, if we are to understand aright the rapid formation and diffusion of his glory as a poet. Leopardi was indebted above all to the emotional elements contained in his poetry for his effortless triumph over obstacles, which would otherwise have prevented a writer such as he, of classical education, of classical and learned vocabulary and of classical modesty, from succeeding in that period of fervid literary romanticism. For the tendency was then towards the popular on the one hand and on the other toward the unbridled, the disproportionate, the facile and the verbose, also in Italy. It was due to their emotional and pessimistic content that Leopardi's poems brought him European notoriety and esteem when, owing to hide-bound prejudice, it was believed that nothing of universal value could appear in provincial Italy. From that time onward his name shines among the poets and poetical personages who represent " the sorrow of the world," Werther, Oberman and René, Byron, Lénau, De Vigny, Musset and the rest; and since the systematic philosopher of pessimism paid homage to the Italian pessimist, he was ranged alongside of Arthur Schopenhauer. Comparisons and parallels between Leopardi and Byron, Leopardi and Lenau, Leopardi and De Vigny, Leopardi and Schopenhauer, and others, have provided the theme for countless essays and dissertations.

During the period of the Italian Risorgimento Leopardi was " the poet of the young men," of the youthful liberals who were preparing war and revolution. This is not to be wondered at when we consider the passionate link between emotional romanticism and national sentiment in Italy, the generous discontent and the generous longing for better days, the sorrow of the world and the sorrow of our Italy. For this reason and setting aside the properly patriotic poems of Leopardi, the young men felt that such a man as he was one of them, almost in virtue of that very pessimism of his, and that " if destiny had prolonged his life till the 1848," they would have found him at their side, " comforter and combatant." Yet the very young man of them who said this, destined to become a remarkable critic in later years, after having venerated Leopardi as the bringer of the truth and a master of life, perceived, in 1850, that it was no longer a time to doubt, to imprecate and to moan, that human sorrow is the " seed of liberty," that suffering is necessary, but in acting and in hoping, and that for this reason " Leopardi must be set aside," Leopardi, master of life.

And we too must set him aside in respect of
the new and attenuated form which that erroneous
and deceptive notion has assumed, of Leopardi as a
very great thinker, whose arguments and doctrines
should have their place in the history of philosophy.
The sense of delusion produced by the publication
of Leopardi's *Correspondence* will be fresh in many
minds. So these doctrines (it was said), to which we
had attributed speculative value, were nothing but
the reflection of the sufferings and unhappiness of
the individual? So they were merely reflections of
the infirmities with which he was afflicted, of family
restrictions and cramped economic conditions, of
vain longings for the love of a woman who would
none of him?

But there was no true reason for awaiting these
biographical or autobiographical revelations in order
to become aware of the quality of Leopardi's speculation. Whenever and inasmuch as philosophy is
pessimistic or optimistic, it is always intrinsically
pseudo-philosophy, philosophy for private use, for
the reason that everything can become the object of
approbative or disapprobative judgments, good or
evil can be uttered of everything, except of reality
and life, which itself creates and uses for its own ends
the categories of good and evil. Hence praise
attributed to or blame inflicted upon reality has no
other foundation than that of a movement of passion,
occasioned by good or bad humour, by cheerfulness,
lightsomeness, intolerance, caprice, by favourable or
unfavourable happenings. True and serious philosophy neither weeps nor smiles, but is concentrated
upon the investigation of the forms of being, the
activity of the spirit; its progress is marked by the

I

ever richer, more varied and definite consciousness that the spirit acquires of itself. The philosophers who call themselves optimistic or pessimistic draw their sole importance as philosophers from, let us say, the logical or ethical or other such contributions which they make to philosophy outside and beyond their pessimistic or optimistic attitudes. That is their only claim to enter into the history of thought, which is always the history of science and criticism.

But Leopardi makes only a slight contribution to philosophy thus understood, and his observations are scattered, lacking depth and system. He thus stands outside creative philosophy, being without speculative tendencies or training. He also arrived at no new, closely thought-out truth of importance in the theory of poetry and of art, although he was led to meditate more than once upon their nature. " Are the things I say " (he asked naïvely in the dialogue of Timander and Eleander about those questions of evil and suffering) " leading truths or are they merely accessories ? " He replies to himself with the remark that " the substance of all philosophies is to be found in them." A like error is committed by the many who to-day deplore in solemn philosophemes life as sorrowful and life as evil and believe that they are thus philosophizing and, what is more, philosophizing as to the highest truths. Were this the case, philosophy would have accomplished its task many centuries ago, indeed ever since man was man, because such emotional propositions have always been uttered by man and belong to the common stock.

It is also well here to dispose of another exaggeration, which appeared at the moment of the publication of the *Zibaldone*, in which Leopardi was in the habit of annotating his thoughts over a period of years. There can be no doubt that much is to be learned from Leopardi in relation to the practice of the art of literature, especially in our days, when the discipline of writing has been so much neglected; but there is as much to be learned from other writers who, like him, studied their art, and to quote one of them of equal stature, I may mention Foscolo, as well as another who abhorred him and whom he abhorred, Tommaseo, profoundly versed, however, in the secrets of style and of language. Others, too, there are of lesser build, such as Cesari and Puoti, exact and subtle-minded, as purists are wont to be, and much, too, is to be learned in other ways from Manzoni and his followers.

All were masters and models in something, none a master or model in an absolute sense, because Leopardi could not be a " model " to anyone but himself (this is clear), and anyone who wishes to avoid being merely a commonplace imitator must create of himself and for himself his own model. Utterly vain are therefore the disputes which have arisen as to the direction which Leopardi is supposed to have indicated to Italian literature, but which has not been followed and which should now be followed. Leopardi's language and style suited him well; but since they could not be adopted by his contemporary Manzoni, because Manzoni's spirit was not that of Leopardi, this proved equally impossible for the generations of Verga and of Carducci which followed.

The above remarks have had for object, as is my wont, to eliminate problems either without existence or extraneous to the consideration of Leopardi's poetry, which is the only subject that occupies us here. It is rather a question, however, of returning to the study of this poetry, so closely and subtly studied in Italy, and especially by that youthful patriot of the '48, Francesco De Sanctis, who was among the very first to place it very high and to link it to the movement of European poetry.[1] He resumed his studies of the " poet beloved of my youth " when he was an old man and near his end, and began to write a book about him, which is among his most profoundly meditated and accurate works, but unfortunately is only half completed. Since De Sanctis, the critical examination of Leopardi's poetry has not been neglected and has given good fruit of late years. Nevertheless, there yet remains something to be said as to the general character of his art, and it is worth while stating briefly the point of view from which this poetry will be understood and judged.

What was Leopardi's life ? By this I mean the spiritual process through which man expresses and shapes his own feelings, defines and particularizes his own thought, asserts his aspirations in action, and in a general way develops the germ which he bears within him, realizing more or less completely, yet substantially, his own ideal. To employ a crude but expressive metaphor, his was a strangled life.

As a young man Leopardi was trained with the utmost care and ardour to become a philologist, learned in language, literature and classical antiquity; it was hoped that he would find a place beside the Titans of these studies, such as Mai and Borghesi, perhaps even Niebuhr, Müller and Böckh. He

---

[1] See what De Sanctis says on this subject in his autobiography, and particularly in his lectures of 1842, edited by me in the *Critica*, xiv. pp. 22–25.

sought and awaited the joys of love with the trembling
of a heart open to the noblest enthusiasms and love
of country and humanity, and one feels the gradual
birth in him of poetry in these various encounters
with life, though the dream-world was the most
important factor in this development. But in the
midst of the first ravishment of love and glory, he is
oppressed, bound down and overpowered by a brutal
force, named by him " Enemy Nature," which broke
up his studies, forbade the very beatings of his heart,
and threw him back upon himself, that is to say,
upon his physical basis, obliging him to struggle
every day to support or to alleviate his ill-being and
the physical pains which ruthlessly tormented him.

There was no intellectual significance in his final
abandonment of philological studies, marked by his
handing over his volumes of youthful notes to De
Sinner. Here there was no question, as there might
be for others, of abandoning one sphere of work for
another sphere, offering wider or at least different
opportunities. No, it was due to the imperious
bidding of his eyes, which no longer performed their
office and rendered continuous methodical work
impossible. The same sad necessity, with, in addition, money difficulties, decided his troublous mode
of life, his changing of dwelling-place in search of
more suitable physical and moral conditions and of
work not too ill-adapted to his state of health. Thus
he was always trying new arrangements, none of which
proved satisfactory, obtaining only occasionally and
rarely some respite, an endurable interval during
which he could breathe tranquilly even for a brief
period.

Think by contrast of other lives, not of those of

calm, happy folk, but of such a one as Foscolo's, so full of storms and so heavily weighted with tasks to be performed. Yet it is evident that Foscolo lived and developed, while poor Leopardi did not. The solemn movement of history which brings the whole drama of humanity before the soul of man and moves it to admiration or enthusiasm; sublime philosophy which searches out the human soul, illuminating with its own internal light the dark places and the mysteries of the universe, making reality comprehensible; politics where history is created anew by love and strife; love and the family, which perpetually restore childhood and youth to the world; these and all other forms of human activity were out of his reach, extraneous, far distant : their joys and sorrows were not for him. " A human trunk endowed with feeling and thought," Leopardi was tied to himself, to his physical body alone, given over to the elementary problem of breathing and living. And when he did experience some alleviation, when it became possible for him to resume for a few hours or days some sort of activity, the only possible material which offered itself for contemplation and meditation could not be anything but his own troublous condition, which had become for him a prison in which he was locked up and whence he no longer hoped to issue forth.

Hence it was that the lament for what might have been, yet might not be, for the promise that Nature had not kept, constantly inspired his work. Gradually he arrived at an intellectual judgment, which eventually took the form of a philosophical theory, as to the evil, sorrow, vanity and nullity of existence. This was itself, as we have said, really a lamentation, a sense of bitterness, a masked expression of feeling, a reasoned projection of his own unhappy state. His spiritual horizon was limited to this complaint, to this theory of lamentation and of accusation. The sole fount of inspiration of his imagination, the sole centre of his thoughts, lay in the contemplation and reflection upon this mystery of suffering.

Leopardi has sometimes been looked upon as a poet-philosopher, a point of view which we have shown to be inexact in his case, as it is always inexact in the case of every poet. His fundamental condition of spirit was not only emotional and not philosophical, but it might be defined as an emotional absorption, a vain longing of so desperate a nature, so violent and condensed, as to overflow into the sphere of thought and determine concepts and judgments. Thus, whenever that tendency of soul in him forgot its true nature and comported itself as though it occupied a reasoned doctrinal position and gave forth criticism, polemic, or satire, that part of Leopardi's work which is to be frankly recognized as vitiated made its appearance. Such are the majority of the *Operette morali* and in verse particularly *Palinodia* and *Paralipomeni*.

He had got himself into a blind alley as regards doctrine, engaged in a useless strife. He held that life was an evil and should be lived with the bitter consciousness of this radical evil; but he found other men around him who viewed the matter otherwise than he, because they felt in a different way and were able to dispose of their physical powers, their nerves were calm, their minds well balanced, and the joy of living dominated and animated them. They enjoyed the smiles of hope, were burning for action, drunken with love, and as for sorrows and adversities they resisted them by placing them among the inevitable difficulties to be dealt with, when they were free of them, and when they did arise faced and overcame them. They did not think of death, thus obeying the ancient saying, that death does not concern the living, because they are alive, nor the dead, because they are dead. It was such men as these that Leopardi would have wished to persuade that they were wrong and that they should join him in despairing. But there is no reasoning possible with feeling.

Years ago one might have read an inscription outside a little rustic dwelling in the Tyrol to the following effect (the German verses may still be in their place for aught I know); they ran as follows : " I am living, but for how long ? I shall die, without knowing where nor when. I go I know not whither and I am astonished that I am so gay in spite of all that. Lord Christ, protect my house ! "

Leopardi was not astonished, but he was angry that men should be so gay in spite of all that. He called them cowards and tried to confound, to shame and to convert them, that is to say, to infuse into them in the form of arguments his personal state of soul, having recourse, with this object in view, to irony, sarcasm and the grotesque. Those among the *Operette morali* with this mission were necessarily altogether frigid : they contain vain attempts to produce comic effects (which cheerfulness and serenity of the imagination can alone produce, not the spirit of strife and ill-humour); their characters are nothing but names; their dialogues are monologues; their language, although extremely laboured, has no depth and often smacks of academical vain parlance.

In verse and prose he mocked the faith of the new age, the incessant growth and broadening of the human spirit, progress; he mocked at liberalism and attempts at reform and revolution, at economic and social studies, and at the philosophy of the new times, which was beginning to see the light among the great thinkers of Germany; he mocked at philology, which allowed itself to break through traditional groupings and to discover relationships between Indo-European languages, and indeed at every single thing which gave signs of vitality, of ardour or of invention. At times, when reading the dialogues of the *Operette morali*, certain other *Dialogetti*, tinged with the reactionary colour of Count Monaldo's pen, keep returning persistently to the mind (and I am not the first to have experienced this impression, for I now see that Pascoli also had done so). One is sensible of the likeness, not only in a common literary predilection for that academic style, for the so much-abused imitations of Lucian, for those " News from Parnassus," but also, in their narrowness of spirit, their obstinate, reactionary tone, their antipathy for what is new and living. One feels as though one were assisting at the apparition of the vision to the eyes of Renzo, when the lineaments of the features of Gervasio appeared upon those of the sick and raving Tonio, where " the plague, which had taken from him all vigour both of body and of mind, had at the same time revealed in his face and in his every gesture a small concealed germ of resemblance to his enchanted brother."

There is something unhealthy in that prose and in those palinodes and paralipomena. De Sanctis himself was led to talk of the " evil laughter " which one hears in its pages and of the " dagger thrusts," which the writer tries to give, " with the joy of an avenger," and of " unfriendliness for the human race," in which one is " the man refused by fate."

And here we may well pause a moment to consider the wonted lack of understanding which exalts such writings as these to the position of works of pure imagination, thought and art. But let us hasten to add that the " evil laughter," the bursting forth of rage, is really to be placed to the account of that most cruel stepmother of Leopardi, Nature, to the account of Leopardi sick (Ranieri's book, more realistic than is generally admitted, refers to this), and if it obliges us to certain critical reservations, yet constrains us to human pity, and, in any case, is incapable of altering our already recorded admiration for the nobility of Leopardi's character. The scoffer at liberals had all his friendships among liberals, the contemner of mankind had no other longing than to love and to be loved. Ah, if one ray of sunlight had chased out of his blood the poisonous malady, dissolved the torpor which aggravated it ! He would have at once gone out afoot and with astonishment yet greater than that which he sung in the *Risorgimento*, would have looked upon the world with new eyes and seen the dark clouds of his imagination disappear in the distance, while the powers of creative application, crushed down in his sickly body, would have spread themselves abroad in generous abundance.

If, therefore, we wish to discover the pure, healthy Leopardi writing as an artist, we must seek him, not in his polemical, ironic and satirical moods, with their echo of evil laughter, but where he expresses himself seriously and is really moved. This Leopardi

is to be found in certain places among the same
Operette, such as, for instance, in certain pages of the
Timander and Eleander, so much akin in tone to the
best letters of the *Epistolario*. In this connection,
we must observe that the question that has been
mooted and is still in the air concerning Leopardi's
" prose," which by some is held to be of classical,
marmoreal quality, by others artificial, and as to
which others again dispute whether it suits or does
not suit Italian literature—is in the last clause without
meaning and in the two former ill stated. Leopardi's
prose is indubitably vicious where the conception
itself and the tone are wrong, and where he is found
making vain efforts and borrows false graces, but it
is most beautiful where it is truly founded upon
thought.

Here and there also in the *Paralipomeni*, in strident
contrast with the rest of the poem, Leopardi relaxes
his tone of ironic tension and forced merriment, and
expresses himself with simplicity, as in the well-
known octaves on Italy or in the apostrophe to the
beauty of Virtue, verses which remain in the memory.
Yet, in addition to the criterion of diffidence as to
Leopardi polemist and ironist, we must retain yet
another in mind, relating particularly to Leopardi
when he is serious and moved, to the Leopardi quite
full of his sorrow and of his sorrowful thought.

There can be no denying that this condition of
spirit, since it is the extreme point and conclusion of
an internal process, has something in it of the static.
For this reason, it presents itself as a dogma believed
and inculcated in its objective form, and in its subjective form, as though it were an epigraph upon his
own life, henceforth closed. It would seem that

here too there can be no true lyrical quality, which must always be epic and dramatic in its nature as well as lyrical, a multiplicity assembling itself to form a unity, an external world discovering itself as an internal world.   The exposition of a series of thoughts, of a pessimistic catechism, and the assertion of a desperate resignation, of a renouncement or of a denial, are this side of or beyond poetry.

For this reason, there is a large amount of didacticism in Leopardi's poetry; scattered more or less everywhere with its prosaic tone, sometimes even filling an entire composition such as the *Epistola al Pepoli*, or almost a whole composition, such as the *Ginestra*.   To compare it with Dante's didacticism in the *Paradiso* is a mistake, because it frequently resembles rather the tone of Dante's verses on nobility and other such themes, when he abandoned the sweet rhymes of love to which he was wont to attune his thoughts.   Such are the verses of the *Ginestra* : " A noble nature is that which burns to rise higher," etc. At other times, the didactic tone is dropped and it is rather an oration, an indictment, a series of questions such as are put to an accused person whose place is taken by nature, virtue, the mystery of things—such as in the *Bruto* or in the *Canto notturno*.

Not less frequently also, we find in Leopardi the assertion of suffering as a historical fact, a recognition or repetition that such is the case.   This is manifested in a certain dryness of tone, in summary fleshless diction, which are not life itself in action, but the reflection of life as in a compendium, its reduction to the conceptual form.   The brief poem *A se stesso* may serve as an instance of this epigraphical style, which it does not seem possible to describe as lyrical :

" The extreme deception of my own eternity has perished. It has perished. I am well aware of our dear self-deceptions, but now not only hope, but desire also is extinguished." Here, as elsewhere, the tone is so sorrowful, so heart-broken, so desolate, so free from all coquetry of suffering, that it cannot fail (and never has failed) to produce a profound impression and to inspire a sort of reverence. But, on the other hand, there is no gainsaying the fact that here, as in other similar cases, we have rather a notation of feelings or sentiments which do not extend beyond the sphere of the individual. On a very few rare occasions we meet with the opposite procedure, when Leopardi tries to express directly the full emotion : once in the case of the amorous emotion from which he extracted the burning desire expressed in the *Consalvo*, and on another occasion when his soul is thrown open to the commotions of life, in the *Risorgimento*. But in the *Consalvo* there is something of those solitary ravings about love of which Ranieri was sometimes witness. In the *Risorgimento*, the motion of the soul fails to finds its adequate and proper form of expression and the author allows it to run in the channels of the brooklet of Metastasio's little half descriptive half musical strophes.

Where, then, is the poetry of Leopardi ? you will say : it is neither here nor there, nor in any other place either. Do you wish to suggest that Leopardi was not in any sense a poet ?—Well, conscious critical opinion in general has already pointed to the places where the poetry is to be found. It received coldly the *Operette morali ;* it refuted the arguments of the *Paralipomeni* and the *Palinodia ;* it accused the

Ginestra and other poems of being prosaic. With the utmost positiveness and by the mouthpiece of De Sanctis, and despite the shouts of patriotic fanatics from Settembrini to Carducci, it recognized further that the early poems are rhetoric of the schools, that of the crazy or minatory poems only a few traits are to be retained, that in the case of those that remain there are reserves to be made.

It directed admiration especially to the so-called " idylls," both early and later, and to the " great idylls." It seems to me sufficient to avoid making this statement into an exclusive and comprehensive approval of certain particular compositions and to understand it in its ideal and profound sense, in order to obtain the criterion by which to discern the true poetry of Leopardi.

Leopardi, as we have said, was " shut off from life," but not so that, in his early youth, he had not dreamed and hoped and loved, enjoyed and lamented, nor that later in life, at certain moments, he did not feel himself alive and his mind again open to the emotions of life. In these moments, when he again felt himself forming part of the world, either by remembering things of distant years or by immediate recollection, his poetical imagination was stirred : for poetry may be what you will, but it can never be cold or acosmical. Such moments of inspiration are the *Sera del di di festa*, the *Vita Solitaria*, the *Infinito*, the *Sabato del Villaggio*, the *Quiete dopo la Tempesta*, the *Ricordunze*, the *Silvia*. Then his words take on colour, his rhythm becomes soft and flexible and full of harmonies and intimate poetry, the emotion trembles as it reflects itself in the dewdrop of poetry. The effect is the more powerful, inasmuch as those moments of life, those glances at the surrounding world, not in order to reject, but to receive it sympathetically, those bursts of desire, those hopes of love, that tenderness, that suavity, have in them something almost furtive and are snatched from the jaws of a hard destiny, which presses closely in his steps, and from the chill feeling that is to come so soon. They are expressed with the reserve, the modesty, the chastity of one who says things which he is no longer in the habit of saying. Hence their particular charm, hence the slight touch of carmine on the pale cheek of this poetry, which makes much vigorous highly coloured literature seem pale indeed by comparison.

Who does not bear in mind and heart the images which come then to flower, those divine images, those girlish faces, those aspects of the country-side, of humble folk at their work? Silvia at her loom, singing in odorous May, her mind full of a beautiful dream, and of the young man who stays his writing to lend an ear to the sound of that voice, linking his dream with the girl's dream? Those evenings in the father's house, the starry sky, the song of the frogs, the glow-worms wandering among the hedges, the voices of those within the house alternating with one another, while thought and desire sail away into the infinite?—The tranquil village of a Saturday night with the girl standing there, the flowers for her adornment on the morrow in her hand, the old woman who babbles of the past, the boys jumping and shouting, the labourer returning to his frugal table as he thinks of the morrow's repose, the smith and the carpenter, who hasten to complete their work, while all the world sleeps, betrayed by the light that filters through the chinks of the workshop;—

the evening of the feast-day, so full of sadness, with the memory of the song which one can still hear dying slowly away in the distance;—the solitary margin of the lake, " crowned with still flowers," near which he sat down and abandoned himself to his thoughts, becoming motionless as motionless nature;—the impression of life reviving after the tempest; and others similar, all of them eternal and ever new creations? And then there are such cameo-lines as " When beauty shone resplendent in thy laughing fleeting eyes "; and those perfect lines : " The wind comes bearing with it the sound of the hour striking on the tower of the town "; " Soft and clear is the night and free from wind. . . ."

Those other moments, when Leopardi takes refuge in the intellectual world so dear to him, and, so to speak, loves love and death together, as in the most beautiful *Pensiero dominante* and in *Amore e morte*, rise to the level of poetry together with these memories of life. Although their form is meditative, they are not didactic; and the *Aspasia* is not didactic but dramatic, in which, after the shipwreck of his last love, he finds refuge on the firm shores of the intellect and recovers his strength by explaining to himself what had happened and in making a theory about it. The old passion still vibrates in his soul, but he believes that he has gone beyond it and is able to dominate it by means of his calm thinking.

It is true that Leopardi's work is rarely or never entirely poetic. Almost always, he becomes didactic or rhetorical, or dry and epigraphical in the way already described. In the *Sabato del Villaggio*, the poetic scene which should have suggested by its very poetical touches the thought of joy awaited, which is the only true joy, the joy of the imagination, is commented upon critically and weighed down with allegory, which takes the form of a rhetorical exhortation addressed to " the merry little boy." Even in the *Silvia* itself, which is perhaps his masterpiece, that " Hope," which appears at the close, has in it something of the abstract, and some interpreters and many readers (although they are wrong as a matter of fact) have been led to merge this Hope in Silvia, reviving her by means of this fusion, and making the poet have a young girl and not an allegory as " dear companion of his new age " and with her " so many delights at once," of love, of pleasure, of works and of experience. These poetical passages of one tone into that of another or of poetry into what is different from poetry, these lapses into aridity could not be demonstrated otherwise than by examining each element separately. This examination has in great part been made by De Sanctis in his unfinished work on Leopardi, and by more recent students. It is also possible to see more clearly into what is called the poetic sytle of Leopardi by means of such an examination : language, syntax, metres. Leopardi has always the choice and exquisite style of the humanist, for whom it would be impossible to have recourse to words and modes of expression suitable to poets of other origin and formation, in the sense of being more sociable and popular in their appeal. He is, however, able to show himself simple and immediate, without abandoning that refinement of choice and solemnity of tone. Elsewhere, however, he is dominated by literary formulas as regards certain rhythmical arrangements and phraseology, even accepting Metastasio and the Arcadians as

K

guides. See, for instance, *Amore e Morte*, where we find : " Things fair as these are not to be found elsewhere here below; nor in the stars," and further in the *Sabato del Villaggio*, where not only the " young hopeful " but the " nice little girl " and the " dainty little bouquet of roses and violets " are effeminate and unworthy of the rest.

All this goes to prove—and this shall be my last critical and methodical remark on Leopardi in these brief notes—that we must not allow ourselves to be deceived by the perfect correctness, propriety and style of Leopardi's poetry, but look beyond that and observe that if we never find emptiness of thought and feeling beneath that impeccable form, we do nevertheless find now the poetically strong and now the weak, now the complete and now the incomplete, and come to the conclusion that the poetry of Leopardi is much more subject to these variations than is generally suspected or believed. There is in it something arid, prosaic, merely literary, and something also of sweetest, purest and most harmonious; and perhaps that very obstacle, preceding or following the free movements of the rhythm and the imagination, makes us better able to experience the miracle of poetic creation.

XI

ALFRED DE VIGNY

Two thoughts occupied the mind of Alfred de Vigny in his early years, suggested by his double experience as a writer and as a soldier: the one concerned the relation between the rights and duties of the artist and society, the other the frequent disaccord between the duty of the soldier and his conscience as a man. But both alike were rather the anxious self-tormentings of a delicate sensibility than theoretical questions: for in what respect is society wanting towards artists in the matter of duties? Indeed, what *special* duties does society owe to the artist? It certainly has a duty towards art, that of compelling itself to enjoy and to understand it. But its duty towards artists is the same, neither more nor less, than that owed to all its other members.

If it be urged that artists are as inexperienced as children and as irritable as invalids, assuming but not admitting this to be the case, it is to be feared that if they be placed under guardianship and treated like sick folk or children, we should destroy them as artists in thus attempting to guide and to cure them. Thus it might almost be held more advisable to follow the severe but more profitable treatment suggested by Jean Paul and blind them like finches, and let them wander about in the shadows for love of the poetry which their sufferings will produce! De Vigny's question was indeed without head or tail; he nursed illusions as to the place of art in the spirit, holding that the artistic life is superior to the practical and political, and that those who make " des choses impérissables " of a sheet of paper or a canvas or a block of marble or a sound are " les premiers des hommes." What he wrote on this argument can therefore have no other value than as a document of the romantic cult of genius, or as a personal document throwing light on De Vigny's searchings of mind.

The contest between military and human duties is also without greater consistency, being but one of many instances that occur in life where internal difficulties and struggles must be conquered and composed by the individual, and if he is found to be unable to get the better of them or if the victory leave him broken and exhausted, this means that he is ill adapted to the military profession, as was the case with De Vigny. Here, too, the poet's thought is to seek, for the army seemed to him to be a paradox, " une sorte de nation dans la nation," as though the same could not be said of any other profession, industry or commerce, of art or the Church. De Vigny cut the Gordian knot by remarking that " la philosophie a heureusement rapetissé la guerre, les négociations la remplacent, la mécanique achévera de l'annuler par les inventions."

Though these problems have no theoretic existence, yet they represent real distress, real illusions and real suffering, and consequently the books that they inspired, *Stello*, the play *Chatterton*, the collection of anecdotes, *Servitude et grandeur militaires*, although of slight theoretical import, are none the less full of fine observation and emotional quality. The play is less happy, for its plot has in it something cold and artificial, which becomes evident in the execution; but the pages of *Stello*, where an acute psychological analysis of the terrorists of '93 is to be admired among other things, and above all the military anecdotes with their portraits of those old *troupiers*, who have incurred death as a matter of professional duty, and in obedience to orders have shot a young man whom they had torn from the arms of his wife—afterwards permanently insane in consequence—who have bayoneted a youth as he stood by his white-haired father and who afterwards have failed to console themselves for what their conscience tells them has been a crime and await and almost seek for death—such pages as these penetrate profoundly the soul of the reader. The sad seriousness of feeling manifests itself in the naked, incisive style, all things and thoughts, disdainful of ease and brilliance. Napoleon, whose well-executed attitudinising De Vigny despises, appears in one of these stories. He is depicted in conversation with the Pope at Fontainebleau, an expert in knowledge of the human heart, who throws in his face the word " Comedian ! " on one occasion, and on another " Tragedian ! " And when the great man turns round to speak to the modest official in whose mouth De Vigny places the story, he too refuses to be carried away by the able acting of Talma's pupil : " Je sentis pourtant que c'était là une force fausse et usurpée. Je me révoltais, je criais :—Il ment ! Son attitude, sa voix, son geste ne sont qu'une pantomime d'acteur, une misérable parade de souveraineté, dont il doit savoir la vanité. Il n'est pas possible qu'il croie en lui-même aussi sincèrement ! Il nous défend à tous de lever le voile, mais il se voit nu par-dessous.

Et que voit-il ? Un pauvre ignorant comme nous tous, et, sous tout cela, la créature faible." *Servitude et grandeur militaires* is the high-water mark of De Vigny's art in prose, although he made somewhat feeble attempts at historical fiction and drama with *Cinq Mars* and *La Maréchale d'Ancre*. In the verse of his first period, along with a good deal of imitation and mere metrical exercise, are to be found elements and traits of composition which are astonishing in their purity and originality. The little poem *Éloa* gives evidence of inexperience in writing, and here and there falls into the trite; nevertheless, there is poetic inspiration in the angelic purity of Éloa (made of a tear of pity that fell from the eye of Jesus !) when she hears with horror in heaven of the guilty and rejected Lucifer, she is not repelled, but on the contrary stimulated to aid him in his misfortune :

> " Son premier mouvement ne fut pas de frémir ;
> Mais plutôt d'approcher comme pour secourir ;
> La tristesse apparut sur sa lèvre glacée
> Aussitôt qu'un malheur s'offrit à sa pensée :
> Elle apprit à rêver . . ."

Le Cor, which renders the sound of the horn heard among the mountains ("Dieu ! que le son du Cor est triste au fond des bois ! "), and recalls the heroic legend of Roland at Roncesvalles, is not triumphantly, but tragically heroic. Heroic sadness also dominates in the story of the old commander lamenting his fine ship which fought and was sunk to the bottom of the sea at Aboukir (*La frégate " La Sérieuse "*). But the masterpiece of this first series is without doubt *Moïse*, written by De Vigny at the age of twenty-five. Moses ascends the mountain already in sight of the Promised Land,

while all his people await below in the plain; he sings
the hymn of glory, and as he does so feels himself
bend beneath the yoke of his own power and greatness.
He is weary because of all the humanity that God
has denied him when raising him above it to be
his instrument to dwell in a desert, without love,
friendship, confidence or companionship. He confesses this to God in a sort of song with repeated
refrains, praying for death over and over again :

> " Sitôt que votre souffle a rempli le berger,
> Les hommes se sont dit : ' Il nous est étranger ' ;
> Et les yeux se baissaient devant mes yeux de flamme,
> Car ils venaient, hélas ! d'y voir plus que mon âme.
> J'ai vu l'amour s'éteindre et l'amitié tarir ;
> Les vierges se voilaient et craignaient de mourir.
> M'enveloppant alors de la colonne noire,
> J'ai marché devant tous, triste et seul dans ma gloire,
> Et j'ai dit dans mon cœur : ' Que vouloir à présent ? ' ;
> Pour dormir sur un sein mon front est trop pesant,
> Ma main laisse l'effroi sur la main qu'elle touche,
> L'orage est dans ma voix, l'éclair est dans ma bouche ;
> Aussi, loin de m'aimer, voilà qu'ils tremblent tous,
> Et, quand j'ouvre les bras, on tombe à mes genoux.
> O Seigneur ! J'ai vécu puissant et solitaire,
> Laissez-moi m'endormir du sommeil de la terre ! "

And when God consents and he is carried away
from before the eyes of the people, his successor,
the new leader, already advances to fulfil the same
mission, also condemned to a like desolation. He
advances, thinking of the work which he has under-
taken, pale for the sacrifice to which he is consecrated :

> " Marchant vers la terre promise,
> Josué s'avançait pensif, et pâlissant,
> Car il était déjà élu du Tout-Puissant."

This is the most grandiose representation ever given
of the hero's function in history; he is worthy of
Michael Angelo, this leader of peoples, representing

the historical heroes of poetry in the same years as Hegel devoted some pages of his *Philosophy of History* to historical heroes.

These works followed one another in brief sequence, but after their appearance De Vigny published nothing for about thirty years, though he was always working in and with himself, keeping a private diary and composing lyrical poems at long intervals. These latter saw the light posthumously in a collection entitled *Les Destinées*.

What are these lyrics contained in *Les Destinées*? They are his different attitudes towards the great categories of the soul and of reality, of pain and death, of love, of science, of poetry, of spiritual nobility, of destiny, of divinity. The female has betrayed and mocked him, she has played with his heart; consequently, he represents her as Delilah and man as Samson : the latter good and always in need of the stimulus of encouragement in his work, of comfort in his disappointments; the former, of baser clay, impure, astute, availing herself of man's confidence to glut her vanity and serve her caprices (*La colère de Samson*). But in addition to the female, that mystery of iniquity, there is the woman, that spiritual mystery terrible as an enemy drawn up on the field of battle : woman who is weak and is strong, who is subject to impulse and also to weakness, but who yet has nothing of man's cowardly prudence; woman who thrills and vibrates at the cry of the oppressed, arms herself and urges on to battle (*La maison du berger*). We are rent with pain and death awaits us : shall we vilely weep, moan and call upon the gods ? No : we must push onward with head erect, we must do our duty energetically, we must suffer and die without a word (*La mort du loup*). Is our soul, which has been made free by Christianity, thereby released from the pressure of its ancient destinies? Each one's destiny weighs always upon each, and freedom is the new duty of combating destiny (*Les Destinées*). Brutal forces dominate man and submerge him; but his thought escapes them and he is able to fix it in speech or to confide it to writing before he dies, like the captain of a ship in imminent peril of shipwreck, who encloses his observations and scientific discoveries in a bottle, which he throws into the sea and which is eventually found and tells the whole thought of the shipwrecked one (*La bouteille à la mer*). Nowadays, aristocracy does not depend upon a sword or rank and office at Court, but upon the pure Spirit, the book, poetry (*L'Esprit pur*). He who flies from the vile life of cities finds peace and solitude in Nature. But Nature remains external, intent upon following her eternal and changeless law, careless of man as of every other animal or plant which appears upon the earth, and finds in earth its tomb. It is not the things that are changeless which merit our love and our emotion, but those that pass away (*La maison du berger*). Vain are anxious questionings of God, to know the meaning of the world, of the soul and of the body, of good and evil, of life and death, of peoples and of history, for God is silent before our interrogations; the just man so unjustly rejected must now abandon prayers and henceforward answer coldly and with silence the eternal silence of the Divinity (*Le mont des Oliviers*).

This collection of lyrics has been praised (we have mentioned only the principal ones) as " philosophical poetry " and to De Vigny has been attributed the merit

of having been the first or among the first to found
"philosophical poetry" in France. With no wish
to indulge in subtleties, but desirous, maybe exces-
sively, to remove all danger of judgment going
astray, I would wish to recall the fact that "philosophical poetry" is one of those formulæ in which
substantive and adjective contradict one another,
for a poem can never be philosophy, that is, a dialectic
of thoughts. Having stated this, there can be no
harm in allowing vogue to the popular definition of
De Vigny's poetry, understanding it as used meta-
phorically, that is, as attributed to poetry which
moves among the *novissima*, the ultimate things;
though it would seem to be more apt to call it dramatic
or epic poetry occupied with the drama or epic of
the modern spirit, in the sense that it no longer has
Greeks or barbarians, Franks or Saracens, for pro-
tagonists, but God and Nature, Good and Evil, Joy
and Sorrow, and other such-like opposites and
antinomies.

The same writers who have described De Vigny's
poetry as philosophical have considered it to be pessimistic; and this is less incompatible just because pessimism introduces a subjective and sensational tendency,
that is to say, material for poetry, into the meditation of
the great problems. But does this description really
satisfy us? Is not "pessimism" perhaps too general,
too coarse a term, to be applied to a state of the soul
so complex and so individual as that of De Vigny's?
If religious faith be removed, there yet remains
religious inclination towards nature and God; if
faith in the objectivity and fecundity of the good and
in the necessity of historical and social process, there
yet remain firm will for good and social duty; if

faith in war and in its perpetual and intrinsic ethical value be removed, admiration for bravery and self-sacrifice remains; if faith in the redeeming virtue of thought and poetry, there remains the worship of genius; if faith in love be removed, there remains the tender feeling of love. And so we may proceed, through all degrees of things worthy and beautiful. What will happen? What has been removed would urge the soul towards scepticism, indifference, inertia, boredom, or towards bored and stupid pleasures; but what remains saves it from falling over this precipice, directing and elevating it towards religion, virtue, heroism, science, poetry, love. But since matter and aliment are lacking to all these things, the soul faints like an empty form, which once was filled and is therefore not empty in the same way as those others for which a content has been artificially created, but never really possessed or really sought. This is the singular condition of De Vigny : a desolation arising from the negation or failure to understand the rationality of the course of things; a tenacious adhesion to all that is lofty and noble, though all perhaps is vain, but yet all is to be accepted and promoted as a debt of honour, for dignity's and pride's sake, as a sentinel defends a lost position or a knight a hopeless cause.

It may be said that there is some analogy between the poetical inspiration and the person of De Vigny, a gentleman of ancient lineage, who, like others of his class, either did not wish to accept or did not succeed in accepting the new ideals, nor yet was able to turn back to the past, not only in fact, but even, which is more serious, in desire and imagination, since the impact of the new times had shaken, in his spirit also, the bases of old ideas and habits. Thus he is to be found rejecting in his diary, alike " le droit divin et la souveraineté du peuple " as contradictory absurdities, or satirizing and inveighing in turn against charlatan democracy and the absolute Czar. In his practical life, he is remembered during the July days of 1830, unable to take sides with the King or with the revolutionaries and finally arriving at this decision :—If the King mount his horse and come out to face the revolt, I shall wear his badge and stand beside him.—Such an attitude has in it something sublime, but a sublimity that is somewhat strained and empty, bound also by a well-known psychological law to approach to a slight extent its opposite; and we must confess that sometimes, though rarely, when we come upon certain movements of De Vigny's poetry, we are affected with a slight smile, to which his malignant contemporaries were also liable and did not always succeed in restraining; a flash and it is gone, because those movements are the extreme point of a true anguish of soul and of a real elevation of heart and mind. See him picturing his ancestors, soldiers and courtiers :

> " J'ai mis sur le cimier doré du gentilhomme
> Une plume de fer qui n'est pas sans beauté . . .
> Dans le caveau des miens plongeant mes pas nocturnes,
> J'ai compté mes aïeux, suivant leur vieille loi . . .
> Si j'écris leur histoire, ils descendront de moi."

And see him before God. God does not reply to his vain questionings, and he rises, frigid and offended, from his knees :

> " Si le Ciel nous laissa comme un monde avorté,
> Le juste opposera le dédain à l'absence,
> Et ne répondra plus que par un froid silence
> Au silence éternel de la Divinité."

Does it not seem here as though De Vigny were treating God as a gentleman would treat a king who had failed to behave as a king, before whom he consequently resumes his rights as a peer, almost demanding satisfaction by arms, no longer regarding him as a subject does a sovereign, but as a gentleman does a gentleman ?

Arising thus, as it does, from an original and distinct spiritual form, the poetry of De Vigny presents itself as possessed of the characteristics of internal necessity : literature has no share in this, and if ever it does appear, we are at once sensible of it as a defect. For De Vigny was not one of those writers known as well-endowed, quick-witted, copious, regular : in his writing we are often sensible of a certain effort, his composition is often maladroit, there are obscurities and deficiencies in his style. Yet only a schoolmaster could condemn him for such defects, which even have a certain sympathetic attractiveness for poetical readers. Why ? Because, if we wish for profound, intense poetry, we must resign ourselves to what is almost always linked with it, namely, signs of fatigue, the expression which does not always succeed in achieving clarity or self-possession, intermittences and omissions. De Vigny knew and boasted shortly before his death that he had striven to hold aloft with the great masters " l'idéal du poète et des graves penseurs "; and as early as in his nineteenth year he had already, in a letter to his friend Count de Moncorps, expressed his contempt and abhorrence for facile poetry :

" la haine
Que nous professons tous pour les vers faits sans peine ;
Le vers le plus obscur d'un auteur sérieux
A plus de vraie mérite et vaut plus à nos yeux

Que l'inutile amas de légères paroles
Qui forment le tissu de ces œuvres frivoles,
Qui sans rien peindre au cœur cherche à nous éblouir. . . .

Later on, in *La maison du berger*, he burst out in invective against the " Vestal of the spent fires," the Poetry which had lost her fine seriousness, or which allowed her robe of priestess to be lifted and herself to be drawn on to the knees of old drunken Anacreon, or who should sing at the banquets of Horace, or should wanton laughingly with Voltaire. His very effort, his weak voice, the slight hesitation in his speech, the rather delicate, mannered and tenuous elegance occasionally to be observed in him, have also something of the aristocratic.

But this aristocrat has the energy of the lofty Muse, this painter with the palette whose colours do not catch the eye knows how to draw figures and situations with a few potent living touches. Jesus on the Mount of Olives vainly cries out thrice to Heaven : " My Father ! "

" Le vent seul répondit à sa voix.
Il tomba sur le sable assis, et, dans sa peine,
Eut sur le monde et l'homme une pensée humaine. . . ."

Delilah is carried in triumph and placed on the altar, hard by Samson bound and blinded by deed of her :

" Et près de la génisse au pied du Dieu tuée
Placèrent Dalila, pâle prostituée,
Couronnée, adorée et reine du repas,
Mais tremblante et disant :—Il ne me verra pas ! "

The wolf, defending its mate and children, notwithstanding the hail of blows that are showered upon its body and the wounds that they make, finally strangles the mastiff that has attacked it, then ..

" Il nous regarde encore, ensuite, il se recouche,
Tout en léchant le sang répandu sur sa bouche,
Et, sans daigner savoir comment il a péri,
Refermant ses grands yeux, meurt sans jeter un cri."

The bottle, thrown by the shipwrecked sailors on the waves, wanders upon the ocean :

" Seule dans l'Océan, seule toujours !—Perdue
Comme un point invisible en un mouvant désert,
L'aventurière passe errant dans l'étendue,
Et voit tel cap secret qui n'est pas découvert.
Tremblante voyageuse à flotter condamnée,
Elle sent sur son col que dépuis une année
L'algue et les goémons lui font un manteau vert."

He embraces the woman beside him, weak and broken as he, with a long look which gathers every particular of her beloved person :

" Oh ! qui verra deux fois ta grâce et ta tendresse,
Ange doux et plaintif qui parle en soupirant ?
Qui naîtra comme toi portant une caresse
Dans chaque éclair tombé de ton regard mourant,
Dans les balancements de ta tête penchée,
Dans ta taille dolente et mollement couchée,
Et dans ton pur sourire amoureux et souffrant ? "

This " philosopher " poet, when he utters a solemn thought in the course of his poetry, presents it and venerates it in words of religious enthusiasm, free of all vulgar unction or pompous eloquence. The Just Man :

" L'examen de soi-même au tribunal auguste
Où la raison, l'honneur, la bonté, l'équité,
La prévoyance à l'œil rapide et la science
Délibèrent en paix devant la conscience
Qui, jugeant l'action, régit la liberté."

The virtue of Poetry :

" Comment se garderaient les profondes pensées,
Sans rassembler leurs feux dans ton diamant pur ? . . ."

Woman :

> " Ta pensée a des bonds comme ceux des gazelles,
> Mais ne saurait marcher sans guide et sans appui.
> Le sol meurtrit ses pieds, l'air fatigue ses ailes,
> Son œil se ferme au jour dès que le jour à lui. . . ."

And De Vigny has also in his poetry such great image-making lines as these :

> " Les grands pays muets longuement s'étendront . . .,"
> " Ton amour taciturne et toujours menacé . . .," etc.

and mighty gnomic lines, such as :

> " Aimez ce que jamais on ne verra deux fois . . ." ;
> " Fais énergiquement ta longue et lourde tâche " ;
> " La Femme, enfant malade et douze fois impure " ;
> " Lui, qui doute de l'âme, croit à ses paroles," etc.

Such writers as the luxuriant Hugo and the diffuse and fluent Lamartine reveal their intimate poverty, when compared with De Vigny, author of but a few poems composed with but little mastery. When, too, one turns one's gaze upon the crowd of those others, one is disposed to conclude that as Alfred de Vigny is among the greatest poetical writers that have ever appeared in France, so he is probably the greatest French poet of the nineteenth century.

XII

MANZONI

Giovita Scalvini, in his essay of 1829 on the *Promessi Sposi*, noted that in this romance there is something uniform and insistent, that we do not feel ourselves " wandering freely amid the great variety of the moral world," and are often aware of being " not beneath the great dome of the firmament," which covers " all multiform existences," but beneath that of " the temple which covers the faithful and the altar."

This judgment, although later repeated or renewed by others, who deprived it of its vigour and truth by imparting to it their party passions, was due to an undeniably clear impression by its first author. In my opinion, it deserves to be more profoundly studied and more minutely defined, because it throws open the way to the correct critical interpretation of one of the greatest masterpieces of our literature.

Whence comes this sense of narrowness which one seems sometimes to experience when reading the *Promessi Sposi*, but more especially when Manzoni is compared with other poets ? We are not made to feel any of what are called the human affections and passions in their full force and in their full development in that romance. The effort towards the truth, the obsession of doubt, the desire for happiness, the ravishment of the infinite, the dream of beauty and dominion, the joys and sorrows of love, the drama of politics and history, the ideals and memorials of peoples and so forth, which supply material for other poets, are not to be found here.

It is not because the author had no experience or knowledge of these things that they are absent; but he has surpassed and subjected them to a superior will, for he has risen above the tumult and has reached calmness and wisdom. And what wisdom! Not the wisdom that feels sympathetically the different human passions, yet remains above them, assigning to each its place and arranging them harmoniously. No, Manzoni's is the wisdom of the moralist, who sees nothing but black and white, on one side justice, on the other injustice; on one side goodness, on the other evil; here innocence, yonder malice; reason on the one side, wickedness and fatuity on the other; approving the one and blaming the other, often with the subtle considerations of the casuist. The world, so various in colour and sound, so closely related in all its parts, so inexhaustible and so profound, becomes simplified, not to say impoverished in his vision. One only of the innumerable strings of the soul vibrates here and the very fact of its being alone gave Scalvini the impression of the uniform and persistent. Manzoni's inspiration seems to have been : " *Dilexi iustitiam, odivi iniquitatem.*

This character of the feeling that dominates in the *Promessi Sposi* comes clearly into view, not only when we place it side by side with the works of foreign and Italian contemporary poets, such as Goethe, Foscolo and Leopardi, but also when we compare it with the earlier works of Manzoni himself. These should not now be looked upon rather as sketches or parts of the future masterpiece as has usually and too exclusively been the case, but be taken in themselves, as presenting motives and forms which are no longer to be found in the romance. In them are to be heard notes that Manzoni did not wish to touch again; and if we take the word " poetry " as is usually done, as applying to certain particular tones of passion, we must then declare that in those representations lies the true *poetry* of Manzoni, whereas in the *Promessi Sposi* the long period of reflection and of *prose* is already begun.

I think in the first place of the *Adelchi*, which is a work of genius, notwithstanding, rather indeed owing to, the contradictions discovered therein by the critics or by the author as his own critic. I am well aware that Manzoni's theologico-moral system was already completely developed at the time, together with his anti-historical conception of history, as is proved by various passages of the critical statement that accompanies the tragedy. But what had been definitely fixed and established in the mind was not so established in the soul, and for this reason the most diverse and opposite sentiments are in desperate conflict in the poetic reality of the tragedy, life is there tumultuous. In Manzoni's theoretic conception of life politics have no share; there is only morality. In the *Adelchi*, on the contrary, politics assert their own originality and value, exciting our admiration with or without the approval of the author, as does every well-grounded assertion of strength, which is always admirable. Old King Desiderio follows the tradition of his forbears against the Franks and against the Popes whom they protect, closing the road to Rome to the Lombards. He is

further incensed with Carlo owing to the sufferings
of his daughter and the shame inflicted upon himself
by an unjust repudiation. Who can blame him?
Not even the poet, notwithstanding that he had
esteemed it possible to blame him in the historical
statement in the name of abstract justice. Carlo
defends the cause of the Popes against their Lombard
oppressors : does the hero of the Church preserve
his purity of hands and soul by doing this, as abstract
justice and morality pretend? Politics do not allow
him to do so, " the lofty reason of State," as he calls
politics, induce him to dismiss Ermengarda and take
another woman in her place, careless of treading
underfoot the innocent on his fatal path. He experiences, it is true, something like remorse, but this in
reality more closely resembles a momentary and
superstitious dread at having committed the crime,
which it seems to him has brought with it bad fortune.
Politics cause him to accept the betrayal, clasp the
hand of the traitors, praise and reward them, although
despising them at heart.

And these traitors of King Desiderio, are they
merely wicked, egoistic and cowardly? They too
are led by politics, by the craving for independence
and freedom, the tendency towards individualism and
feudalism which was part of the social conditions of
the time, the consciousness that the cause of the
Lombard kings is a lost cause. Why should they
aid King Desiderio to win the victory? In order
to be more securely held in check and tyrannized
over by him? Why should they go against the will
of God's Church? The bond of fidelity is a poor
refuge, as in all historical events, when opposed to
the necessity of defending their own freedom and

safety, imperilled by the ruin of the State. The soldier Svarto, who wishes to emerge at all costs from obscurity and to obtain, not riches, but power, and exhibits cleverness and energy in seeking this end, is of the stuff of dominators and, like the youthful Bonaparte, " serves indocile, shivering as he thinks of the kingdom."

Feeling and expressing all these jarring passions, the poet certainly feels more intensely the burning of the wound he bears in his breast and hence asks of himself anxiously : " Why ? Why is society so constituted that either one must do or suffer wrong ? Why does a ferocious force, which takes the name of right, possess the world ? Why are we condemned to suffer the injustice sown by the hands of our ancestors and now the only harvest offered by the earth ? " He asks himself this, but like a poet refrains from answering the question, because the very person who torments himself with such questioning is all the same obliged himself to engage in combat, and to exert the utmost of his strength to gain the victory and to abase, tread down and destroy his adversary.

This contradiction is unsolved, and, as set down by Manzoni, insoluble. It has given us the figure of Adelchi, which the author judged at a later period to have been " unhappily intruded " among the other characters and the critics to be " anachronistical," but which is, on the contrary, a supremely poetic creation. The lament of the poet makes itself heard in this personage, thrown into the midst of a world with which the whole soul is in conflict, yet which imposes and asserts its superior strength.

Adelchi dies, he can do nothing else; but he is

forbidden even to seek or to desire death : he dies, but while he is fighting to escape and to preserve himself for recovery and revenge, according to the commands of historical necessity rather than to the promptings of his own heart.

Another contradiction : the Latin people have been conquered and reduced to a state of servitude by the Lombards. Manzoni's moral judgment reproves conquests and oppression and consequently rejects the apology made on behalf of the Lombards as a powerful people, capable of creating a new and reinvigorated Italy. For Manzoni they remain nothing but " the guilty race," whose prowess depended upon its numbers and whom it was but natural to attack. But he has pondered the history of the Middle Ages, and lo ! a different inspiration sends its message to his soul, a different vision appears to his imagination and dictates to him the wondrous chorus of the *Scented porches, the falling market places*, where the prevailing feeling is clearly blame of passive inert peoples, however innocent they may be, and exaltation of the barbarians, the heroes who make history, making it by seeking their own advantage, which advantage is justice, " the reward reserved for the strong."

The whole epic of the barbaric conquests arises luminous and sublime from that poem : the ferocious conquerors are men, and as men they too have gentle feelings hidden away in their hearts, something sacred to protect, something sweet to offer up in sacrifice : " They passed in their throngs over the land, singing joyous songs of war, but in their hearts they were thinking of the pleasant life of the castles ; in rocky valleys on lofty crags, they kept vigil throughout the cold nights, but they were thinking of the intimate confidences of love."

There is also in the *Adelchi* the figure of the deacon Martino, surrounded with the aureole of a sacred mission. He represents the opening out of the path, the unexpected and easy surmounting of obstacles which seemed to be insurmountable, in the enterprises which God wills and history commands. It seems as though nature herself, those very mountains which oppose and yet invite him, those solitudes which he alone among living men can traverse and yet live, are accompanying his arduous mission with a religious rite. Then there is also love, there is Ermengarde, Manzoni's only creation of love, but the few essential lines of the portrait he gives us are worth volumes from other poets less chaste than he.

Ermengarda has been repudiated by her husband and returns to the paternal mansion with the sign of contempt for her and hers marked upon her forehead. She returns thus covered with ignominy to the home she had left enfolded in the homage and love of all, overflowing with hope and joy. But Ermengarda does not gather strength from the thought that comforts and warms the hearts of her folk, who are already gazing upon her as a king's daughter and sister, rising above the admiring throng no vain brow, but one " beautiful with glory and revenge." Nor does Ermengarda resign herself to the God in whom she believes, seeking repose in Him, the God Who receives and succours the unfortunate and rewards those who have been unjustly persecuted. She loves him who has driven her away from his side and has made her suffer. She loves in womanly wise all the past of that love, her past of the woman of his love and of his choice, her past as queen : she loves the kisses and caresses, the feasts, the pomps, the admiration of the people and the envy of the other women. The poet feels the passion which shakes her to the inmost fibres, to the very roots of her being. He sees " *Vénus tout entière à sa proie attachée* " : her giving of herself up, her tenacious clinging to the man she adores : " My love is terrible, thou knowest it not yet : oh ! I have not yet shown it all to thee as it is ; thou wast mine ; *I was silent sure of my delight*, nor would this modest lip have dared declare to thee the full intoxication of my secret heart." In her delirium of trembling passion and jealousy she addresses with desperation him who once loved her. He had enjoyed some pleasures, of which she was the cause, and all this is still present to her. She turns her thoughts with extreme tenderness and a glimmer of hope towards the gentle, pious Bertranda, his mother, who had desired the marriage and certainly wishes it still to continue and has power over her son, and in her arms she feels " a life, a bitter joy which seems like love." Finally, she sets aside these thoughts and turns to God, prepares for death, and dies. The second very lovely chorus of the tragedy sings of this awakening, this repose in God. Religion has not broken up and destroyed earthly love ; it appears as the consoler, almost a new love, less bitter and more pure, to fill the void left by the other love.

The other, earlier tragedy, the *Carmagnola*, is on the whole a feeble work, composed under the evident influence of Goethe's *Egmont*, with which it shares the defects. It is developed like a historical anecdote put on the stage and the parenetical chorus itself, which is feebly linked to the action of the drama, is inferior to the two marvellous choruses of the *Adelchi*. One can, however, discern here the same conflict as in the *Adelchi* between politics and morality, between reality and a transcendental ideal. Here too it remains undecided.

Carmagnola, generous and confiding, believes that loyalty and free speech will enable him to dominate and overcome the tortuous and suspicious policy of the signoria of Venice, and thus incautiously hastens to his doom; Marco, the friend of Carmagnola, is sure of his friend's innocence and is yet obliged to be silent to stand aside and let him fall into the toils laid for him, because the country of which he is a citizen and which he denies in his heart, yet which he cannot do otherwise than obey, while calling for death, which alone gives peace; both these are characters differently situated, yet serving to compose the figure of Adelchi in the later tragedy. Like him, they represent the protest of the poet against a world that he fails to understand, but which stands above him in its might, the world of history. " What matters it to me that thou art great and glorious ? " says Marco, as he gazes upon Venice, " I had two great treasures, my virtue and my friend; and thou hast taken them both from me." Such is his confusion, when he feels the shock of the forces which he fails to understand, that he is led to accuse himself, his own will and intellect, and it seems to him that nothing would have availed him against that external crushing force : " O ! God, that seest all things, reveal to me my heart : let me at least see into that abyss I have fallen, whether I have been the more foolish, or the more cowardly, or the more unfortunate." Here too religion supervenes, to console and to purify; Carmagnola by means of religion frees himself from the bitter passions of the man who struggles in the political arena : " And thou, Philippo, wilt enjoy it ? What matters it ? I too have experienced these impious joys : I know now what they are worth. . . ." And he bows to death : " Death ! The most cruel enemy could not do otherwise than accelerate it. Oh ! men have not invented death . . . it comes from heaven, and heaven endows it with such powers of consolation that men can neither give nor take away. . . ."

We must also note for our objects, in addition to the tragedies and their choruses, that one among the sacred hymns which rises to a far greater height than the others, the *Pentecoste*. Here Manzoni does not strive, as in the others, to sing the myths of the Church, accepted by him as a devout believer, but disobedient to his imagination as a man of culture and a critic ; he sings of a spiritual renovation of mankind in the formation of the Church : a becoming and not a become, as Catholicism later came to mean for him. The less there appear in this hymn of such pictures as abound in the others, flights of angels, crucifixion, resurrection, with an element of post-Tridentine Catholicism, the more there is of impetuosity, of ardour, of sacred enthusiasm. And we must remember the *Cinque Maggio*, where the final religious catharsis, which certainly did not forbid the emotional representation of Ermengarda's love, does not forbid that of the sublime profane greatness of the hero Napoleon. He is not the defender of the Church, but the warrior and conqueror and emperor, arisen to conciliate the aspirations of two ages, and whom the poet nevertheless recognizes as the son elect of God, who wishes to stamp upon him a wider tracing of his creative spirit.

Anyone placing himself in the centre of these earliest works and remarking the conflicts which they contain and which are poetry, is led to think that Manzoni might well have accentuated and amplified more and more the historical or dialectical aspect of his spirit, its passions and affections, and have left his religious faith above or beside them. The narrowness noted by Scalvini was not due to his faith, but, on the contrary, to the consequences which Manzoni deduced from it, the rigidly moral point of view to which he believed it right to assign the first place as master of his soul. If it had been possible for Vico, whom he had studied during this first period and whom he had always living and present in his mind, to be at once a pious believer and a great realistic historian, Manzoni might also have been a believer and a poet of passion, as he had already shown himself to be, and as he was capable of becoming ever more completely. Manzoni's was on the whole a romantic soul; he was not merely a moderate literary reformer in the name of certain romantic doctrines.

But we have said : " he might have," as a way of making understood what was then his state of mind. He could not really do this, because all his mental and moral qualities urged him to give a different direction to his imagination. On the one hand, then, he was always bound to chasten his various feelings and passions, to depress, to veil and to leave visible only that part of them consistent of moral effects; on the other, to proceed to free himself from the incubus of history, of history as something serious, as the sole reality or as the reality of which it was necessary to take account. Instead of history, he would have preserved the simple notation of historical facts as resulting from good and evil, and rather from evil than from good, looking upon them rather as mere proofs of human unhappiness, stupidity and folly. This implied that he would have gone more and more in the direction of the transcendental both in sympathy and imagination, he would have inhabited the world beyond as the sole form of the rational life, while regarding the world below as a vale of error and of trial. The end of this passage is represented by the *Promessi Sposi*, which is to be described as the work of Manzoni's full maturity, the work in which he attained the completest coherence, but rather from the moral than from the poetical point of view.

This coherence was certainly practical and moral and not logical, representing a sureness and firmness of outlook independent of logic because a critical consideration of Manzoni reveals his manifold rifts. I shall not delay to point them out here, whether because they have already been brought to light by myself and others criticizing Manzoni's theories as to history, art, language, the moral life, and so on, or because a critic of Manzoni's philosophy would easily lose himself in general considerations, such as a criticism of Christianity and of transcendentalism, and more especially of Catholicism and neo-Catholicism. These contradictions would also be discovered in the *Promessi Sposi* by anyone who had sufficiently bad taste to treat that work as reality rather than fable and attack it—which would be about the same thing as to attack a Greek god resplendent in his white marble—because there too all is willed and set in motion by the Omnipotent, and nevertheless individuals are conceived as *causæ sui*.

Manzoni's victory over human feelings and affections in the *Promessi Sposi*, which he has subordinated to ethical feeling, does not result in these feelings and affections being abolished or cancelled, but by subjecting endows them all with a like impress, or if another image be preferred, clears and colours them, throwing the light of a single torch, the torch of morality, upon the shadows which surround them. Hence his peculiar mode of drawing characters, of setting them in action and of narrating events. When critics have lamented that the characters of the *Promessi Sposi* have not the immediacy, the spontaneity and the freedom from restraint of Shakespeare's characters, they have fallen into a misunderstanding, even if they are called Francesco de Sanctis. The personages of the tragedy are Shakespearean, for Adelchi has something of Hamlet and Ermengarda belongs to the family of the Ophelias, Cordelias and Desdemonas. But the personages of the *Promessi Sposi* cannot be Shakespearean, the Lucias the Christophers and the Innominati, owing to the great diversity of sentiment in this work from the tragical cosmic sentiment of Shakespeare. For this reason, in the best of circumstances, such a comparison does not point to a high and a low level of artistic achievement, but to a difference in quality. Everything must be well defined in the *Promessi Sposi*, because, whereas in Shakespeare the world is in the power of the forces that form it and transform it, in Manzoni it is supported and corrected by the moral ideal.

In the *Promessi Sposi*, notwithstanding the marvellous descriptions of countries, of aspects of nature, of journeys (suffice it to recall Renzo's flight to join Adda or his return to his own country and stay at Milan), there are no landscape effects to note, such as are to be found even in the works of minor Italian artists, contemporaries of Manzoni, such as Tommaseo. I am pleased to see that Momigliano, the most recent historian and critic of Manzoni, has understood that " whoever has penetrated into the spiritual organism of Manzoni and therefore sees the whole reflected in the parts, feels the breath of faith even in the page descriptive of the storm, forerunner of the end of the pest." I should not, on the other hand, be prepared to admit that the *Promessi Sposi* is a religious poem, as is now quite the fashion to proclaim it, or at any rate not without making the reservation that it is a poem inspired by religious morality, the world perceived by a firmly convinced moralist, which amounts to a more restricted definition of the above saying.

In this respect, Manzoni's method of treating love has especial importance. He clearly shows that he had descended into the abyss to which it may lead and had cast upon it the profound regard of the searcher, as is to be seen in the episode of Ermengarda, but now in the *Promessi Sposi*, he has for love a feeling of vigilant suspicion, tinged with disdain. I find it said by him in a posthumous publication that love should not be treated of in such a manner as to lead the reader of the story to indulge himself in that passion : there is more love in the world than is necessary and we should not re-kindle it with our books.

In the *Promessi Sposi*, love is either nothing but a natural feeling, which morality surrounds and renders innocuous and purifies by means of the priest's blessing upon the blessed union—in this case it is spoken of with indulgence and compassion and the smile we have for the childishness of children, as in the case of the innocent yet very dangerous loves of Renzo and Lucia; or as in the case of the nun of Monza, where love is a violent passion and is represented as an evil leading to perdition draped in black: " The unfortunate nun replied."

As a fact, love is the irrational-rational, the most direct symbol of life, a mingling of self-love and of self-sacrifice, of voluptuous delirium and of fruitful toil, of weakness and of strength, a fount of purification, or a vortex of impurity : in love, man is dominated by nature, yet he affirms himself to be man as he lifts his gaze to heaven. If we look at love from the point of view of passionate love, we shall look at it from the opposite point of view to that of Manzoni and of the moralist, who judge it according to their conscience and moral will. Another poet of the will and of searchings of the conscience, Pierre Corneille, profoundly different from Manzoni both in historical surroundings and in mental qualities, but here resembling the author of the *Promessi Sposi*, exhibits a like avoidance of the representation of love.

It is thus plainly understood that the personages of Manzoni's new drama, the *Promessi Sposi*, should answer to his new form of inspiration and incorporate the moral activity in its thesis and antithesis. But for this very reason, we are wrong in holding them, as is often done even by De Sanctis, to be

" constructed," that is to say, " constructed " according to types and therefore not poetical but intellectualistic. The fact remains that they are not typical, but perfectly individualized, each one with his proper elements of humanity, his own defects, his own faults, his own virtues. Lucia is a good religious soul, but in her eternal search for the right path she sometimes allows herself to be persuaded and disarmed by others without feeling that displeasure which she should feel. She proposes, for instance, to fulfil her vow to the Virgin, but all the same does not succeed in removing Renzo from her heart. Fra Cristoforo turns his fervent blood to good account, though it once led him to commit homicide, and sometimes restrains himself with difficulty. The cardinal Federico Borromeo, strong as he is, yet feels his own weakness and the miserable and terrible condition of mankind, which never altogether succeeds in equating being and the duties of being; wise as he is, he shares in the prejudices of his time.

Don Rodrigo, who represents the other extreme, brings to the persecution of Lucia almost as much punctilio, or misplaced sense of honour, as of brutal caprice. He has the gifts of a perfect gentleman, master of his acts and deeds, and feels remorse in the depths of his soul for the evil which he is led to commit. Similarly, the father of Geltrude, so hard and merciless in his treatment of his daughter, is not a wicked man but a maniac as regards the splendour and beauty of his own house. Where, indeed, is there any trace of the typically good or evil in all these personages ? At the utmost, it is possible to detect here and there, but very rarely, in Manzoni's way of presenting them, some slight excess of insistence, an insignificant work, such as is found in every work of art. The truth is that the accusation of typicity or abstractness bestowed upon Manzoni's virtuous or vicious personages is nothing but a new form of the erroneous comparison of his art with some other form of art. Whoever wishes to test the truth of this assertion should place himself at the centre of Manzoni's inspiration and then attempt to think of a way in which his characters could have been better embodied and made to live. He will find that he will never be able to conceive of them as different from Manzoni's conception and realization. Every placing of the accent elsewhere will turn out to be discordant; every heightening of the colour or retouching of the design, a blot. We turn away with horror from the idea of some who would like to hear the story of the love and crime of the nun of Monza told in the language of a Flaubert or a Zola or to see a little of the sensuality that another Catholic writer (a Catholic of a fantastic kind), Fogaz- zaro, has poured into his romances, introduced into the *Promessi Sposi*.

The critics who tend to diminish to a greater or less degree the value of Manzoni's lofty characters, lofty in good and evil, are really making use of another standard of comparison of an internal nature : that which they draw from another order of characters to be found in the *Promessi Sposi*, which they call " medium " and in whom they see the best of his art. Such are the more or less comical personages, or rather those that are comically treated, of whom Don Abbondio is the chief. The number and vivacity of these last are really great, and when we consider them after having considered the series of

M

the others, it would seem as if Manzoni possesses the soul of a La Rochefoucauld, indeed of a Voltaire, who should have become more dexterous and alert in discovering human frailties owing to experience as a confessor and inquisitor and perhaps a tormentor of himself, but who has not by any means lost on that account his gaiety and vigour of comic imagination. And all this on the top of a soul equal to that of a Bossuet or a Bourdaloue as he reveals it in the treatment of his chief personages.

This coupling of contraries finds its explanation in Manzoni's form of spiritual culture, for he was first an encyclopædist and a man of the enlightenment and afterwards a Catholic not without traces of Jansenism. He may thus be said to have harboured a double historical heredity in his singular temperament. This double heredity found a common basis in moral polemics in the name of reason or rationalistic religion and developed logically as though from a single root, because moralism, when it posits an ideal, posits at the same time the images of those that incarnate and of those that oppose it, of those that would wish to incarnate it but do not succeed, or do not incarnate it but pretend to have done so, by means of fictions in relation to others and sophisms in relation to themselves, and so on through an infinite series of instances and degrees; and for this reason we find bracketed on one side the noble or the base, and on the other the comical. But it is difficult, when the mind is fixed upon the one class, to include the other at the same time, or to allow equal merit to both classes.

Manzoni was further always disposed to accomplish the second of the two tasks, and did so gladly, because, as he observes at a certain point in the narrative, " we are all ready to do the things we feel we can do," and having thus quieted his conscience by means of a logical justification, he indulged very freely in satire and irony. We find this especially marked in the character of Don Abbondio, whom he pursues from the beginning to the end of the story, turning him about first on one side and then on the other, never leaving him in peace, and in general in his promptitude everywhere to seize upon tentative attempts, struggles, second thoughts, hidden intentions, the most fugitive and subtle and complicated movements of egoism, of vanity, of fear, and the tortuous complications of passionate reasoning, thrusting them into clear light, which prevents them from concealing or veiling themselves any longer.

Even history is carried away by this comic vein: history which in the first period of Manzoni's art had excited a serious interest in him, as history of the barbaric invasions or of dark Venetian policy or of Napoleon's triumphant warlike course across Europe. But now he proceeds to describe a time which lends itself better to ridicule, the decadent state of Italy when it came under Spanish rule, " both crude and affected." In Manzoni's eyes, that period, which was not without its positive factual value, shows itself, rather than anything else, as a welter of extravagances, follies, blunders and bad reasonings. He treats it, as he had treated Don Abbondio, with the same ferocity of implacable derision, and it is chiefly due to him and to his extreme application of Voltaire's methods that the seventeenth century has assumed a grotesque burlesque aspect in the eyes of readers.

But can we truly say that Manzoni had greater

aptitude for the comic than for the serious, the moving and the sublime ?   Did he succeed in it better ?   Do the anecdotes and portraits of Don Abbondio and of Don Ferrante, of Donna Prassede and of the avuncular Count, of Perpetua and Friar Galdino and of the worthy tailor with a smattering of letters and the like, succeed in throwing the scene of Fra Cristoforo's pardon or the night of crisis of the Innominato or the lofty colloquies of the cardinal Frederick or the terrible and piteous description of the plague into the shade ?   Is not the fact rather that the method of the comical and serious parts is intrinsically the same, the pathos of the moral judgment ?   Is not the preference generally shown for the comic parts of the *Promessi Sposi* due to no other motive than the greater facility for laughter in comparison with the concentration of mind required for the contemplation of duty and of suffering ?

Not only is the artistic value of the two elements that flow together in the *Promessi Sposi* equal, but they are in relation and harmony with one another. And he who arranges them thus harmoniously is the author, too critical not to be autocritical, too acute and too satirical an observer of others not to be diffident towards himself, too full of the sense of ridicule not to avoid with care the ridicule that would result from emphasis, preaching, pious unction, from any sort of exaggeration.   Hence the tone of the *Promessi Sposi*, so simple yet so measured, able to rise to the sphere of the most sublime emotion, but careful always to place the foot upon firm ground in order to avoid falling from the heights, which should be climbed gradually and gradually descended.   The perfection of this book even among the most carefully written and finished works of all literature, the fact of its containing no affectation, nothing mannered or commonplace, nothing unfounded or indeterminate, nothing affixed to it from without, is due to this. It has been said and we have all repeated it without examination, that the historical portions of the romance are too extensive; but here also I am glad to see that Momigliano has contested the traditional opinion. De Sanctis, who likewise shared it, afterwards confessed that those portions seemed to him so beautiful that he would not have dared remove them. It is clear also that if they really were excessive, we should and could always place them at a distance, while continuing to preserve them and to admire their beauty.

The truth of the matter is that the historical portions, here as in every really poetical work, are only historical in appearance, and become dissolved and merged in the two constitutive elements of the romance. Some of them, such as the narratives of the famine, of the plague and of the passage of the marauding soldiery, are one with the serious, sad and troubled portions of the story, and the others, of a satirical and ironical character, go to the formation of Manzoni's vast satire of human follies, which serves as an appendix to the *Praise of Folly* of Erasmus.

It is to be noted that this great book has not obtained the place which it deserves in the literature of the world, though for the Italians of the nineteenth century it possessed the same value as the *Jerusalem Liberated* for those of the eighteenth. This becomes evident when we read the histories of Italian literature written by foreigners. One possible reason for this is the habit of considering abstract forms or kinds as being things in themselves and of primary importance, and of singularizing the novelties and revolutions which take place in them. Regarded from this point of view, the *Promessi Sposi* appear to be, and are often considered as being, nothing but a romance of Walter Scott, from whom Manzoni borrowed, not only the idea of the historical romance, but also certain devices of composition, such, for instance, as the introduction of comic relief and of characters with a *tic*, such as Don Ferrante and Donna Prassede, who have many similar but far less subtle counterparts in Scott's stories. But the shell is the shell and poetry is the living being that dwells within, and which makes its home there, alters the shell to suit a change of taste and bears the shell with it on its way. Scott put into the shell as a rule his rather slender tale told to amuse the company, but Alessandro Manzoni put into it all human tragedy and comedy, as comprehended by a man of subtle and reserved moral consciousness.

XIII

BERCHET

WHEN the national liberal Revolution had become an accomplished fact in Italy, readers and critics rapidly acquired distaste for the political and patriotic poetry of previous decades. "Political poetry, bad poetry," they said, and perhaps the equity of this statement might be questioned, because bad poetry is written about all the passions, even about those which seem, like love, to be the most poetical, and all have need of one thing to become poetical, and of one thing alone : to be converted into poetry. It is, however, certainly true that the nineteenth century, especially the first half of it, owing to democratic dissensions and consequent national conflicts, produced much mediocre or bad "political poetry" everywhere, even in Italy, which was not among the countries least disturbed by these conflicts.

In carrying out the severe sifting above-mentioned, the critics sometimes remained doubtful and hesitating before a little book of few pages, which contained the most celebrated Italian popular romances, the *Poesie* of Giovanni Berchet. They were doubtful, that is to say, as to whether they should or should not throw it away into the abyss of oblivion, the rag and bone bag of history, together with so many other volumes of plays, stories and lyrics. A like hesitation persists to-day, because some continue to attach a value to these poems, while others accuse them of allowing themselves to be led astray and seduced by noble, by sacred memories, which are, however, extraneous to a true understanding of art. Yet I am of the opinion that even the second of these would not venture to affirm, if asked, that the poems of Berchet are nothing but rhetoric, mere verbal exaggeration and imposture. They would be bound to admit the incontestable fact that genuine emotion vibrates in these few verses, composed in a few years by an exile of 1821, who showed by keeping silence for a long period that he had nothing else to say, and thus afforded a proof that if he had formerly been led to write verse, he was impelled to do so by an overwhelming force.

For what reason do Berchet's poems now cause to arise a doubt after a first reading as to their poetic consistency, or even urge impatient readers towards a hasty condemnation? Berchet was a poet, or rather he was poetically moved, in the years that followed upon the unsuccessful revolution of 1821. He was melancholy and in exile, amid hardships yet buoyed up with hope, sometimes angry with fate, at others enthusiastic, plunged in anxiety for the fate of Italy, which for him took the place of the lady of his heart, to whom he dedicated his deepest tenderness and devotion. But although he was a poet, he was not sufficiently a poet, his interest in poetry itself was not equal to his inspiration, he lacked ardour in seeking out and rendering perfect the expression of his own feelings, the passion of the artist for the one word, unique and without any possible equivalent. Quite full of the religion of Italy, it seems as if he did not wish to betray this cult even by the cult of art, art that is wont to be so jealous a mistress! It resulted from this that when the breeze of poetry rippled the surface of his soul, he did not await the gradual effect of the inspiration, he did not accompany it with meditation and re-meditation, re-searching and testing it at every point with patient care; no, he availed himself of obvious and ordinary modes of expression, of simple expedients, of images, phrases and words which were merely general and conventional, contenting himself with approximations and patchwork. The melodramatic, limpid, easy, externally musical style was usual in old Italian literature; into it could easily be poured fixed formulas which would be carried along in its limpid flow, together with worn-out expressions and crudely prosaic utterances, just as a rapid torrent conveys its cargo of yellow leaves, dead sticks, and straws. This melodramatic style had not been entirely destroyed by romanticism, which to some extent appropriated and introduced into it or made common new metrical combinations and a predilection for galloping metres and for oxytone rhymes.

Stylized personages, such as the Virgin, the hermit, the troubadour, the apostle of liberty, the ardent patriot, the brave warrior, and so on, were also elements of the melodramatic-romantic style. Beginnings by hypotyposis and abrupt interrogations, development by means of symmetrical pictures, not less symmetrical polymeters and other such things, formed part of the same style. Berchet availed himself of all these methods : he divided the *Profughi di Parga* into three parts, of which the first part consists of sestets of ten syllables of alternating lines without rhyme or imperfectly rhymed. It describes the attempted suicide of one of those fugitives who is dragged out of the waves into which he had thrown himself by an English traveller. The second part is in *terzinas* of ten syllables, to each of which series are affixed two little strophes of six syllables with alternating proparoxytons and oxytones. This describes the misadventures of Parga, told by the mistress of the fugitive-suicide. The third, composed of octaves of ten syllables, mixed with oxytones, in which is recounted how the Englishman vainly offered his aid to the desperate fugitive, who rejects the tendered hand of help and remains implacable in his hatred of England, which had sold his country. In like manner, the *Fantasie* make alternate the two different orders of images which come in dream to the Italian exile, the images of Italy combating and triumphing over the Germans at Legnano, and those of the Italy of the poet's time, a degraded and spiritless slave. Such spectacles as these, together with the feelings that animate them, are placed side by side by means of an obvious artifice.

The poem of *Clarina* is intended to portray the sufferings of a young girl, whose betrothed has been torn from her side and sent to wander an exile in foreign lands, owing to Charles Albert's betrayal of the Carbonari in '21 and the failure of the intended national liberal Revolution. Nothing could be more melodramatic than this representation, in which the young girl figures as " an unhappy virgin " and her affianced as a " warrior," a " fugitive," a " vagabond," and we may cite the following as the quintessence of theatricality : " Beneath Dora's poplars, where the water is more nun-like, at the last hour of every day

is heard a sound of sorrow." Pause and explanation :
" It is Clarina, whose life is gnawed by the pangs of
love."

The other poem, *The Hermit of Cenisio*, presents a
foreign tourist, who climbs the Cenisio and gazes
from it upon the land of Italy, with joy that promises
joy. A hermit appears and warns him that a tone
of lamentation is suitable to one approaching the
land of sorrow, proceeding to describe the oppression and the torments inflicted upon the Italian
people. Upon hearing this, the stranger turns back,
preferring his own inclement northern land to Italy,
so joyous with her sun-rays and her vineyards, but
so sad in the adversity of her inhabitants.

Remorse follows third and reveals to us an Italian
lady left alone and avoided by all the other guests in
the midst of a banquet and reception. She hears
with horror these words murmured around her :
" She is the woman of our tyrant, the wife of the
foreign man ! " At night time she dreams horrible
dreams and her days are rendered miserable with the
refrain : " Vile are thou that has woven a mantle of
infamy; may it remain upon thy back ! Groan as
thou wilt, thou vile one, none shall ever relieve
thee of it ! "

In *Matilde*, the fourth poem, another young girl
wakes up from her sleep with a start, the prey to an
incubus : she has dreamt that she is to be given as
wife to an Austrian : his ugly face is before her in
all its repulsiveness : " His coat is white, there is
myrtle on the crest of his helmet; black and yellow
are his lower garments . . . execrable colours to all
Italian hearts."

The *Troubadour* symbolically represents the exile

in the guise of a youthful troubadour who has dared to raise his eyes in admiration of his master's wife and has been banned and driven forth " into the gloomy forest all alone, conquered by the cruelty of fortune. . . ."

Julia, the last of the poems, describes the palpitating anguish of an Italian mother, who has a son in exile and assists at the drawing of lots for the other conscripts, which will bear away from her the other son, to serve in the Austrian army, and perhaps meet face to face his own brother in arms as an enemy. Here too the process is the same : " Wherefore this throng in the temple ? " . . . " Who is this motionless woman unlike all the rest ? " . . . " She is Julia, a mother. . . ."

All this is " popular " poetry as it is called and certainly obtained complete popularity and deserved to obtain it, by reason of the purity and nobility of the sentiments that inspired it. Granted the style, it would be impossible to better it, and Berchet's words were murmured religiously by Italians panting for liberty, hating the foreigner, ardent for winning back what they had lost, by means of a national war. Even to-day those words have not grown cold : one feels the breath of passion beneath them. With what accents he expresses his hatred and contempt for the oppressors, who lord it in their arrogance under the protection of international treaties ! " It is not the strong man that defies us in the light of day, it is the peasant who proceeds securely to cut the throat of the she lamb that he has bought." What an accent of hatred there is in his abomination of the cold egoistical English policy ! " But everywhere, in front and behind us, harken to the complaint of infinite peoples, of other peoples that Anglia has betrayed, of other peoples that Anglia has sold ! " or the imprecation hurled at the Italian prince, in whom confidence had been placed and who had deserted the national cause : " Carignano, thy name is exe- crated among all peoples. . . ." And with what sacerdotal elevation he represents Italy in the revo- lutionary throes of the '21, when it seemed as if God had caused the serene dawn of hope to rise for her : " the desire of three centuries He has turned for thee into will ! " Hark to the fierce eloquence of war : " On, on, Lombards, thrust your swords into the gross, heavy German . . ." and the reproach to shame cowards : " Frederick ? He is a man like you, his sword is of iron like yours; he went forth to fight with it, though his flesh like yours is but mortal." And the severe admonition to those who imagine and argue, when the time has come for solemn willing and acting. " Now the die is cast. If there be any that still speaks prudently of doubts, if he does not feel victory in his heart, he thought of betraying you in his heart ! "

There is too the gaze fixed on the better times to come, which will follow the victory, the coming age of purity, of austerity, and of holy joy, when Italians will at length feel themselves : " willing and potent, as God created them." The mothers will raise a stronger race : " And ye, mothers, bring forth a race that shall be sober, ingenuous, modest and industrious, for liberty never weds bad habits, nor ever sets its foot in dirt."

Since the conception of " popular poetry " is one of the most hybrid, having sometimes served to designate original vigorous poetry, it will be well

to state clearly, with a view to avoiding such confusion, that the popularity described as the characteristic of Berchet's lyrics is the same as that of
much other poetry of the romantics. It consists, as
regards its external form, in a complex of fixed types
and phrases of literary origin, in a poor and unprecise
vocabulary, in rhythms which are easily retained in
the memory, and internally, of a kind of didacticism
and oratory based upon feeling.

But is all of Berchet contained in the work recorded
above and in popular poetry thus understood? Did
his emotional soul express itself only and always in
didactics and oratory? Is there nothing else truly
artistic and poetical in him? Something, which
communicates a certain ideal afflatus even to the
oratorical and didactic passages? There is: and in
my view this serves to explain the hesitancy as to
placing him in the same bundle as the other occasional
poets, and the affection manifested towards him by
certain lovers and critics of poetry.

Beside and amidst his patriotic oratory and didactics
is to be found in Berchet what may be termed the
lyricism of the exile. Here take actual form and life
his nostalgia, his deep love for his own country,
increased through absence, his tenderness for everything that can recall Italy, his dream of an Italy,
strong and great and free, his torment of doubt,
equal to the ardour of his desire, as to whether the
Italians will really be able to redeem themselves, to
rise up in combat and to conquer, defying dangers and
renouncing their ease and pleasures. The *Troubadour*
is something more than a simple poem to set to music:
it tell us of the anguished separation from places in
which we have dreamed and loved.

> " Scese—varcò le porte ;—
> stette ;—guardolle ancor :
> e gli scoppiava il cor
> comme per morte." [1] . . .

There is something more in the *Fugitives of Parga*
than the accusation and malediction of English
policy.   There are lament and longing unassuaged for
the land of his childhood; there is the lime (the tree
of nostalgia !), which points out from afar that there
at the mountain side are the houses of beloved Parga,
the lime tree that stands alone :

> " Se mai vien ch'io risalga secura
> a posar sotto il tiglio romito,
> che di Parga incorona l'altura." [2] . . .

The most beautiful page of the little poem is that
in which the population, which has been handed over
by the English to the Musulmans, prefers exile in
mass, and renders no longer sacred, in being obliged
to abandon it, that place which is sacred to it.   It
was during the " bitter-holy " days of Christ's passion
that this took place, and the population came together
to pray in the temple :

> " Poi, gemendo il novissimo addio,
> surse : e l'orme dei suoi sacerdoti
> taciturna la turba seguio." [3] . . .

Coming to the cemetery, to that corner of the earth
where, " beneath the weeping boughs of willows, sleep
the forefathers of Parga in their tombs, the bones of
our parents."

[1] " He descended—he crossed the threshold; he stood still; he
looked at them again : and his heart broke as though he were dying." . . .
[2] " If it ever happen that I return in all security to rest beneath the
solitary lime-tree which crowns the summit of Parga."
[3] " Then moaning forth a last farewell, the crowd arose and followed
the footsteps of its priests in silence." . . .

Those bones were taken from the tomb, piled up and burned upon a pyre, almost in sight of the enemy's vanguard, in order to remove them from the insults of the unbelievers. Then the crowd went down from the little city amid the lamentations, the cries and the pious acts of the women :

> " Qui toglievasi un'altra dal petto
> il lattante, e, fermando il cammino,
> con istrano delirio d'affetto
> si calava al ruscello vicino,
> vi bagnava per l'ultima volta
> nelle patrie fontane il bambino.
> E chi un ramo, un cespuglio, chi svolta
> dalle patrie campagne traeva
> una zolla nel pugno raccolta." [1] . . .

Finally the wretched population arrives at the beach and enters the boats :

> " Noi salpammo.—E la queta marea
> si coverse di un lungo ululato." [2] . . .

We see also other aspects of this condition of soul. The exile is moving among new people, new customs, he is called upon to form new relations and friendships :

> " Accolto in mezzo i liberi
> al conversar fidente,
> ramingo tra gli schiavi,
> chiuso il pensier prudente." [3] . . .

and he always has " his country in his heart." There among the strangers, his country's tragedy arouses

---

[1] " Here another took the suckling from her breast and staying on her way, with a strange movement of frenzy dipped her babe into the little stream for the last time, dipped it into the fountain of its fathers. Another pulled a branch, one bore a sprig from a bush, another coming from the paternal glebe, carried in her hand a clod of earth.

[2] " We weighed anchor and the quiet tide was covered with a long lament."

[3] " Received by free peoples and trustingly admitted to confidential conversations, or wandering among peoples enslaved, his prudent thought closed in his bosom." . . .

but slight or remote interest and sometimes it is
quite ignored.   What information can possibly have
reached a citizen of the remote north concerning the
recent history of Italy ?

> " Un dì a lui sull'aure algenti,
> là lontan, su l'onda baltica,
> dell'Italia andò un rumor,
> d'oppressori e di frementi,
> di speranze e di tormenti,
> di tumulti annunziator.
>
> Ma confuso, ma fugace
> fu quel grido, e ratto a sperderlo
> la parola uscì dei re,
> che narrò composta in pace
> tutt'Italia ai troni immobili
> plauder lieta e giurar fé." [1]

The news was vague, colourless and altered at
will; a feeling of indifference, the result of ignorance,
corresponds to it.   But he, the exile, is the apostle
of his country : he tells of its heroic deeds and its
misfortunes, makes known its loves and its aspirations,
explains its thought.   Above all, he describes it as
tortured, quivering, unreconciled, ready to rise up
for action, and announces its imminent revolt and
the war of independence.   Hope has become faith
in his mind; the words, which he has so often uttered
to himself and to others, have acquired the solidity of
things as to which it is impossible to doubt.   Nevertheless, doubt comes to insinuate itself : it arises
perhaps from the unsatisfactory news that has reached
him as to the present state of mind of Italians at home;

---

[1] " One day a rumour came to him from Italy, borne upon the cold
winds to that distant land by the Baltic wave, telling of oppressors and
enthusiasts for liberty, of hopes and torments.   But the sound was
confused and the word that came from kings seized upon it and
destroyed it, telling of all Italy at peace and ready to swear glad fealty
to the unshakable throne."

N

or, yet more, from unexpected and unpleasant memories that arouse images repressed and almost suffocated, which now claim to be real and assert their value. He feels as though he had somehow returned to Italy; it is dawn : he sees again the well-known fields and recognizes the places where he was happy as a child and explores them all with his eyes and finds them all in his heart; he is already pleased at the reception awaiting him, already he is clasping his brothers to his breast in a fraternal embrace, his brothers full of like hopes, desires, and resolute will to himself. But the men he meets are not Italians prepared for war, menacing, already rising against their aggressors, bursting free from their bonds—such as his imagination had long presented them to himself. They are peasants hastening to the sowing and to the vines, peasants, brutalized with hardships and closed to every other thought than that of gaining their daily bread : " they show their stupid faces tinged with misery; they move shoeless and in rags over the soil of plenty."

They are workmen and citizens, who care nothing for politics or country, anxious only as to their own affairs, their own ease, their own pleasures :

> " Dai fumaiuoli annunziansi
> ridesti a mille a mille
> i fochi dei castelli,
> dei borghi e delle ville.
> Dove piú folto è d'uomini,
> a due, a tre, a drappelli,
> escono agli ozi, all'opere,
> sparsi per la città." [1] . . .

---

[1] " The chimneys announce that thousands of fires are lit in castles, towns and suburbs. Where the throng is thickest they come forth, by twos and threes in groups, scattering themselves through the city, intent upon their pleasures or upon their toil."

At such a contrast between the ideal and the real (what seems to him at that moment to be the real but is itself an incubus due to his anxiety and to his immense love for his country), at so crude and unexpected a delusion, the returned exile is as it were stupefied, and sorrow and contempt rise to his lips, as he murmurs bitterly to himself :

> " Son questi ?   È questo il popolo
> per cui con affannosa
> lena ei cercò il periglio,
> perse ogni amata cosa ?
> È questo il desiderio
> dell'inquieto esiglio ?
> questo il narrato agli ospiti
> nobil nel suo patir ? " [1]

As a contrast, in another vision, the image of a foreign country becomes united to the idolized image of the Italian people : the landscape is that which recalls the peace celebrated at Constance, the peace that sealed the Italian victory over the Germans of Barbarossa. We feel, in the touches with which the little German city is depicted, that the poet has received it into his soul, has penetrated it with his sympathy. It is a landscape all shining with snow and purest water, a dear little city to be venerated for its antiquity and its suave domestic intimacy. Here the recognition of Italy's rights against the barbaric rule of the German will shine brightly, the little city will always recall in its name that austere triumph :

> " Dinanzi una cerulea
> laguna, un prorompente

---

[1] " Are they such as these ? Is this the people for sake of whom he sought out danger with eager breath, and abandoned all he loved ? Is this the longing of the restless exile ? Is this the people of which he told his hosts that it was enduring its sufferings with nobility ? "

fiume che da quell'onde
svolve la sua corrente.
Sovra tanta acqua, a specchio
una città risponde :
guglie a cui grigio i secoli
composero il color,
    ed irte di pinnacoli,
case che su lor grevi
denno sentir dei lenti
verni seder le nevi :
e finestrette povere,
a cui nei di tepenti
la casalinga vergine
infiora il davanzal." [1]

There is a great crowd in that city now, as though it were a feast day, a tramping, a waiting, and armed barons preceded by heralds pass through its streets, trumpets peal and glad news is declared. Silence falls in a moment upon all : the crowd opens dividing itself into two wings; a small and modest company arrives and advances : " Not escorted by soldiers, nor by splendour of heraldry, they are few in number and only notable for their black and prudent eyebrows, they move with slow foot amid the blond folk. They walk two and two, wrapped in their simple cloaks of dark hue."

He regards them with passion and insatiable admiration : " What frank and discreet gestures ! What dignity of countenance ! They intone among themselves a spiritual song, which they alternate joyfully." And all of a sudden he perceives the words of that song, and utters an almost childlike cry of

---

[1] " Facing us is a blue lagoon and a rushing river that draws its current from the waters of the lake. A city is mirrored above those many waters : its spires are grey with age, its houses have pointed roofs upon which the snow must weigh very heavily during the long winters, and poor little windows which the homebred maiden decorates with flowers on sunny days."

jubilation : " Oh, 'tis the dear tongue of dear Italy." . . .

In this part of his work, Berchet surpasses popular oratory and didactics, he caresses his feelings with his imagination and contemplates his own soul as a spectacle, an act proper to the poets.

XIV

Among the many kinds and varieties of literature is one which would be well defined by means of a verbal paradox, as *prosaic poetry*. It is not, as might be supposed, poetry that is a failure, but a thing of itself, having its own value, and called poetry solely because it assumes metrical form, whereas in reality it is prose. Metrical form is indeed suitable and natural to it, but here it does not fulfil the same office as in true and proper poetry, affording a new proof that the presence or absence of the verse (as indeed of every other characteristic taken in a material sense) does not give a sure indication of the presence or absence of poetry. I should like to add that the majority of jocose, gnomic, satiric and such like poets whom we meet with, especially in French and Italian literature, are to be included among prosaic poets, were I not restrained by the warning just uttered concerning the impossibility of judging from without and by means of material elements. And indeed there are joke and joke, satire and satire, didactics and didactics, the one poetical the other prosaic, because there is always *le ton qui fait la chanson*, and the material that appears to be identical in the abstract belongs to the one or the other class according to the spirit which breathes within.

How does prosaic poetry come to be? It does not

give an impression or an emotion which rises at once and directly to the sphere of contemplation, but it gives an impression or an emotion, which is quickly converted into a reflection, into an observation, into an oratorical proposition fit to impart this or that tendency to the mind of him who makes it or to another mind. Metrical form offers itself spontaneously as a means to this end, being efficacious in providing such a discourse or warning or invective with rhythm, in attracting attention to it, making it easy of communication and easily remembered. The composer of qualities, which have been obtained from poetry or rather from literature, works upon them, if he is an artist, and obtains very pleasing effects, although he never obtains that effect which is proper to beauty, and which further is excluded from his particular purpose. Almost all men of good taste and culture are able to make some elegant contribution to prosaic poetry, and at one time, when verse-making was taught in schools and this acquired virtuosity was among the duties of social intercourse, the output was copious indeed : even to-day anyone accustomed to literary production finds little difficulty in turning out an epigram or a few jesting verses, whereas he might perhaps find it impossible to write a single line of poetry.

Giuseppe Giusti is to be broadly included in this class as among its most eminent votaries. He was the author of comic poems and satires, which enjoyed great success in Italy between 1830 and 1848, and continued to echo through the succeeding decades, growing gradually, however, weaker and more weak. He often seemed annoyed at his reputation as a comic and satiric poet, discontented with himself and with his fate. He insisted upon being at bottom sad at heart, his jesting was not his best work, he declared, for he drew his sorrowful laughter from his disdain; obliged to be satirical, he grew weary of it and suffered, for he was not without feeling a restless longing for the beauty of truth; he aspired, he said, to an arduous ideal of art, which he hoped one day to attain. But this potentiality or general attitude towards poetry, existing more or less in every man, is not excluded by the definition we have given of prosaic poetry; we only wish to make it clear that in such a form the potentiality does not become converted into actuality, but remains a psychology not further probed or developed, or an antecedent which gives way before reflection, observation and practical tendency. The very protests and confessions, which Giusti never ceased making, show that he was conscious of the limit set to his gifts and that sometimes he hit himself against it.

This limit is clearly demonstrated by the paucity of his serious, amorous or emotional compositions, which are not without delicacy of feeling and elegance of form, but do not surpass in quality thoughts put into verse. The very popular sonnet upon the statue of Bartolini, *La fiducia in Dio*, which is the most perfect composition of this group, will serve as the best example : " Almost forgetting the bodily burden, borne off to Him who willingly pardons, she abandons where she kneels gently her fair body and therewith all her honours. A weariness of pain, a celestial calm, seems to be diffused all about her; but on her brow, which has intercourse with God, shines the immortal ray of the soul. And she seems to say : if every pleasant thing deceives me and I feel my

restless life flying from me, O Lord, my spirit trusting
to Thy paternal bosom has recourse to and repose in
a love that is not of this earth."

It is simple, limpid, facile, and coherent : yet one
cannot help thinking how well it would look in an
album or a gift-book as a laudatory commentary upon
a gracious piece of sculpture or as a manifestation of
sympathy for that sweet little form of a young girl
sorrowing and imploring. Were anything else sought
for there, a certain void would become evident. But
then, why seek for anything else ?

A yet clearer perception of Giusti's limitations is
to be found by paying attention to some of his satirical
poems, especially upon that one which has been
celebrated as his masterpiece, the *Sant-Ambrogio*,
where he seems to have merged his two founts of
inspiration, sentimentalism and political polemic. The
poet has entered a church during service and has
found himself in the centre of a group of Austrian
soldiers who are assisting at Mass. He is already
seized with repugnance, when those soldiers, whose
appearance is so odious to him, begin to sing, and
in the harmony of the song and the unhappiness and
nostalgia there expressed, he suddenly feels a new
tenderness insinuating itself into his heart and completely filling it; these enemy soldiers are poor
human creatures accustomed to suffer like himself;
he is almost ready to open his arms and embrace them.
But this emotional discovery of common humanity
in the midst of divisions which estrange men from
men does not of itself form the true lyric. Giusti
was capable of really experiencing that feeling, but
he was not capable of fecundating it, of living it
completely in the imagination and of making it the

centre of a world, as would have been the case with a poetical poet.

And now behold that emotion become for him a sentimental anecdote, which he tells with an active mind and a cold heart, to the extent of joking about it, commenting upon it, adding to it satirical salt, drawing from it political allusions and versifying it in simply rhymed octaves, which rather provide the reader with matter for sage reflection than carrying him off into a sphere of sublime human sentiment. Giusti lets fly here a new arrow of many-coloured feather against the foreign tyrant, but he does not send that golden shaft towards the sun, by means of which, in Carducci's words, the poet " looks and enjoys and asks nothing more." He begins : " Your Excellency who eyes me with severity because of those few satiric verses of mine and writes me down an anti-German because I put thieves in the pillory, pray listen to what has just happened to me as I was strolling about one morning and chanced to enter out of hand Sant-Ambrogio in Milan."

What is really dominating the spirit of the writer is the thought of the advantage he will be able to obtain for his political polemic from the narrative of the sentimental adventure that has befallen him. And in order the better to prepare that effect, he addresses his discourse to a high official of the Austrian Government in Italy or of an Italian Government with Austrian leanings. He is thus able to make the practical conclusion more ironical, for his sensation of love for the Germans becomes a strong desire that, for the benefit of all, they should leave Italy. The salient point is thus given : " A German canticle moved its wings slowly, slowly on the sacred air, and seemed to me to be the same lament of grave, solemn and flexible sound such as I always feel within my soul : and I am astonished that so exquisite a harmony could reside beneath such cuticles, in those foreign simpletons made of wood."

And impressions in the form of analysis follow the narrative; they are not without sentimental emphasis :

> " Sentia nell'inno la dolcezza amara
> dei canti uditi da fanciullo : il core
> che da voce domestica gli impara,
> ce li ripete il giorno del dolore :
> un pensier mesto della madre cara,
> un desiderio di pace ed amore,
> uno sgomento di lontano esilio,
> che mi faceva andare in visibilio." [1]

Hence, the following considerations :

> " Costor—dicea tra me—re pauroso
> degli italici moti e degli slavi
> strappa ai lor tetti, e qua senza riposo
> schiavi li spinge per tenerci schiavi." [2] . . .

The finale of the poem is gay in tone, as of one ashamed to have been discovered in tears who hastens to escape from them with a laughable image; but, in reality, the narrative and discursive tone prevented the direct effusion of pathos : " Here, if I do not fly, I embrace a corporal with his grand corporal's *bâton* made of hard cherry-wood, planted there firmly like a peg run into the ground."

Given the end which the author proposed to himself,

---

[1] " I heard the bitter sweetness of songs heard as a child in that hymn. The heart learns them from those at home and repeats them on the day of sorrow : a sad thought for the dear mother, a longing for peace and love, a *malaise* of distant exile, which ravished me."

[2] " 'A king who fears Italian and Slavonic risings,' I said to myself, ' and deprives the Slavs of their homes, and sends them here as slaves to hold us in slavery.' "

the *Sant-Ambrogio* may be said to realize the conception to the full.   Perfect in like manner, or almost so, are other compositions of Giusti, among which, suffice it to cite *Delenda Cartago*, the *Istruzione ad un emissario*, the *Congresso di Birri*, the comic scene of the *Discorsi che corrono*.   There exists a work which examines the artistic development of Giusti with subtlety, from the period of the first " frolics " to these works of his mature talent.   It is a pleasure to me to recall and to send readers to it, because we owe it to a young student of great promise, who died young, Tommaso Parodi, and also because it has enjoyed little popularity, although in my opinion the best critical essay upon the argument that exists.   The one thing lacking to the youthful critic was the daring required to arrive at our conclusion, that is to say, the denial to Giusti of inner poetical inspiration.

The fame too of Giusti began to decline, as we have mentioned, after '60 and '70.   When I was a youth, his verses were still largely much read and known by heart; then the reprints became less frequent and severe or at least reserved and sober judgments were uttered concerning him.   He certainly could not be reproached, in common with other versifiers of the Risorgimento, with being facile and careless—for he was an admirable versifier and his rhymes are rich, as well as an artist, conscientious to the point of being sometimes involved and hesitating from excessive labour—but he was blamed for a certain provincial narrowness, for his subject matter as being too occasional and contingent, and for the scarcity of form and colour in his satirical figurations.

But the true reason for the decline of his fame lies in his above-mentioned character of prosaic poet.

All prosaic poets enjoy greater fame among their contemporaries than with posterity, whereas the opposite is the case with poetic poets. Prosaic poets are orators in their own way, and orators arouse but little interest, once the occasion that moved them to exercise their power of words is passed. Each generation likes to have its own epigrammatists, satirical writers, caricaturists and preachers, which does not prevent those of former times from retaining their artistic value and from exciting admiration, when we return to contemplate them in the way suitable to their work. This is the more the case, seeing that the human comedy of different times is also the human comedy of all times, and old gnomic, epigrammatical and satirical writers, are still always able to supply us with some caricature, some witty saying, efficacious when employed in the polemics of our own day.

XV

HEINE

A GOOD part of the critical literature concerning Heine is occupied with the controversy concerning the judgment to be given as to the life and character of the man and as to the meaning of his artistic work. It is asked whether he deserves the gratitude of his compatriots, to be expressed by the erection of a public monument, obstinately denied to him hitherto. It would seem that both points of the controversy are better left alone : the first, because it is of little advantage and the reverse of pitiful to torture the soul of the dead poet, rousing it from its eternal repose, in order to investigate weaknesses and errors which were paid for with long and atrocious sufferings, and as regards the second, because it is connected with political tendencies of the sort that for a long time contended or prevailed in Germany.

This however is not so, and beneath the appearance of an inquiry into the life and political intransigence, nothing less is in question than the character and value of Heine's poetry. If the poetry had shone before the eyes of all as belonging to the sphere of great and lofty poetry, the poet would have been absolved and redeemed in a far more appropriate manner than by the physical sufferings of the man; and political partisanship would be silent. Foscolo had an anything but unblemished record, and Manzoni

was among the heads of a party that wished to make
of liberal Italy the faithful and favourite daughter of
the Papacy; yet no moralist, no political adversary
has appeared to deny to them admiration and gratitude,
both human and national. If any dare do so, owing
to sourness of temperament or momentary blindness,
resulting from particular contingencies, he was quickly
repressed and reproved by general opinion. The
bitter censures of Foscolo by Tommaseo aroused
reprobation and disgust as odious malignity, and the
republican, anti-clerical, anti-Manzonian Carducci
ended by reverently inclining himself before the statue
of Alessandro Manzoni, conquered by the generosity
inherent to his character.

It is possible to regard these controversies concerning Heine disinterestedly, but in another sense;
by taking up and examining directly what is sought
for in them indirectly, in the consequences rather than
the causes, in the particulars rather than in the whole :
in other words, by asking simply whether Heine were
a poet, and, if so, of what sort. In our answer to
this question we shall both illustrate his moral
character and the unwillingness of his compatriots to
place him among the great ones, for whom their heart
should beat.

Undertaking such an examination, it will be best
first to clear away the image of Heine as a profound
thinker, all the more profound inasmuch as he concealed the depth of his thought with the mystery of a
smile, and as the assertor of noble ideals, all the more
powerful because armed with the powerful and
terrible arm of irony. This image arose outside
Germany, and culminated in Italy with the well-
known portrait of Heine contained in one of Carducci's

lyrics. Years ago a learned Frenchman wrote a book on *Henri Heine penseur*, which should be read in order to come to a precisely opposite opinion to that suggested by the title and the work itself, that is to say, a Heine who is a *non-penseur*, whose thoughts were never either coherent or original. It is not very difficult to explain that it should appear otherwise outside Germany, because Heine was born and educated at a period of extraordinarily rich German culture, rich in every sort of philosophy and criticism. Its treasures reduced to small compass were on the lips of all, so that a vivacious intelligence such as his, acute and adaptable, became to a certain degree interested in them, and made use of them to a very large extent as decoration, especially impressing in this way the ignorant and curious readers of Parisian reviews. The conversations and discussions between students in the university of Göttingen sufficed to supply him with sufficient philosophical furniture to astonish anywhere but in Germany. Something not dissimilar happened later in the case of a weak philosopher, Schopenhauer, who was everywhere known, thanks to his limpid style and to the pessimistic pose which it pleased him to assume. He seemed to be a very great philosopher, although he merely repeated the discoveries of his predecessors, combining them anew and weakening them in the process. And as Heine had decked himself in Germany with the thoughts of Kant, Schelling and Hegel, and of the romantic historians and philologists, so with an equal promptitude he availed himself in France of the political democratic writers, especially of Saint-Simon and his school. He never achieved a serious philosophical, moral or political elaboration of himself; nor can we rank as serious with that seriousness which stamps every thought, every emotion, every act, and makes itself felt in the style, his faith in the ideal of which he declared himself the champion.

He certainly professed something that can be called an ideal; but it often happens, when we examine its external manifestations, that a suspicion arises as to its being due to the dictates of art—an artistic necessity—for it is very vague and indefinite, adapted to his Jewish origin, his Rhenish birthplace and to his long residence as an exile in France. Indeed, it is difficult to conceive how a sociable spirit like Heine's, always intent upon joking, making fun of others and laughing at or deriding them, to caricature, to elegant buffoonery, and very exquisite in the enjoyment of such tastes, could have continued to satisfy so uncontrollable a need without something that should serve as an ideal. The very vague ideal of liberty, of brotherhood, of progress, of rationality and even of God in heaven afforded him an excellent vantage-ground from which to throw his stones with vigour and success. And what a large and handy target for a jesting spirit was provided by things that had become or were antiquated, although still sound and useful institutions, such as absolute monarchy, semi-feudal nobility, a devout and zealous middle-class, the police, corporals and barracks, and the like! But since his love for the ideal was not profound, so his hatred for its negative aspect, the counter-ideal, was also lacking in profundity. This is evident from his frequent lapses into sentimentalism for the old world, and from his incapacity to refrain from pointing out the ridiculous side of

o

men and things democratic. But the convincing proof of this lies in his mode of manifesting his aversion and raillery by means of descriptions so grotesque and happy thoughts so comical as to be a clear indication that he was really enjoying himself rather than hating. Extreme German patriots, and believers in the Hohenzollern monarchy do him too much honour when they grow indignant at his quips and sarcasms : they would do more wisely in simply laughing at them, when, as is almost always the case, they are gracefully turned and neatly delivered. But sincere lovers of liberty and democracy, such as Carducci, show proof of little discernment in accepting Heinrich Heine as of their faith : he is at best a disloyal ally, with his heart elsewhere.

He was, as we have said, at heart devoted to jesting, and this was the fundamental form of his mind, constantly maintained, not liberty, democracy, pantheism or theism. Now is it ever possible, when one loves pleasantry so much, to become pure and great in such a thing as poetry, which has in it something almost religious. It may be answered : Why not ? Is it not now held to be axiomatic that poetry arises from any sort of soul state, and that the poetic form is poetic, not the quality of its abstract content ? Is this not the directive principle of these very critical essays ?—No doubt it is : but doubt exists as to whether the jesting state of soul is a genuine state, of the sentimental and passionate sort from which poetry arises, or whether it is not on the contrary a mode of activity which has passed beyond both the ingenuous soul state and poetry itself. The intention to exhort or to incite, for instance, is not a state of soul, but an act of will, which produces oratory and does not contain poetry within itself as an end, but looks back upon it as a presupposition. Jesting is produced in identical conditions : it is a practical mode of obtaining pleasure in company and by oneself, by combining images in an unexpected form and by striking the notes of that scale of psychical reactions known as laughter.

This attitude is altogether different from and in a certain sense even opposed to the attitude of the poet, who fixes his regard on the depths of his own self, striving to portray what he finds there and to reflect an aspect of the universe in the spasm of its becoming. The wit makes us expand our chests with laughter and leaves our heads free; the poet fills our heads with images and our breasts with emotion. The poetical disposition is that of serenity, joy, buoyancy, but not the act of jesting, or only when it is lowered to the level of psychical material and included as an element in a representation. Here the jester may even look upon himself with pity, exactly like Giusti's saltimbanco, " who is dying with hunger, but amuses the crowd with his frank and hilarious appearance."

Jesters are artists in the manner of orators (and it can be shown that they are a sub-species of these), because they must make use of poetical images in the development of their activity, which does not lead to a poetical image, but to a practical effect, and since they reduce poetry to the level of a means or an instrument, they are not poets. The distinction between poets and artists is as well employed in the case of jesters and of orators as it is ill employed in æsthetics to indicate two different artistic groups or two forms of poetry or two opposed poetical tendencies. With what care tellers of laughable anecdotes study inflections, suspensions, suggestions; with what lively and appropriate expressions and mimicry do they portray physiognomies with a view to the final effect ! When we hear them thus diverting the company, we admire and proclaim them " artists."

In this art, Heinrich Heine was a master, and we still laugh at his witticisms, and enjoy the delightful imagery with which he gives them force and relief, although so much has happened in the world since his time. Only a jester largely provided with poetical small change could obtain such results. He pursues Atta Troll, the German Philistine, but Atta Troll never rises to the level of a poetical personage, but remains always a jesting comparison. But to depict him as Heine does requires a soul sensible of the most varied emotions and a plastic imagination, as for example in the cave where he has retired to sleep with his one male child and his daughters :

> " In der Höhle bei dem Jungen
> Liegt der Alte, und er schläft
> Mit dem Schnarchen des Gerechten ;
> Endlich wacht er gähnend auf . . .
> Gleichfalls an des Vaters Seite
> Liegen träumend auf dem Rücken,
> Unschuldrein, vierfüssige Lilien,
> Atta Trolls geliebte Töchter." . . .

He almost touches one's heart for those bearish virgins, as he jests, the beloved daughters, who are sleeping beside their father, with their four feet in the air, " purest innocents, lilies with four paws " !

In *Die Stadt Lucca* he banteringly describes the sway of philosophy in Berlin and employs these images :

" Ich schilderte ihm nun, wie in der gelehrten Karawanserei zu Berlin die Kamele sich sammeln um

den Brunnen Hegel 'scher Weisheit, davor nieder-
knien, sich die kostbaren Schläuche aufladen lassen,
und damit weiter ziehen durch die märkische Sand-
wüste." . . .

We are on the point of submitting to the enchant-
ment of that well of Wisdom, of those camels which
collect around it and kneel down in order to allow
themselves to be burdened with the precious skins of
water before seeking the desert, and we think of an
Oriental scene.

A little further on in the same volume we come
upon the following :

" Nach der Messe gab's noch Allerlei zu schauen
und zu hören, besonders die Predigt eines grossen
vierstämmigen Mönchs, dessen befehlend kühnes
altrömisches Gesicht gegen die grobe Bettelkutte gar
wundersam abstach, so dass der Mann aussah wie ein
Imperator der Armuth." . . .

What a picture is this great, big, strong mendicant
friar, who raises the daring, commanding countenance
of an ancient Roman above the rough cowl of the
monk, and looks like an Emperor of Poverty! A
few strokes complete the living portrait.

The *Nordsee* cycle is full of jests about the mythology,
suggestive of the council of the gods in the *Secchia
rapita* and the *Scherno degli dèi ;* but Heine's realism in
the midst of his caricatures and strange fancies is
really wonderful. The Sun, or rather the Lady
Sun, a fair dame who has made a marriage of con-
venience with the old God of the sea, circles splendidly
adorned in the sky during the day, as though it were
a promenade or a ball in Society; but in the evening,

when she returns home, there are scenes with her consort, reproaches and abuse on one side and weeping on the other, until finally the old man becomes desperate, jumps out of bed and rises to the surface of the sea, in order to take the air :

" So sah ich ihn selbst verflossene Nacht
Bis an die Brust dem Meer enttauchen.
Er trug eine Jacke von gelbem Flanell,
Und eine liljenweise Schlafmütz',
Und ein abgewelktes Gesicht."

Just the image of an old husband, tired and ugly, absurdly clad and broken down in appearance.

Nevertheless, if there were nothing in Heine but this fine art of wit adroitly wielded, it would be difficult not to agree with those who deny that he is a true poet, and there would also perhaps be something to say as to his moral character, recalling Pascal's saying : *Diseur de bons mots, mauvais caractère*. But Heine possessed a true, free and proper vein of poetry, beyond the virtuosity of his little pictures and portraits, with their minute poetical emotional quality employed to a practical end. This true vein of poetry has wrongly been regarded as histrionic and sentimental with affectation, because what appears with the first manifestations of a soul, reappears in less favourable conditions, maintains itself tenaciously up to his last days, is expressed in little lyrics pure and transparent as a drop of dew and in innumerable passages of verse and prose of singular freshness, cannot be so described. This fount of inspiration might be called the poetry of childhood, of a childhood sensible of the pleasure of the paternal hearth and home, which listens with wide-opened eyes to fables and legends and becomes plunged in the reading of old histories, abounds in admiration for olden warriors and wise men, loves with the lovers, beats with its wings around the heads of the blond queenlets, shudders at terrible events, and asks to see the ruins of the castle, once upon a time witness of so many wondrous deeds, the marble effigies upon the tombs, the images upon the altars, and regards with rapture the hoary old peasant crossing the road when told that once upon a time he was a man of war and adventures.

This feeling was never so keen as during Heine's years of childhood, when he first felt the nostalgia of the past and wished for its return. This attitude of mind provided a basis for a whole literature, not only in Germany, but throughout Europe. Few, however, experienced it with an intensity equal to that of the little Jew from Düsseldorf, who might have been expected to remain indifferent to what was to some extent extraneous to one for whom the regretted, dreamed-of past was not the past of his own people. The suavity of childhood and of the images that attract the spirit of childhood in its opening out to the world, always accompanied Heinrich Heine, like the memory of an innocent exchange of love experienced for the first time, which for ever distils its sweetness, softening the bitterest hearts and those most hardened by the trials of life. He hears old ballads sung and exclaims :

> " Ein Traum war über mich gekommen ;
> Mir war, als sei ich noch ein Kind,
> Und sässe still beim Lämpchenscheine
> In Mutters frommem Kämmerleine,
> Und läse Märchen wunderfeine,
> Derweilen draussen Nacht und Wind." . . .

This is his true dream of love and happiness, his idyll. A little masterpiece of moving, soldierly devotion, *Die zwei Grenadiere*, belongs to his youth, inspired by the already legendary figure of Napoleon. To his youth belongs also *Die Wallfahrt nach Kevlaar*, and many other exquisite things like *Die Lorelei*, or the little strophes of the three king magicians :

> " Die heiligen drei Kön'ge aus Morgenland,
> Sie frugen in jedem Städtchen :
> —Wo geht der Weg nach Bethleem,
> Ihr lieben Buben und Mädchen ? "

But delicate love-tales, glad and sad, are still to be met with among the poems of his maturity, so full of irony and laughter.   Such, for instance is the *Schlachtfeld bei Hastings*, or that of the monk who succeeds in raising the most beautiful corpse from the tomb by means of a terrible incantation.   She sits beside him and they look at one another without speaking :

> " Ihr Blick ist traurig.   Aus kalter Brust
> Die schmerzlichen Seufzer steigen.
> Die Todte setzt sich zu dem Mönch,
> Sie schauen sich an und schweigen."

This affection for myths and legends, for domestic and paternal customs and for the figures that express them, forms the poetical parts of *Atta Troll*, of *Deutschland* and of the *Götterdämmerung* and of his writings on history and on German literature.   It has been said in his defence that, however irreverent he may seem towards his own country, yet he dearly loved it, as is proved by these most tender effusions. But he never loved his country on its political and ethical sides, but only his country as the country of his childhood, as the symbolic whole of the suave impressions once there enjoyed :

> " Wie der Winterwandrer des Abends sich sehnt
> Nach einer warmen, innigen Tasse Thee,
> So sehnt sich jetzt mein Herz nach dir,
> Mein deutsches Vaterland." . . .

he exclaims, jestingly as usual, but revealing his real mode of feeling in the jest.

In order to understand his love poetry well, we must replace it in the yearning for childhood, because he never conceived of love as a passion, which, by merging itself in the loftiest moral interests, colours them with itself, or by entering into conflict with them, produces an interior drama or tragedy. For Heine, love was always a game, an agreeable game, the only refuge in the prosaic modern world, deprived alike of God and devil, obscure and cold (" Und wäre nicht das bisschen Liebe, So gäb' es nirgends einen Halt "). It was a game in which one wins sometimes, but more often loses, sometimes again coming out scratched, disabused and in tears, but which always remains interesting and amusing. Hence he spontaneously adopted the form of popular poetry, which was another of the literary tendencies of his day, akin to him through its elementary point of view, its rhythm and even its syntax and its elementary adorations, its proposals, its sighings, its accusings and complainings, which is represented in the *Intermezzo*, in *Die Heimkehr*, and here and there in his other works. Love wove there also its fables, as in the unforgettable :

> " Die Lotosblume ängstigt
> Sich vor der Sonne Pracht." . . .

and :

> " Ein Fichtenbaum steht einsam
> Im Norden auf kahler Höh." . . .

But even when he sang of his little cousins who would have none of him, and admired beauties of a lesser purity than her who had inspired :

> " Du bist wie eine Blume,
> So hold, und schön und rein." . . .

and narrated less innocent adventures, such as the nocturnal journey in the post-chaise, the joking and laughing with his fair neighbour and how, when it was dawn :

> " Doch als es Morgen tagte,
> Mein Kind, wie staunten wir !
> Denn zwischen uns sass Amor,
> Der blinde Passagier." . . .

and gyrated between the Hortenses and the Clarisses, and the game from the sentimental that it was became sensual and the sighing youth gave way to the dissolute, it still remained the same.

Listen to his dangerous conversation with Hortense :

> " Wir standen an der Strasseneck,
> Wohl über eine Stunde ;
> Wir sprachen voller Zärtlichkeit
> Von unserem Seelenbunde.
>   Wir sagten uns viel hundertmal,
> Dass wir einander lieben ;
> Wir standen an der Strasseneck,
> Und sind da stehn geblieben.
>   Die Göttin der Gelegenheit,
> Wie'n Zöfchen flink und heiter
> Kam sie vorbei und sah uns stehen,
> Und lachend ging sie weiter."

Finally, Heine's satire, jest and irony owe to the poetry of childhood, in addition to so many particular images and inventions, its most effective and most usual tone, that of a malicious youngster who notices everything and looks as if he is astonished and unaware of the sharp darts that he is running into the flesh of other people. He persisted in this practice to the end, without ever allowing himself to be caught by juvenile indignation or to be overturned by passion. For him this was no difficult matter, because it was the part that best suited him and best contributed to the effect of his jesting.

But the latter of these, perhaps, did less good service to his poetry than it received from it. And even in the more lyrical portions of his work the line is frequently crossed that separates simple emotion felt and jesting : his style acquired a witty mode of expression, which prevented the appearance of powerful lines and those of great musical charm. Certainly the comic spirit was of use to him in getting rid of the idols to which he had sacrificed in his youth. As he said, he had long frequented in his youth the Kiffhäuser, the Venusberg and other " catacombs of Romanticism," and had left documentary proof of his romantic leanings in several sentimental compositions such as the *Junge Leiden*, and especially in two tragedies, one of which belongs to the Moorish-Spanish style, and the other to that of the dramas of destiny dependent upon spectres and fatal vendettas, both, that is to say, to the literary mode. Further, the forms of the popular song, on the other hand, restored and endowed in Germany with the highest culture and refinement, became easily diverted into the jocose, and the jocose removed from them what of rough and absurd they contained, which elsewhere, as in Italy, ended with the parodies (the " heroic Anselm [1] "). But on the whole, Heine, freeing himself from romantic inflations, maintained the romantic

[1] The *Prode Anselmo* is a graceful Italian parody of the romantic ballads.

conception of irony, and made a very wide use of it, especially in *Atta Troll* and in *Romancero*, thus falling back into jesting and rendered incapable of more profound inspirations, or when they appeared dissolving them at once in jest. Not that the new romantic poems fail of frequent felicity in the comic vein. The good-natured bantering tone of the poem on mediæval genealogies in *Schelm von Bergen*, of noble race, descendant of the village executioner, made a gentleman by arrangement, with its solemn conclusion will certainly please :

> " So ward der Henker ein Edelman
> Und Ahnherr der Schelme von Bergen.
> Ein stolzes Geschlecht ! es blühte am Rhein,
> Jetzt schläft es in steinernen Särgen." . . .

Admirers will also be found for the luxurious mock-heroic Ali Bey, who frees himself from the embraces of the ladies of his harem to mount his horse and speed to battle, and with the expression of lasciviousness still lingering on his countenance, lops off the heads of Christians :

> " Während er die Franken Köpfe
> Dutzendweis herunter säbelt,
> Lächelt er, wie ein Verliebter,
> Ja, er lächelt, sanft und zärtlich." . . .

Many other similar poems will also please; only they do not, as many believe, express a more complex mode of feeling, when they behold this and such-like romantic-ironic poetry, but, on the contrary, a feeling that has been surpassed and rendered superficial, its place being occupied by light laughter : the poet, as a matter of fact, here becomes eclipsed—he goes out like a candle. Nor does he rise again in the *Letzte Gedichte*, where physical anguish, destruction, terror of the tomb, desperate clinging to the pleasures of life, are all poured forth, but always in those witty, amusing modes which had become for him habitual. I do not recall what German has said of Heine that he was a " Harlequin of pain," but perhaps that is saying too much, and it would be better to say a " painful Harlequin," because we feel pain too immediately in him and not sufficiently poetically, incarnated alternately in that witty being, accustomed to face life with epigrams and the martyred dying creature of so many poems.

Such was Heinrich Heine, and regarding him thus, it becomes quite comprehensible that others do not succeed in admiring and loving him with complete abandonment, and object to making him a hero of national poetry; because he (and he would not have looked upon the comparison as offensive) too often reveals " the cloven hoof," which is not the attribute of a poet.

XVI

GEORGES SAND

WE read to-day with effort the hundred and more
volumes of Georges Sand, which made our grand-
mothers shiver and grow pale, and the re-reading of
them fails of giving pleasure, like a game that has
ceased to amuse, because the trick of it has been
discovered.

When I see recent æsthetic critics and æstheticians
really thinking that poetry coincides with social
manifestations and practical achievements and proceeding to treat of it as a historical product of the
same quality as they, I am astonished that they are
not struck by these great examples of decadence and
by their failure to perceive the impossibility of reviving
as poetry what never was really poetry, and not
having been born as such, cannot be made to live
again as what it never was. We know that in the
fervour of interest aroused by certain works, no very
careful choice is made of epithets of praise, the more
so, because these epithets are mutually interchangeable,
and it thus comes about that what has only given an
agreeable stimulus to the fancy, has moved or brought
conviction to certain minds or has reinforced their
persuasions, is called " beautiful."

But time passes, social and practical interests are
displaced and others appear, former pleasures grow
wearisome, and behold to the eye of the connoisseur
what is truly beautiful still shines forth, and other

things, which once seemed beautiful or were called
beautiful, but are no longer supported by the forces
which rendered easy the illusion, grow pale and wan
and become merged in obscurity.   Then the historical
critic, or rather the critic who fails of being historical,
who proceeds to discourse of art without faith in the
idea of art busies himself with supplying equivalents
for the lost pleasure, of which he vaunts the fame.
For example, he will try to make the novels of Georges
Sand again agreeable, by presenting their authoress,
the fruitful writer, " l'Isis du roman contemporain,
la bonne déesse aux multiples mamelles toujours
ruisselantes," and by assuring us that " il fait bon se
rafraîchir dans ce fleuve de lait."   But the wise reader
enjoys the graceful image and does not indulge in the
milk.

Or he will draw attention to the curiosity aroused
by the personages of the novels, when considered
historically : " Comme ils ne sont plus du tout nos
contemporains, leur fausseté ne nous gêne plus : nous
ne voyons en eux que les témoins du romanesque d'une
époque; et même nous finissons par les aimer parce
qu'ils ont plu à nos pères."   But the reader who in
that case wishes for poetical beings and not mummies
and other such historical curiosities does not allow
himself to be seduced by the two different orders of
objects.   I too am fond of romantic books, and
particularly of those illustrated, among which I possess
Les femmes de Walter Scott and *Les femmes de Georges
Sand* (how many lovely faces ! how many superb
queens of the heart !) and I contemplate them with
a smile, but that smile does not express purely artistic
satisfaction.   Or, again, the same critic will count
upon a renewal of interest in Georges Sand as the

result of satiety and reaction from the different kind of conventionalism of naturalistic and veristic fiction. This may be successful (and it certainly was so in the celebrated case of Rostand's *Cyrano de Bergerac*, which is a *pastiche* in the manner of Hugo and of Dumas the elder, cooked in a moment of disgust for verism and middle-class commonplace), yet such a reversion, since it is determined by external and contingent motives, shows itself to be unstable like the others.

Georges Sand was undoubtedly one of the most noteworthy representatives of European moral life in the twenty years prior to the revolution of 1848. She represented this practical side of life chiefly and energetically by means of a strange Utopia, which may be termed " the religion of love." This Utopia, owing precisely to its religious element, was distinguished from the *sensiblerie* of the eighteenth century, and bore the mark of the new times, times without a God and yet desirous of a God. From the point of view of this religion, the value and meaning of life are to be found in love, just in love, understood sexually; and Eros is the god, although the rhetorical phraseology of the day preferred to formulate its thought with a certain degree of unction and spoke of " love " as "coming from God."

Love, being the highest and indeed the only act of the religious cult, does not recognize any law as superior to itself : as soon as it appears, it has the right of obtaining satisfaction, " the right of passion." And it is sovran : it does not tolerate a division of its kindgom with other affections : every other passion must serve it, receive orders from it and submit to it. It is also unique and eternal; and when it seems to vary in its objects, the fault lies with society, which embarrasses it with its foolish and tryannical laws, or with material accidents, which trouble it, for in its essence it is constancy and fidelity. He who loves without return should respect the passion for another object in the beloved, and love ordains self-sacrifice, in order that passion may celebrate the sacred rite in full joy and freedom : in making this sacrifice, duty is performed, the heroism of the perfect lover is attained.

What had been the tragedy of Lélia ? Precisely this. She had loved a man in every way most worthy of love, but she was loved by him in the way men love who are otherwise busy, that is to say, at intervals. Horrible ! " Il y avait pour lui dans l'accomplissement du devoir social, des satisfactions d'amour-propre plus vives, ou du moins plus profondes, plus constantes, plus nécessaires, que *les saintes délices d'un pur amour.*" She has been deluded, and remains for ever desolate and desperate. " Je n'eus plus rien à mettre à la place. Tout me parut petit près de ce colosse imaginaire. L'amitié me sembla froide, la religion mensonge, et la poésie était morte avec l'amour." The mainspring of life had been broken. " Qu'est-ce que l'amour ? n'est-ce pas un culte ? et derrière ce culte, l'objet aimé n'est-il pas le dieu ? Et si lui-même prend plaisir à detruire la foi qu'il inspirait, comment l'âme peut-elle se choisir un autre dieu parmi d'autres créatures ? Elle a rêvé l'idéal, et, tant qu'elle a cru trouver la perfection dans un être de sa race, elle s'est prosternée devant lui. Mais maintenant elle sait que son idéal n'est pas de ce monde."

And what is the tragedy of Jacques ? He loves the youthful Fernanda, and marries her ; but after a time, Fernanda is loved by another and returns his love.

P

Jacques is also a faithful adept of the new religion. How, then, could he dare to protest, blame, condemn, in the name of an inferior morality, when that sacred flame is burning which is the supreme, sole, true morality ? " Aujourd'hui elle cède à une passion qu'un an de combats et de résistances a enracinée dans son cœur; je suis forcé de l'admirer, car je pourrais l'aimer encore, y eût-elle cédé au bout d'un mois. Nulle créature humaine ne peut commander à l'amour, et nul n'est coupable pour le ressentir et pour le perdre. Ce qui avilit la femme, c'est le mensonge ": lying is in this case impious, because it denies the true God. What will he do ? " O Fernande," he exclaims, feeling social blame and malevolence surrounding him, " j'aime mieux faire rire de moi que de faire couler tes larmes; j'aime mieux les railleries de l'univers entier que ta haine et ta douleur ! " He will put an end to himself, leaving the field open to the two loving souls : he will do so in such a way as to make it impossible for them to suspect that he has killed himself for them. " Ne maudis pas " (he writes to his sister) " ces deux amants qui vont profiter de ma mort. Ils ne sont pas coupables, ils s'aiment. Il n'y a pas de crime là où il y a de l'amour sincère."

In this manner of feeling, Lélia and Jacques, elect, sublime beings, bring their own sublimity to the highest possible point. Jacques knows everything, can do everything, courageous on all occasions, strong of arm, he would be capable of accomplishing the loftiest undertakings; yet he throws superbly all these many gifts, so rich and rare, at the feet of love. Lélia is at the same time Tasso, Dante, Shakespeare, Romeo, Hamlet, Juliet, Corinna and Lara : " elle réunit toutes les idéalités parce qu'elle réunit le génie de

tous les poètes, la grandeur de tous les caractères."
On seeing her, the Goddess in her becomes manifest.

" Au dessus de tout s'élevait la grande figure isolée
de Lélia. Appuyée contre un cippe de bronze
antique, sur les degrés de l'amphithéâtre, elle con-
templait aussi le bal, elle avait revêtu aussi un costume
caractéristique, mais l'avait choisi noble et sombre
comme elle : elle avait le vêtement austère et pourtant
recherché, la pâleur, la gravité, le regard profond d'un
jeune poète d'autrefois, alors que les temps étaient
poétiques et que la poésie n'était pas coudoyée dans
la foule. Les cheveux noirs de Lélia, rejetés en
arrière, laissaient à découvert ce front où le doigt de
Dieu semblait avoir imprimé le sceau d'une mysté-
rieuse infortune, et que les regards du jeune Sténio
interrogeaient sans cesse avec l'anxieté du pilote
attentif au moindre souffle du vent et à l'aspect des
moindres nuées sur un ciel pur. Le manteau de
Lélia était moins noir, moins velouté que ses grands
yeux couronnés d'un sourcil mobile. La blancheur
mate de son visage et de son cou se perdait dans celle
de sa vaste fraise, et la froide respiration de son sein
impénétrable ne soulevait pas même le satin noir et
les triples rangs de sa chaîne d'or."

Such is Lélia, composed as a statue, with suitable
paludament. But she traverses the world, crosses
countries and deserts, ascends mountains, pouring
forth her great soul in magnificent gestures, magnetic
glances, feverish ardours, extraordinary actions, great
sayings, blaming God, society, but never herself,
and becoming in turn Werther, Faust, René, Oberman,
and in turn rebel, heroine and saint.

All this scenography and choreography of the

sublime deceives nobody now. Jacques does not hide himself from our eyes in his misery as an idle man, who has never succeeded in understanding that to live is to place before oneself an end, to work (in the romantic engravings before me, he is represented as lying flat upon cushions, smoking an exceedingly long pipe with an air of sadness and the look of an erotic maniac !). He has an appearance of false refinement, without moral consciousness and is therefore incapable of demanding and arousing it in others; he looks like a hero with a dash of the criminal about him. If we wish to be indulgent we can at the most compare him to a poor neurasthenic who reasons about his madness.

Lélia also is a maniac, to whom perhaps the wisest remark ever made is uttered by her sister, a prostitute (for we are led to understand that she has a sister who exercises that social function and does not feel the less sublime on that account !) : " Eh bien, dit Pulchérie, puisque vous ne pouvez vous faire religieuse, faites-vous courtisane." Leone Leoni is altogether a criminal, both in fact and soul; but he has received " from God " the gift of " knowing how to love," and therefore a charming woman allows herself to be dragged by him into abjection and crime, and cannot separate herself from him, and when he abandons her, comes running back again at once at his call, because " the hand of God " has for ever united them in love !

The erotic ideology of Sand is to be found to-day among many women, who yield to every caprice of their senses and imagination without let or stay, and are not only incapable of remorse and humility, but, on the contrary, are the more exalted in themselves and believe themselves to be unconquered champions of liberty and sincerity, noblest martyrs to irresistible passion. They offer themselves to people as such, and since they are ferociously egoistic at heart, they wish it to be understood, and give it to be understood, that they are models of devotion, of tenderness and of sacrifice, really believing themselves to be fascinating, but showing themselves to be tiresome and annoying to their neighbours.

Sand once chanced upon a gentleman, in the course of her romantic adventures. He was a young and competent Venetian doctor of medicine, whom she drew into her strange course of life and love and took with her to Paris, but soon tired of him. The young man, who was dignified and serious, did not run after her, but returned to his studies. " My presence embarrassed her " (wrote the good soul as an octogenarian, recalling his remote adventure in which he had involuntarily acted as Octave between Jacques-Musset and Fernande-Sand); she found this Italian in the way with his clear good sense, which made short work of that *uncomprehended sublimity* with which she was wont to surround her *weariness of a love affair*.

The novels of Georges Sand were often accused of immorality, that is to say, of unhealthy action upon readers, and certainly the advice they gave, since it was due to sensual desire and unconfined passion, led to setting alight passion and sensuality and supplied them with a sort of theoretical justification. This woman writer troubled many souls and brought or contributed to bring disorder into many women's brains, and continues to produce like effects, through the echoes of her books, which are numerous. Her influence has been especially great in Russia, as

Dostoievski bears witness. He recounts how "something immense, unheard of, definite solutions of human problems," were expected of her in the near future, and concludes that the Russian people was the people made for her, because "the adoption of all the spiritual interests of humanity is the especial mission of that people." This eulogy sounds not less grave for Russia than for Georges Sand, since she would thereby be rendered responsible for having contributed to educate Russian brains in clear thinking and limpid feeling.

When we recognize (with her sensible lover the Italian doctor Pagello) the altogether sensual and pathological origin of Sand's theories, of her religion of love, and admit the accusation of immorality brought against them, we have already implicitly granted that they are without doctrinal or philosophical importance, and without any value as truth. Truth, however bitter it may be and pessimistic it may seem to be, is always moral and a source of morality. Sand was unable to extract truth from her nervous spasm, which she expressed in formulas possessing only the semblance of being theoretical. But her ideology did not even become poetry and art, when translated into the form of fiction, because art too is truth and demands sincerity towards one's self, a superior sincerity which vanquishes one-sided practical interest and penetrates to the recesses of the soul, dissipating or clearing the clouds that obscure it. Sand's was not a profound mind, she had no strong internal life, although inclined to taciturnity and to remaining shut up in herself, absorbed, as her contemporaries said; but she was absorbed in dreaming; in weaving the web of her imaginings, as the woman she was. And being a woman, she never conceived that art should be respected, but always held it to be the natural outlet for her own sensibility and for her own intellectuality. As woman again, she brought practical sense into the things of art, domestic economy and commercial knowledge, aiming always at making above all what is called the romance, the pleasing book, and at making many of them, because many produced much fruit. She observed reality, but who does not ? She even observed it with attention; but her work consisted, as she said, in " idealizing it." And it is well to record what she meant by that idealization, in order to avoid thinking of the severe process of purification or of true and proper artistic creation in that connection, and in order to see of what slight importance is the customary contrasting of her fiction as " idealistic " with " veristic " fiction. She understood it in the following manner, as the construction of a personage who should incarnate the principal feeling or idea of the novel, and represent the passion of love. To this personage she ascribed " toutes les puissances dont on a l'aspiration en soi même, ou toutes les douleurs dont on a vu et senti la blessure," and an " importance exceptionelle dans la vie, des forces au-dessus du vulgaire, des charmes et des souffrances," and so on. This process, alto-gether practical, of the fancy which is pleased and wishes to please others has also been wrongly taken for the poetic soul, and it has been said and repeated that Sand " grâce à cette richesse inépuisable d'imagination et ce don expressif du style, est restée un poète qui a peu d'égaux, un des plus grands poètes de sa race et de son temps," and her " lyricism " has been much praised, her romances being defined as " lyrical romances." " Lyricism " is well said, in so far as it is not intended to mean the " lyrical," but the verbose rhetoric of passion. On the other hand, it is generally admitted and recognized (and " lyricism " should here avail as *fiche de consolation*) that Georges Sand's novels are defectively composed or lack composition, but it is not observed that this was due in her case to the lack of vigorous thought, or rather of an inspiring poetic motive, owing to which she abandoned herself to chance as regards personages and events, which might be this or the opposite, and since they had little cohesion, it was not difficult for her to change or turn into its opposite this or that one of her novels, to change the fate of *Indiana* or of *Lélia*, making Indiana and Ralph marry or making Lélia die in a convent. She frequently also began her narratives, such as *Mauprat*, with force and vigour; but when we anticipate that a theme from such a beginning should attain to its full significance in the course and ending of the story, we find her losing herself in the conventional, in intrigues and in trivial adventures.

Lyricism as " setting " and the " agreeable " side of romantic love are to be found in all her works in different proportions, sometimes the one, sometimes the other preponderating. In *Lélia*, which is her greatest poetical effort, the former predominates : here everything sparkles and echoes, so that the eye becomes, as it were, dimmed, the ear seduced and deafened. The personages of *Lélia* are neither allegories nor poetical individuals : they are not allegories, because they lack definite concepts, nor poetical individuals, because they lack definiteness of character. This poem in prose, this feminine *Faust*, also fails to resolve itself into a succession of lyrics, because instead of lyrics, it abounds in emphasis and declamation. This is not even so when a lyrical poem is expressly attempted, as in Lélia's song, *à Dieu* : " Pourquoi, pourquoi nous avez-vous fait ainsi ? Quel profit tirez-vous de nos souffrances ? Quelle gloire notre abjection et notre néant ajoutent-ils à votre gloire ? les tourments sont-ils nécessaires à l'homme pour le faire désirer le ciel ? L'espérance est-elle une faible et pâle fleur qui ne croît que parmi les rochers, sous le souffle des orages ? Fleur précieuse, suave parfum, viens habiter ce cœur avide et dévasté ! . . ." What predominates there is the effort after the extraordinary, the romantic in the bad sense, eyes rolling, violence of gesture and an empty brain. Lélia, Trenmor, Sténio go in a boat :

" Trenmor tomba dans une profonde rêverie. Ses compagnes imitèrent son silence. La belle Lélia regardait le sillage de la barque où le reflet des étoiles tremblantes faisait comme des menus filets d'or mouvant. Sténio, les yeux attachés sur elle, ne voyait qu'elle dans l'univers. Quand la brise, qui commençait à se lever par frissons brusques et rares, lui jetait au visage une tresse des cheveux noirs de Lélia, ou seulement la frange de son écharpe, il frémissait comme les eaux du lac, comme les rosaux du rivage ; et puis la brise tombait tout à coup comme l'haleine épuisée d'un sein fatigué de souffrir. Les cheveux de Lélia et le plis de son écharpe retombaient sur son sein, et Sténio cherchait en vain un regard dans ses yeux dont le feu savait si bien percer les ténèbres, quand Lélia daignait être femme. Mais à quoi pensait Lélia en regardant le sillage de la barque ? " . . .

We remain awe-struck before this company of sublime beings. Here is a sublime kiss :

" Lélia passa ses doigts dans les cheveux parfumés de Sténio, et attirant sa tête sur son sein, elle la couvrit de baisers. Rarement il lui était arrivé d'effleurer ce beau front de ses lèvres. Une caresse de Lélia était un don du ciel aussi rare qu'une fleur oubliée par l'hiver, et qu'on trouve épanouie sur la neige. Aussi cette brusque et brûlante effusion faillit coûter la vie à l'enfant qui avait reçu des lèvres froides de Lélia le premier baiser d'amour. Il devint pâle, son cœur cessa de battre ; près de mourir, il la repoussa de toute sa force, car il n'avait jamais tant craint la mort qu'en cet instant où la vie se révélait à lui."

And this is sublime charity : " Lélia m'a remis quelque chose qui ressemble à la rançon d'un roi, avec la même simplicité qu'un autre eût mise à me donner un obole."

What really remains of Lélia ? The documentation of a state of mind. We have already assembled the dogmas of erotic religion as laid down in this volume. Other expressions of opinion are also to be collected, such as the negation of progress, because progress cannot " create another sense " nor " render perfect the human organism " ; or Lélia's desire " to die for curiosity " ; or the exclamation of the same Lélia at the end of the story : " Depuis dix mille ans, j'ai crié dans l'infini :—Vérité ! Vérité !—Depuis dix mille ans, l'infini me répond :—Désir ! Désir ! "

The characters of *Jacques* are also dreams of erotic sensuality : the hero himself, mysterious, most perfect, an idler, whose supreme need and occupation is pure love (not love that is pure), and all the more agreeable

to women, since he is capable of sometimes disappear-
ing, so that they may occupy themselves with their
pleasures undisturbed; Sylvia, the sister of this hero,
is herself a heroine and devotes herself to solitude
" par excès de richesse et d'amour " (" Je me sens
dans l'âme une soif ardente d'adorer à genoux quelque
être sublime et je ne rencontre que des êtres ordinaires;
je voudrais faire un dieu de mon amant et je n'ai
affaire qu'à des hommes "); and the couple Fernanda
and Ottavio.

The art is there all the more easy, because the story
is developed by letters, all of them in the same florid
style, letters that are not letters save by means of a
gross artifice, discussing and recounting previous
events and informing the reader of what is necessary
for his information. This is art of a second-rate
quality, like that of the first romance, *Indiana*, which
gave fame to the authoress, and is the type of so many
others of her novels, in which the craftsmanship
predominates. There is not one poetical motive
or idea in the whole of that celebrated romance : the
theme (a young woman married to an old man and
desirous of loving youthfully and of being loved
youthfully) is treated externally and materially, complicated but not developed by means of strange events,
surprises and suicides, crossings of the ocean, and the
like. " Ce cœur silencieux et brisé appelait toujours
à son insu un cœur jeune et généreux pour le ranimer.
. . . Madame Delmare était vraiment malheureuse, et
la première fois qu'elle sentit dans son atmosphère
glacée pénétrer le souffle embrasé d'un homme jeune
et ardent, la première fois qu'une parole tendre et
caressante enivra son oreille, et qu'une bouche fré-
missante vint, comme un fer rouge, marquer sa main,

elle ne pensa ni aux devoirs qu'on lui avait imposés, ni à la prudence qu'on lui avait recommandée, ni à l'avenir qu'on lui avait prédit. . . ."

They are general or commonplace phrases, although in their vagueness and poverty they so much delight women; and the events and characters are casual, without inevitability, among them being a *deus ex machina*, a cousin Ralph, the silent lover, who never allows his feelings to be discovered or suspected, who divines everything that his cousin thinks or intends to do, providentially intervenes at every perilous or desperate moment, and finally bursts into a lengthy discourse, from which we gather that he is just the opposite of what he had hitherto appeared to be. In the first form of the story, the authoress made the two cousins commit suicide together, by throwing themselves into a cascade from a rock; then, as we have said, she pitied and made them marry.

Certainly qualities of a secondary order are very much in evidence in Sand. She is an authoress of extraordinary fluidity and abundance, although giving but slight relief to her characters, and she knows how to tell a story with vivacity. But perhaps the only places where her writing is illuminated with a touch of poetry are her descriptions of " natural scenery," universally praised, which corresponded to a true emotion in her, to a small melody that sang itself in her soul, in the midst of the din caused there by the passions artificially intensified and by ill-thought-out ideas, and in the midst of conventionalisms and expedients of the craft. Something of the florid, rhetorical and verbose is to be found in them also; but sometimes these are able to render rather success fully the feeling of waiting, of melancholy, of abandonment, of purification, of gladness, which Sand infused into the spectacles of nature. Lélia in the solitude of the country : " Je restai là tant que le soleil fut au-dessus de l'horizon, et tout ce temps-là je fus bien. Mais quand il n'y eut plus dans le ciel que des reflets, une inquiétude croissante se répandit dans la nature. Le vent s'éleva, les étoiles semblèrent lutter contre les nuages agités. Les oiseaux de proie élevèrent leurs grands cris et leur vol puissant dans le ciel : ils cherchaient un gite pour la nuit, ils étaient tour-mentés par le besoin, par la crainte. Ils semblaient esclaves de la necessité, de la faiblesse et de l'habitude, comme s'ils eussent été des hommes.

" Cette émotion à l'approche de la nuit se révélait dans les plus petites choses. Les papillons d'azur, qui dorment au soleil dans les grandes herbes, s'éle-vèrent en tourbillons pour aller s'enfuir dans ces mystérieuses retraites où on ne les trouve jamais. La grenouille verte des marais et le grillon aux ailes métalliques commencèrent à semer l'air de notes tristes et incomplètes qui produisirent sur mes nerfs une sorte d'irritation chagrine. Les plantes elles-mêmes semblaient frissonner au souffle humide du soir. Elles fermaient leurs feuilles, elles crispaient leurs anthères, elles retiraient leurs pétales au fond de leur calice. D'autres, amoureuses à l'heure de la brise, qui se charge de leurs messages et de leurs étreintes, s'entr'ouvraient coquettes, palpitantes, chaudes au toucher comme des poitrines humaines. Toutes s'arrangeaient pour dormir ou pour aimer."

The savage Mauprat, after certain words uttered by Edmea, goes out at night into the open and feels love and charm for the first time : " Je traversais un lieu découvert où quelques massifs de jeunes arbres coupaient çà et là les vertes steppes des pâturages. De grands bœufs d'un blond clair, agenouillés sur l'herbe courte, immobiles, paraissaient plongés dans de paisibles contemplations. Des collines adoucies montaient vers l'horizon, et leurs croupes veloutées semblaient jouer dans les purs reflets de la lune. Pour la première fois de ma vie, je sentis les beautés voluptueuses et les émanations sublimes de la nuit. J'étais pénétré de je ne sais quel bien-être inconnu ; il me semblait que pour la première fois je voyais la lune, les coteaux et les prairies. Je me souvenais d'avoir entendu dire à Edmée qu'il n'y avait pas de plus beau spectacle que celui de la nature, et je m'étonnais de ne l'avoir pas su jusque-là. J'eus par instants la pensée de me mettre à genoux et de prier Dieu ; mais je craignais de ne pas savoir lui parler et de l'offenser en le priant mal. Vous avouerai-je une singulière fantaisie qui me vint comme une révélation enfantine de l'amour poétique au sein du chaos de mon ignorance ? La lune éclairait si largement les objets, que je distinguais dans le gazon les moindres fleurettes. Une petite marguerite des prés me sembla si belle, avec sa collerette blanche frangée de pourpre et son calice d'or plein des diamants de la rosée, que je la cueillis et la couvris de baisers, en m'écriant, dans une sorte d'égarement délicieux :—C'est toi, Edmée ! oui, c'est toi ! te voilà ! tu ne me fuis plus ! "

As is well known, Georges Sand gave herself to the cultivation of humanitarian and especially of socialistic ideals in the second period of the four into which critics are wont to divide her too copious production. She did not think for herself, but accepted and repeated the ideas of the men with whom she formed friendship, so that this part of her fiction is documentary evidence as to the diffusion of social-istic thought prior to 1848. She substituted what she had learned for the vehemence of her personal experiences, towards which she was for the rest inclined owing to her already described mental proclivities, in the first place, from the desire for the extraordinary and sublime, which she scattered abroad over the whole of humanity from the more narrow field of sensual love to which it had been at first confined; and in the second place, from her desire as an authoress of novels to renew her artistic material, menaced with exhaustion after so great an abuse of such themes as " rights of passion," " religion of love," " unrealizability of the erotic-religious ideal."

Her own personal and original notion as to socialism, quite in accordance with the natural eroticism of her mind, was the drawing together and fusion of the social classes by means of fallings in love of ladies and working men. This was certainly a bold conception, because if the middle-class man seeking pleasure is capable of marrying maid-servants and peasant-women, when spurred thereto by sensual desire, woman, in whom vanity prevails, does not let herself go to making such choices and will always prefer the elegant ne'er-do-well to the honest but inelegant proletariat. This, however, is the motive (coldly conceived) of certain of her novels, among which is *Le meunier d'Angibault*, where the honest workman is reluctant to marry the Baroness of Blanche-mont, because he knows her to be rich, and she, when she finds herself ruined by her late husband, addresses a jubilant letter to her beloved proletarian, couched in the following terms : " Henri, qu bonheur ! quelle joie ! je suis ruinée. Vous ne me reprocherez plus ma richesse, vous ne haïrez plus mes chaînes dorées. Je redeviens une femme que vous pouvez aimer sans remords, et qui n'a plus de sacrifices à s'imposer pour vous." The novel is puerile, not only in conception, but in its artistic form, which is all full of *ficelles* and *clichés*.   And what dialogues !   A miller and a workman are discussing, and the workman assumes that he possesses a million : " Je crois que je le distribuerais aux pauvres, comme les communistes chrétiens des premiers temps, afin de m'en débarrasser, quoique je sache fort bien que je ne ferais pas là une bonne œuvre véritable; car, en abandonnant leurs biens, ces premiers disciples de l'égalité fondaient une société. Ils apportaient aux malheureux une législation qui était en même temps une religion.   Cet argent était le pain de l'âme en même temps que celui du corps. Ce partage était une doctrine et faisait des adeptes. Aujourd'hui, il n'y a rien de semblable "; and so on.

Consuelo belongs to the same period, standing between the historical novel—as it was then understood, introducing great historical personages and placing them in relation to other imaginary personages and showed them as immersed in politics, intrigues and love affairs with one another—and the novel of socialistic tendencies. Consuelo is another incarnation of Lélia, an extraordinary woman, daughter of a street singer, herself a singer, but in some unknown manner endowed with the greatest possible knowledge of things in general and of the human heart, of the greatest will-power, of the greatest rectitude, of the greatest tact and practical sense, and in addition acutely intellectual and critical with a mind that meditates upon God and human destiny.   In the novel, the miracles that she accomplishes follow one another : the idealization or idolization usual with Sand, unites with adventures piled upon one another, to compose a perfect novel in supplements.   Here and there are agreeable portions, as, for instance, Consuelo's first attempts in the midst of eighteenth century Venetian life, or the journey she makes from Bohemia to Austria in the company of the youthful Haydn; but its agreeableness is due rather to things in themselves agreeable than to poetical inspiration and refinement of art.   How little capable was Sand of going deeply into anything is to be seen in the figure of Count Albert—the young and noble Bohemian, who by dint of constantly dwelling upon the national history of the Hussites, becomes obsessed by it and continues it in his life, as though it were a vibration of that history in the present.   This figure is well conceived, but quickly becomes superficialized and lost in narratives of strange events, terrifying apparitions and intrigues.

It is true that Sand, in the third period of her production as classified by the critics, having freed herself both from frantic assertions of amorous liberty and from socialistic-humanitarian tendencies, and become serene, is supposed then to have composed at last her masterpieces, the idyllic novels, and to have thus bestowed upon France a kind of literature that she still lacked.   I do not deny that *La mare au diable*, *La petite Fadette*, *François le champi*, *Les maîtres sonneurs*, and one or two like them, are very graceful books, full of gentleness and goodness, far better arranged and proportioned than the foregoing, written with greater care and with an able adaptation of peasant speech.   But, to tell the truth, there does not seem

Q

to be anything poetical that comes to light in these novels, but rather the virtuosity of the expert authoress of pleasing books. A certain preparatory tone makes itself indeed felt in the best of them, *La mare au diable* : we feel there the intention of moving and delighting us with a story of innocence and tenderness. The young Maria is so perfect in all her words and deeds ! She is a country Consuelo. She persuades Germain to please his little son and to take him with him on the trip, and the boy jumps for joy : " Allons, allons ! dit la jeune fille en le soulevant dans ses bras, tâchons d'apaiser ce pauvre cœur qui saute comme un petit oiseau, et si tu sents le froid quand la nuit viendra, dis-le moi, mon Pierre, je te serrerai dans ma cape. Embrasse ton petit père et demande lui pardon d'avoir fait le méchant. Dis que ça ne t'arrivera plus jamais, entends-tu ? . . ." Does she not seem to play the part of the perfect second mother, in order to seduce the little boy ? In the wood, where they are obliged to stop and pass the night, Germain is hungry and proposes to pluck and cook one of the partridges which are intended as a gift for the friend of his father. The following dialogue takes place. " Tu pourrais bien plumer l'autre, pour me montrer.—Vous voulez donc en manger deux ? Quel ogre ! allons, les voilà plumées. Je vais les cuire.—Tu ferais une parfaite cantinière, petite Marie, mais, par malheur, tu n'as pas de cantine, et je serai réduit à boire l'eau de cette mare.—Vous voudriez du vin, pas vrai ? Il vous faudrait peut-être du café ? Vous vous croyez à la foire sous la ramée ! Appelez l'aubergiste : de la liqueur au fin laboureur de Belair !—Ah ! petite méchante, vous vous moquez de moi ? Vous ne boiriez pas du vin, vous, si vous en aviez ?—Moi, j'en ai bu ce soir, avec vous chez la Rebecca, pour la seconde fois de ma vie ; mais, si vous êtes bien sage, je vais vous en donner une bouteille quasi pleine, et du bon encore !—Comment, Marie, tu es donc sorcière, décidément ? . . ." The reader understands at once that his duty is to take the side of poor Marie, obliged to leave her mother and her home, in order to go to work far away ; and since Germain is seeking a wife, why should he not marry this girl, who is so good, so modest, so perfect in every way ? His meeting with the other woman, who had been suggested to him as his wife, results in the complete success of the former. Nor is anything else lacking that may concur to make shine the virtue of Marie and prepare the happy nuptials : the brutal master to whom she is sent wishes to violate her ; she flies and is followed by him, and Germain protects and defends her.

The accuracy of Georges Sand in portraying the life of peasants in this and others of her novels has been contested, and, as is always the case, under the guise of an unjust criticism is to be found concealed another criticism which is just, namely, annoyance at the mannered style of these edifying and consoling narratives. In the *Maîtres sonneurs*, Joseph learns that Thérence is in love with him. " Que me dis-tu là ! s'écria-t-il, et quel nouveau malheur serait donc tombé sur moi ?—Pourquoi serait-ce un malheur ?— Tu me le demandes, Brulette ? Est-ce que tu crois qu'il dépendrait de moi de lui rendre ses sentiments ?— En bien, dit Brulette, tâchant de l'apaiser, elle s'en guérirait !—Je ne sais pas si l'on guérit de l'amour, répondit Joseph ; mois moi, si j'avais fait, par igno- rance et par manque de précautions, le malheur de la fille au Grand-Bûcheux, de la sœur d'Huriel, de la vierge des bois, qui a tant prié pour moi et veillé à ma vie, je serai si coupable, que je ne pourrais me le pardonner." It is not a question of perceiving that the development and moral refinement of Joseph and the other peasants described by Georges Sand are different from reality, but, on the contrary, that the tone is affected, and that in these idylls also the authoress is preoccupied with producing an agreeable work and that for this reason she has turned to the simplicity of rustic life in search of new sources of enjoyment.

And what shall we say finally as to the last manner, that of the fourth period of Georges Sand, when she returned to love stories no longer of the fields but of the city, returned appeased and without the fictions of rebellion and apostolate which had shaken her in the past? The recognized masterpiece of this period is *Le marquis de Villemer*, the story, not even then new, of the young governess or reader, poor, beautiful and proud, who makes the son of the lady who employs her fall in love with and eventually marry her, over-coming all social obstacles in so doing. What a man is that Marquis de Villemer, shy, timid, sensitive, delicate, generous, a well of science, an elect soul, with at heart the ever-open wound of a great love shattered by death! And that ducal brother of his, such a scamp, so dissipated, yet so good and so solicitous as to the welfare of others! And that governess, Caroline de Saint-Geneix, what a model of a woman, uniting the highest moral virtues with the happiest intellectual gifts and the firmest of wills, a new Consuelo, a new *petite Marie*, a new *petite Fadette !* It is one of those novels read with delight by young ladies, married women and gentlemen, and enjoys the favour of good society, being praised there as an *exquise.* If, however, you are simply a lover of poetry, I would counsel you to avoid it and others like it, because they would seem to you to be insipid and would perhaps arouse your indignation at their pretence of art.

Have I perhaps seemed to lack of reverence for a personage so conspicuous, for a writer so remarkable in the spiritual life of the nineteenth century as Georges Sand certainly was ? This would have been at least an act in the worst possible taste. I have only wished (in conformity with my already familiar idea or determination and with the task set to myself in composing these notes) to transfer Georges Sand also from the sphere *Literaturgeschichte* to that of *Cultur-geschichte*, where alone her work can be adequately understood and justice rendered to it. It is useful to acquire the conviction that the history of poetry contains a far less numerous array of poetic and artistic talents than people imagine, when they read the manuals of literary history :

> " Many the fowls that fly, but few and far
> Swans and true poets are." [1]

The others are journalists, orators, conversers, narrators, composers of moving or pleasing works, but they are not " swans," or poets.

[1] Ariosto *Orlando Furioso*

XVII

FERNÁN CABALLERO

I BELIEVE discoverable a truer vein of poetry, even of "idyllic poetry," in the modest Spanish authoress who concealed herself under the name of Fernán Caballero (Cecilia Bohl de Faber) than in the very celebrated Georges Sand. She too was a polemist and a propagandist as ardent as the lady of Nohant, but in a precisely opposite sense, that is to say Catholic, traditionalistic and almost reactionary; yet I find in her a solidity of mind, a simplicity of heart and a liveliness of imagination which the other did not possess, for all her superior facility and virtuosity. In the history of poetry one often verifies the saying that the first shall be last and the last first.

To tell the truth, the very polemic and apostolate of the Caballero seem to me far more securely founded and more seriously justified than the turbid feminism and the superficial socialism of Georges Sand. The old Spain, so great and glorious, so Catholic and so warlike, after having suddenly shaken herself free from the sleep into which she had fallen after having combated French and Napoleonic imperialism with her popular resources, instead of persisting in the character which she had re-asserted with such prowess, began to accept new social and political forms, as presented to her by many of her national writers, and, accepting their point of view and beginning to vacillate

230

in her ancient faith and habits, seemingly accepting as just the criticisms and satires directed against her by foreign writers. This work of the innovators, liberals and free-thinkers was a defiance of her sacred past, which still formed the lively and actual present of so great a part of the Spanish people : Fernán Caballero took up the gauntlet.

You, the illuminated, enemies of superstitions, you who mock at popular customs, at sanctuaries, at miraculous paintings, at ex-votos, at sacred tattooings and the like, have you ever understood them as they are, symbols of the moral life, which restrain, menace, console and inspire kindly feelings and good actions ? You scorn the clumsy Spanish churches, where the images of the saints are incrusted with silver plating and with other ornaments in bad taste : you think perhaps that those churches are really museums for artists, where the merely devout go to pray ? Do you speak of the ignorance and crudity of the Spanish peoples ? But how is it that you are never aware of the daily proofs of good sense and judgment, of disinterestedness, of sacrifice, of dignity, of noble pride, of the virtues which are the fruit of a long Christian education and of which they daily offer examples ? Do you wish to educate the peoples with your vaporous and litigious philosophies ? Will they ever be worth that serene light, that spring of pure crystalline waters that perpetually pours forth in those that have learned to live and die in the Catechism ? Do you wish to endow the poor with a rebellious spirit in order to raise them to the level of humanity ? But why do you take from them that resignation to their own condition, that love of their own work and of peace, and that religion which generates and maintains all these truly humane dispositions, to substitute for them your preachings of hatred? And above all, you who speak of a people, of the Spanish people, do you really know it? Have you sought out and observed it in real life? And how have you observed it? With the reason? That is not enough. " Todas las cosas de este mundo tienen dos modos de mirarse, el uno con la helada mirada de la razón, que todo lo enfria y lo rebaja, como la luz de la bujía, y el otro con la ardiente y simpática mirada del corazón, que todo lo dora y vivifica como el sol de Díos. Esta luz del corazón se llama Poesia. . . ."

This polemic, which took colour and character from its reference to Spanish life, was a particular aspect and instance of the polemic of historicism against intellectualistic radicalism, with which the nineteenth century opened. Not only had it political value at the time it appeared, but a true ideal value, so much so that we are ourselves constrained to have recourse to it, as coming generations will also certainly be obliged to do. What ideal value, on the other hand, is retained by the much-vaunted claim to follow the stimulus of the erotic imagination, or the desired fusion of the social classes by means of the marriage of ladies with workmen, advocated and maintained by Georges Sand? It will be said that the Caballero did not invent the idea of that polemic in support of tradition. Certainly, and it is difficult to determine who exactly did invent it, because it arose everywhere in Europe as the result of inevitable historical necessity. But she represented it very well, so far as it concerned her, and reproduced it anew in new conditions, by re-living it in herself.

With a view to secure this end, which is the first and most apparent of her work, the Caballero selected " the picture of customs," popular Spanish customs, more particularly Andalusian, and doing this with full spontaneity, she seemed also to conform to a literary example which had found in Scott its greatest protagonist; hence this authoress, whom we shall freely term the Catholic Sand, was hailed by preference as " the Spanish Walter Scott " by her contemporaries. So urgent to her seemed the duty she had assumed of defending the old religious and moral forms of her country, that she always protested against those who looked upon the stories she told as " romances " or " artistic works." More than once she declared, " I have not intended to write novels; I have tried to give a true, exact, genuine idea of Spain and of its society, to describe the internal life of our people, its beliefs, its feelings, its acute sayings; I have tried to rehabilitate things which the ignorant nineteenth century has trodden under its heavy and audacious foot, holy and religious things, religious practices and their lofty and tender significance, ancient and pure Spanish customs, the national character and mode of feeling, the bonds that unite society and the family, restraint in everything, and especially in those ridiculous passions which are affected without being really felt (because fortunately great passion is rare), modest virtues. The so-called romantic part of my work is intended only as the framework of the vast building that I have set myself to construct." She also confessed that her intention not only went beyond art, but even led her to oppose herself to art, sacrificing the logic of what she described as the *donnée*, that is to say, the artistic motive, to the advantage of the moral lesson which she desired to teach.

She wished her stories to be edifying, such as should illustrate themes dear to her or give occasion to the development of such themes by means of examples of good and evil. She was an orator in the good cause, a preacher who did not indulge in artistic subtleties, and when necessary ill-treated art, provided she obtained the end in view. She experienced the greatest satisfaction when she was able to assure readers that the story she told was true, that is to say, had really happened, and that in it was to be found, not only a model, but also a document.

But the orator of the good, far more and far differently from him who aims only at encompassing and persuading his readers for his own utilitarian ends, must attain to his means from poetry, in order to penetrate to the bottom of his readers' souls and touch their deepest chords. And we have heard the Caballero talk of " poetry," when opposing the eye of the heart to that of cold reason, and she had been poetically moved prior to giving herself at a late age, about fifty, to her work of defence and apostolate. She had contemplated, dreamed and idealized much, yet she continued always to regard the world with the feeling of a poet, and as a poet lent an ear to the voices that murmured within her. Those who approached her say that after having spoken with her and breathed the perfume of her goodness, they saw the actions of men and the spectacles of nature in a new way, and felt their heart full of sweet tears and of a longing to accomplish good deeds.

She wished to make people love the country, plants, flowers, the earth rich with a thousand animals

and insects, all of them curious to observe, humble
life, villages with a narrow horizon; but she already
loved these things and spoke of them in accents of
trembling affection. Listen to her impressions of a
village cemetery :

" Era tan profundamente tranquilo aquel rincón
que ¿ lo creerá Vs. ? hasta con la muerte se vivia
alli familiarizado. Ahora bien, hacer aparecer á
la muerte suave, sin que infunda horror ni tedio, ¿ no
es una altura á que pocas veces alcanzan el hombre
religioso más metido en Dios, el filósofo más desen-
gañado del mundo ? La hacienda en que habi-
tábamos, solo estaba separada del cementerio por un
pequeño corralon en que pacian unas ovejas; pues
creed que ningun orror me inspiraba la cercania de
aquel lugar de descanso de los campesinos. Cuando
veia abrir una zanja por los parientes de una persona
difunta (puesto que alli no hay enterradores asalari-
ados), lejos de ver en ellos hombres lúgubres cavando
una negra y pavorosa sepultura para un muerto, solo
me parecian hermanos de la Caridad preparando un
lecho para un dormido. . . ."

Those flocks that browse in peace between the workshop and the cemetery, those friendly faces that dig,
not like grave-diggers, to bury a corpse, but as though
they were making a bed for a sleeper, are the poetic
images with which she clothes her love for the quiet
life of the village.—She studied children and discussed
the best means of bringing them up and educating
them; but she had often stayed her footsteps before
them in pensive questioning as before a sweet
mystery :

" ¿ Qué vé en su mente, él, cuyos ojos aun nada han visto ? ¿ Qué sueño puede reflejarse en esa inteligencia, que aun no tiene conocimiento ? ¿ Qué pensamientos conmueven las sensaciones de él, que, despierto, aun no sabe sentir ni pensar ?

" Confesamos que no podemos darnos cuenta de este problema, y que cuando asi hemos observado á estas inocentes criaturas en nuestros brazos, nos hemos creido rodeados de ángeles ocultos á nuestra percepcion, pero perceptibles á la suya. Con ellos comunican cosas de otro mundo mejor, que olvidarán en este, á medida que huyan los ángeles, con la ino- cencia, la dulzura y la pureza, de aquella alma, que desde temprano sentirá las malas influencias de la parte material á que está unida de por vida.—¡ Adiós, pobre alma desterrada en esa misera cárcel !—le diran los ángeles; y la cara del niño se angustia.—Nos vamos, pero no nos olvides;—y el niño gime y se agita.—Sé fiel á nuestro Padre y Criador, y en breve nos reunirémos;—y el niño se serena.—Y ante su trono cantarémos felices sus alabanzas;—y el niño se sonrie, cual el ángel que le consuela. . . ."

Emotional sentiment and religious faith answer her question, showing her this picture of angels surround- ing the child and softly speaking with him, plaint and smile, agitation and a growing calm again succeeding one another on the face of the child at the words of those dwellers in Paradise. And how should children be educated ? They should above all be treated as children, caressed, their innocence preserved and fear of God taught to them :

" . . . mi máxima es que todos los niños deben ser mimados. Creo dañosisimas esas educaciones antici-

padas que hacen de los niños caricaturas en su moral,
como las levitas y los corsés lo hacen en lo físico.
Cuando un niño me dice : *Beso á Vd. la mano : ¿ cómo
está Vd. ?* me hace al oído el efecto de un loro y á
los ojos el de un enano. Mientras son niños, solo
una cosa hay que conservarles, la inocencia; solo
una que enseñarles, el rezar."

Could a more lively image be found for the loathing
of the artificial training of children in social conven-
tions and commonplaces, for the turning of them into
little men ? "They no longer seem children, but
dwarfs ! " And how does it happen that children
and old men seem to understand one another so well ?

" Las pasiones que agitan la vida del hombre, en
los unos aun no existen, y en los otros dejaron de
existir, lo que produce un estado análogo; unos y
otros nos encontramos en las puertas de la vida :
ellos que vienen y nosotros que nos vamos; ellos nos
dicen : ¡ *Descansad !*, nosotros les decimos : ¡ *Buen
viaje ! "*

She makes a psychological observation on the different attitudes of men and women to pain. How does
she express it ?

" En todas cosas se apoya la mujer en el hombre,
ménos en el dolor, que entonces se apoya en Dios.
El hombre en todas cosas se apoya en si mismo,
ménos en el dolor, en que se apoya en la mujer. . . ."

She suffers from the ill-treatment of animals and does
not neglect the opportunity of protesting and admon-
ishing against this cruelty; but her words are simple
and say so simply what everyone can see around

him, and issue in so heartfelt an exclamation of astonishment that they immediately obtain the result of filling
us with scruples and remorse. Suffice it, she says,
for an animal finds itself side by side with a man, to
suffer a continuous martyrdom :

"No hay animal que exista inmediato al hombre,
cuya vida no sea, con pocas excepciones, un continuo
martirio. Y ¿ es posible que haya ánimo al que esta
idea no atormente ? " . . .

The places that she describes, the villages, the
rustic houses, the vine-arbours, the narrow streets,
the churches, are as it were embraced by her longing
and tenderness. Popular beliefs and religious legends
animate the nature that she contemplates; and she
does not allow herself to be deprived of them, and
defends their mystical interpenetrations :

"La mortigada luz de la luna hacia visible la soledad
y la inmovilidad de la naturaleza rendida por el calor
del dia. Los pinos, salpicados á poca distancia del
camino, formaban con sus delicadas barbajas un
murmullo más suave, más leve, mas misterioso y grave
que el que forman con sus hojas los demás árboles
que parece que murmuran, miéntras el pino parece
que ora.

El mochuelo lanzaba en el melancólico silencio de
la apacible noche su triste voz, esa voz que, según la
poética y religiosa imaginación del pueblo, es la de la
Cruz y que repite desde que en el Calvario presenció
horrorizado la muerte que sufrió el Salvador.

Asociados, si no por convencimiento, por senti-
miento, á esta tierna y conmovedora creencia, con-
cediendo que sea una ilusión, pero vuluntariamente

bajo su dulce imperio, no podemos oir la expresión tan suave y triste de esa ave solitaria de la noche, sin conmovernos profundamente, y persuadernos de que siente lo que espresa. Y acaso ¿ no podria ser que el escalpelo de nuestra fria razón, que nos empeñamos en hacer regulador, árbitro y solo juez de las cosas, asi morales como materiales, haya cortado lazos, destruido armonias y roto comunicaciones entre las partes que existen de las cosas creadas ? Dirán que es inverosimil que las hubiese. ¿ Porqué ? . . ."

A young mother sends her child to sleep in her arms with the following lullaby :

> " Allá arriba, en el monte Calvario,
> matita de oliva, matita de olor,
> arrullaban la muerte de Cristo
> cuatro jilgueritos y un ruiseñor. . . ."

And the writer comments that it is certainly difficult to explain why the nightingales and the finches lament the death of the Redeemer, why the swallow plucks the thorns from His brow, why the Blessed Virgin dries her Child's swaddling clothes on the rosemary bush, why the elder-tree is unlucky, destined to see Judas hanged from its branches. She answers that she listens to these sayings as though to a sort of " distant music," without inquiring into their origin and authenticity, but not without thinking that there have been and are mysterious revelations for souls.

The verses above quoted lead us to say that in the midst of these thoughts, which are in reality effusions of sentiment and abound everywhere in the pages of Caballero, there also abound and there exhale their healthy perfume, memories of popular poetry, apologues, songs, wise sayings, proverbs, Spanish folklore, collected first or among the very first by her, here also following the romantic impulse active in every part of Europe. They contain the imaginings of popular religious feeling, similar to the preceding verses. Saint Catherine's day is being celebrated and the people sing, why she listens and sings in her turn :

> " Santa Catalina ! Mañana es tu dia,
> subirás al Cielo con santa alegria,
> y dirá San Pedro al verte llegar :
> — ¿ Qué mujer es esta que viene á llamar ?
> — Yo soy Catalina, que quisiera entrar.
> — Entra, palomita, en tu palomar."

What a rhythm of joy and festivity, how polite, tender and smiling becomes all of a sudden the warden of the celestial portal, who was at first so rude and disagreeable, when he sees that gentle Catherine is the new arrival ! And with what glad good humour he calls her " little dove " and invites her to enter paradise, which becomes the dovecot prepared for her ! At other times we find fancies half farcical, half malicious, like that of Signor Don Gato, whom his father persuades to become betrothed to a Moorish cat. It begins like an epic romance :

> " Estaba señor Don Gato
> en solio de oro sentado,
> calzando media de seda
> y zapatito picado.
> Llegó su padre y dijo
> si queria ser casado
> con una gata moresca
> que andaba por los tejados." . . .

Those were the dominions of the betrothed princess : the roof ! Or the different nuptials of the flea and the caterpillar :

" La pulga y el coco
se quieren casar
y no se han casado
por falta de pan.

Salió una hormiga
de su formigal :
' Hágase la boda
que yo pongo el pan.' "

And thus the wolf will supply the meat, the cricket the vegetable, the gnats the wine, a hedgehog the bed, a firefly will act as parish priest and a little rat as god-father.   And where will the mother-in-law be found ? She too is found; but with her comes disaster :

" Salió una gatita
de aquella cocina :
' Hágase la boda,
yo soy madrina.'

En mitad la boda
se armó un desatino :
saltó la madrina
y se comió el padrino."

And who that has once read it can ever forget the story of the *negrito*, of the very rich little negro, who lived opposite the house of a very beautiful young woman, of whom he became enamoured. The husband, in order to revenge himself, arranges with his wife to pretend to go away, while she invites the *negrito* to dine with her. He arrives laden with gifts, but hardly are they seated at table when the husband enters armed with a whip and begins to make it play about the shoulders of the *negrito*. The *negrito*, who was already immersed in thoughts of the pleasure in store for him, is surprised and confounded.   He vainly seeks the door to make his

R

escape. And at every lash of the whip, he gave a jump and said :

" Pobre negrito ¡ qué mala fortuna !
que, habiendo tres puertas, no encuentra ninguna."

He pities himself, calling himself a " dear little negro," and as he leaps in the air, finds still time to reflect upon his bad luck, which does not leave him time to solve the technical problem of finding the way out. More often, we find with Caballero simple, picturesque comparisons full of good sense, culled by her on the lips of the people. " Ya " (observes a woman talking of a mother who looks with pride upon her ugly sons), " dijo el escarabajo á sus hijos : Venid acá, mis flores; y grumos de oro llamó la lechuza á los suyos." . . . Think! The beetle calls lovingly to her sons : " Come here, my flowerets ! "

The Caballero found these expressions of a poetic world of joy, of smiling, of vexation, of religion, already formed and included them in her narratives; but by thus finding, selecting, arranging them advantageously, her poetic spirit in a certain way makes them hers, encloses them in her world of dream, changing them into a part of her soul. Sometimes legends and poems act in the manner of solutions to her narratives, as in *Lucas Garcias*, who, abandoned by his wicked father together with his unhappy little sister, sings to her the popular story of the hard-hearted woman who allows her own unhappy sister to die at her gate rather than relieve her want. And then the sister of Lucas Garcias falls into disgrace, leads an evil life; secure in his sense of honour, he leaves her to struggle alone with misery and refuses to have anything whatever to do with her, until one evening, at the door of his house, he hears that song which he had taught her in the years of their youth and which now makes melt his heart of stone :

> " Quien niega el pan á su hermana,
> ese entrañas no tenia ;
> quien niega el pan á su hermana,
> ¡ ese lo niega á Maria ! " . . .

Certainly the stories of Fernán Caballero have evident defects, in part confessed by the authoress herself : they are edifying tales, frequently not so much simple as artless, laxly woven together, verbose, interrupted at every step with reflections, considerations and exhortations. She wrote what seemed to her to be useful for her work as an apostle, but certainly more than her real artistic inspiration warranted. In Spain itself there was no lack of folk who found her stories tiresome and frankly said so, or defined them, like Juan Valera (I find this in one of Caballero's letters) *arroz con leche*, rice and milk ; and now there are some who consider that she wrote badly, that she did not possess *el castizo estilo*, the purged style, that she was a " Balzac *debilitado*," and the like. But Fernán Caballero, spontaneity itself as she was, living intensely the lives that she had created, was able on occasion to tell a story with power and sobriety and to show herself to be a worthy heiress of the Spanish story-tellers, from the author of the *Lazarillo* to the great Cervantes and the authors of the picaresque romances. *La Gaviota* is full of very beautiful things : the character of Marisalada the protagonist, daughter of a fisherman, savage, egoistical, charming with her black eyes and voice of gold, but capable of anything when her passions are roused, to the point of making herself a slave, of defying death, is vigorously rendered, without comment or analysis, all by action. We see her again almost as a girl, lying ill at her father's house, the old sun-burnt fisherman Pietro Santaló, whose breast is as red as the Indians of the Ohio, all hairy, his grey locks dense and matted. This father stands beside her, disheartened, brought low to the point of extinction : he is thinking of his four sons all dead one after the other, and of this only girl that remains to him. A woman of the village, pitiful and charitable, comes in with a doctor she has brought to the bedside :

"— Vamos, Marisalada, vamos, levántate, hija, para que este señor pueda examinarte.
Marisalada no se movió .
— Vamos, criatura — repitio la buena mujer; — verás cómo te va á curar como por ensalmo.
Diciendo estas palabras, cogió por un brazo á la niña, procurando levantarla.
— ¡ No me da la gana !—dijo la inferma, des-prendiéndose de la mano que la retenia, con una fuerte sacudida.
— Tan suavita es la hija como el padre; quien lo hereda, no lo hurta—murmuró Momo, que se habia asomado á la puerta.
— Como está mala, está mal templada—dijo su padre, tratando de disculparla."

Marisalada recovers : one day her aunt Maria begs her to sing, and she, with her accustomed rude savagery, refuses :

" En este momento entró Momo mal enjestado, precedido de Golondrina cargada de picón.

Traia las manos y el rostro tiznados y negros como la tinta.

— ¡ El rey Melchor ! — gritó al verlo Marisalada.

— ¡ El rey Melchor, el rey Melchor !—repitieron los niños.

— Si yo no tuviera más que hacer—respondió Momo rabioso—que cantar y brincar como tu, grandísima holgazana, no estaria tiznado de piés á cabeza. Por fortuna, don Federico te ha pro-hibido cantar, y con esto no me mortificarás las orejas.

La respuesta de Marisalada fué entonar á trapo tendido una canción."

These small extracts suffice to indicate of what a narrative style Caballero was capable. And what shall we say of the betrothal scenes of Marisalada with the worthy open-hearted doctor Don Federico, and of that other in which she lets her handkerchief fall at the feet of the torero Pepe, and of many others like them ? And what of the other characters, inhabitants of the village, like Friar Gabriel, monk of the abolished monastery, who remains, taciturn guardian of its precincts, thinking of the past and awaiting its return, as by a miracle ? What, again, of Rosita or *Rosa mistica*, and Don Modesto, the veteran, commander of the demolished fort of San Cristoforo, with his uniform cleaned and cleaned again, until it has lost its colour, too wide and too short, with which he lives as though identified with this, the last vestige of his dignity ? Listen to the lilt of any one of Don Modesto's dialogues. Take this one, for instance, between him and *Rosa mistica*, an old maid with whom he dwells, giving rise to ill-natured comment and to *Rosa mistica's* awakened

apprehension for her own reputation, as to which she
converses with Don Modesto :

" — Pero entre Usted y yo — dijo el Comandante —
no hay necesidad de poner no talique. Yo, con
tantos años á cuestas ; yo, que con toda mi vida no
he estado enamorado más que una vez . . . y por
más señas que lo estuve de una buena moza, con que
me habria casado á no haberla sorprendido en chicoleas
con el tambor mayor, que. . . .
— Don Modesto, Don Modesto — gritó Rosa
poniéndose erguida. — Honre Usted su nombre y mi
estado, déjese de recuerdos amorosos.
— No ha sido mi intención escandalizar á Usted —
dijo Don Modesto, en tono contrito." . . .

Like characters and scenes are to be found strewn
among others of her romances, stories and sketches,
and some of them are enchanting. Let us take the
story of Don Gil, chorus master in Seville (*Cosa
cumplida*), with the soul of a child in his enormous body,
the volume of which grows and grows for several
years irresistibly, so that he succeeds in being at once,
" en lo moral el hombre más feliz y en lo físico el
hombre más gordo del mundo." When to Don Gil
was accorded the office which he was destined to fill
during his whole life,

" desde entonces debió notarse en su expresivo
rostro la mezcla más graciosa de la bondadosa y
sencilla alegría de un niño y de un buen alma con la
dignidad y prosopopeya de un padre grave y de un
alto funcionario. Alternaban á veces ambas cosas
en su semblante con tal rapidez que se esplayaba aun
sobre sus labios su infantil y alegre risa, cuando ya

sus ojitos negros desde su concavidad lanzaban una mirada grave, austera, y con infulas de imponente."

We almost seem to see him walking about his church :

" Andaba derecho y la pelada cabeza erguida; su barriga aparecía entonces en toda su majestad prominente; su sotana respingaba muy sobre sí por delante, mientras á la espalda barría humildemente el suelo : su semblante en tales circunstancias aparecía impasible; no levantaba los ojos sino para echar una mirada iracunda á algun monacillo descuidado. Nada le sacaba de su paso grave y composado, á no ser algun irreverente *ladrón* en un cirio : al aparecer este sacrílego, Don Gil perdía toda su compostura y su moderacion, entrando al punto en un furor que solo era comparable al de Orlando. Cogía la caña del apagador con los brios con que Hércules empuñaba su maza, y exterminaba al descarado delinquente, como aquel al leon de Nemea."

But one must hear him sing ! When he goes to pay a visit to the family which had befriended him in his childhood, he finds himself suddenly and unexpectedly before a mirror and is troubled and almost terrified at his own enormous bulk, but ends by laughing at it. Then, all of a sudden, he gives us a specimen of his singing :

" Era aquella muestra de canto-llano arrancada á Don Gil por la pasión que á él tenía, pasión que no sentia sino como la siente el artista por su arte, el sabio por su ciencia : esto es con solemnidad, con veneración y con respeto."

His life was the most contented and the happiest that can be imagined :

" No se cuidaba de política ni de cosa ninguna, fuera de su iglesia y de su casa. Para él era el mundo un cáos que no definía : solo sabia que existían *el ingles el francés* y *las Indias*. . . . La comida, que era buena, ¡ qué bien le sabia ! el vino, que era malo, lo mismo. ¡ Qué descanso tan completo en su lecho ! ¡ Qué actividad tan grata de día ! ¡ Amar á Díos y servirle, amar al prójimo y ayudarle, y *viva la Virgen !* Esta era su divisa."

Once, in that life of continual joy and peace, he abandons himself even for an instant to an amorous caprice : his wife surprises him joking with a half-witted servant-maid, whom she prudently sends away, taking instead a horrible old woman. But Don Gil preserves a vein of profound tenderness in the midst of his thoughtlessness and gladness of spirit : he becomes attached to a little orphan niece, whom he has taken to live with him, a little dark-haired, pale child with black eyes and splendid teeth. And when the child unexpectedly falls ill and dies, Don Gil dies also :

" En breve se postró. Sentado en su lecho y respaldado en almohadas, porqué no podía estar acostado, clavaba la vista sin cesar en la sillita que había sido de la niña, y que había mandado colgar en la pared; y á poco tiempo dejó de existir, sin que los esmeros y los cuidados de su amante mujer hubiesen conseguido alargar su existencia."

This sketch also contains reflections and exclamations intercalated, though these do not remove anything from the plasticity of the representation. For example, the authoress, having described the daily life of Don Gil, so idyllic, so Catholic, cannot refrain from exclaiming :

" ¡ Oh querido, feliz y excelente Don Gil, de grotesca, pero suave y risueña memoria ! " . . ., e dall'esclamazione passa all'invettiva e alla parenetica : " ¡ Triste filosofía que te quemas las pestañas sobre tus libros y te derrites los sesos en tus cavilaciones, buscando la piedra filosofal, esto es, la *verdad* y la *felicidad* que no encuentras ! ¿ qué éres tú en comparación de aquella tranquilidad de espiritu, de aquella serenidad de alma, que nada busca y todo lo halla ? . . ."

I shall give another instance of this polemic which rises up beside the picture she is painting without spoiling it, of this union of the poetical spirit with the combative spirit. In the romance entitled *Un servilón y un liberalito* is represented a family of poor but very honest people, of *almas de Dios*. One of these poor folk, head of the family, dies quietly as he had lived. The two women who survive accept his death tranquilly and with religious thoughts :

" Una noche, después de haber rezado, se acostó don José en perfecta salud, al lado de su buena compañera : á la mañana siguiente llamó ésta su cuñada doña Liberata, acudió y. . . .

— Hermana, le dijo, mira que me parece que Pepe se ha muerto.

— ¡ Que ! no ; no puede ser ! . . . — repuso ésta acercándose á su hermano ya cadaver. — Pepe ! Pepe ! llamó ; pero viendo que no respondía, se puso á

tentarle la frente y el pulso, hecho lo cual, volviéndose
á su cuñada le dijo :

— Mujer, como que tienes razon . . . muerto esta !

— Nos cogió la delantera, dijo su mujer.

— Ayer me dijo : alli te espero, añadió doña
Liberata. Pero se ha ido sin los santos Sacramentos,
Escolástica.

— Ayer, confesó y comulgó, repuso su mujer;
¿ si le diria el corazón que se iba á morir ?

— Se lo diría al oído el Angel de su guarda, dijo
doña Liberata. Vamos, hermana, á encomendar
su alma á Díos, que es lo que nos queda.

Y ambas cayeron de rodillas, y se pusieron á rezar
con voz tranquila y espiritu recogido y fervoroso, pero
sereno."

Here too the narrator cannot restrain herself, and
having told the story with so much simplicity and
beauty, exclaims :

" ¡ Oh, almas de Díos ! Sencillas, mansas, tranquilas
y conformes. ¡ Almas mil veces bienaventuradas !
¡ Qué lecciones dais á las almas mundanales, inquietas,
apuradas, extremosas, que refinan y alambican el
dolor gastando su buena savia en hojarasca ! "

These exclamations and reflections will perhaps
seem artistically redundant, because they are not able
to add anything to the force of the narrative; they may
even seem extraneous and distracting; but what
matters is that they do not suppress or disturb the
poetical pages written by the Caballero, with which
they are rather on neighbourly terms. As is the case
with almost all female writers, the practical tendency
predominated in the Caballero, rendering her careless

or impatient of artistic elaboration and resulting in the defects noted by us, for the rest sufficiently evident in themselves. But Caballero's work is able to resist this practical tendency and the bad literary effects which result from it, because, differently from other women writers, she did not look with one eye at the paper and the other at the public (as Heine would have put it), she attempted no blandishments, she paid no attention to arranging herself in such a way as to excite or to seduce the imaginations of readers, she did not expand and falsify feelings and passions, nor raise them to the rank of theories, but was animated with a pure and serious conviction, and possessed sound judgment. And above all a spring of poetry was bubbling in her heart, which maintained itself fresh and lively even in the midst of the fervent apostolate which she exercised in the service of her faith as a Catholic of the old Church and as a Spaniard of the old Spain.

XVIII

IF poetry could be identical with life (as some extreme romantics of all times dream), Alfred de Musset would have approached this ideal more nearly than any ever did, and should be numbered among the great poets. For he did not conceive of poetry otherwise than as an efflux from his life and his life as an efflux from his poetry, making them perfectly identical. And in order to arrive at this identity, he gave to his life for unique content what is reputed to be the content most proper to poetry : the drama of love. Not politics then, not country, not humanity, not family, not religion, not search for truth; but only love. Nor was this love of Musset's a spiritual association between two beings in order to achieve a harmony for each, a common activity; no, for this would mean duty and sacrifice and have in it something of prose. Nor was it the love which is complete abandonment of self to another creature, made an idol and reason for life; for this would have savoured of religion and mysticism and would have offered little variety. Musset's love was both comedy and tragedy, the love which claims the faithfulness of the loved one, but reserves the right of being unfaithful to her. But if she in her turn break the bonds of fidelity, malediction falls upon her, and if she remain faithful, then she is overcome with *ennui*, which is worse than a malediction.

What Musset sought, then, was passionate love, with all the volubility and all the contradictions which are of its very nature : love, which is a rose rich in thorns, a rose to be plucked with loud outcry at the pricks, yet the desire that the thorns should be there. Sensibility, imagination and the leisure of a poet are needed for such a love as this, and only a poet can give or receive such love. Poetry should be the echo of this, echo of joy, of enthusiasm, of delirium, and then of delusion and desperation and bitterness and disdain, and then, all over again, of hope, of joy renewed and of new delirium. Always it must be melodious and tuneful, always facile and spontaneous, without any hindrances such as are presented by meditations, condensations, elaboration of verse, rich rhymes. Such things are of the domain of literary men and pedants, cold souls all of them; they have nothing akin with lovers or with blond, pale, vibrating and lamenting poets.

There is something juvenile, almost childish, in this idea both of love and of poetry. And it is for this reason that De Musset has been called the young man's poet. We have all of us loved and cared for him in our youthful days, and some of us have carried nosegays to lay upon his tomb, shaded by the willow-tree, itself both real and poetic. All of us have since in a way felt ashamed of our admiration, talking of him with reservations not untinged with pity. In so doing we have been unjust, in addition to being cruel, because Alfred de Musset represents in a definite classical form one of the eternal tendencies or eternal weaknesses of the human heart. For this reason I am pleased to think that Donnay—well qualified to feel the value of such a kind of life and poetry—has lately devoted a volume to him, which although it does not come to close grips with the critical problem, is indulgent and sympathetic, as it ought to be.

There is no occasion to repeat what happened to Musset in practical reality, as the result of his effort to identify life and poetry, because it is the argument of innumerable biographical and anecdotal volumes. The majority of them revolve around the central event of his love affairs with Georges Sand, which deserve to form the object, not of a dream and an unhealthy curiosity, but of historical consideration (as is now being done), because in them the romantic conception of love tried, neither more nor less, than to actualize itself completely in two chosen champions, such as it would not be easy to bring a second time together, and their catastrophe into the comical and the vulgar appears also as the catastrophe awaiting that mode of conceiving love.   But we are more particularly interested in seeing what happened to poetry during this effort after identification of poetry and life.

We all know what happened, that it became emphatic and rhetorical in the search for spontaneity, all exclamations, apostrophes, interrogations, comparisons made for effect broadening into pictures, the versification certainly fluent but monotonous with something in of the effect of a children's swing :

> " Nous écoutions la nuit ; la croisée entr'ouverte
> Lassait venir à nous les parfums du printemps ;
> Les vents étaient muets, la plaine était déserte ;
> Nous étions seuls, pensifs, et nous avions quinze ans." . . .

Or :

> " Poète, je t'écris pour te dire que j'aime,
> Qu'un rayon de soleil est tombé jusqu'à moi,
> Et qu'en un jour de deuil et de douleur suprème,
> Les pleurs que je versais m'ont fait penser à toi." ./. .

Not a single intense, sculptured or profoundly musical verse ever comes out of all this ; but instead, the verse very frequently dominates the thought, and sounds for sound's sake, as, for example, in this very epistle to Lamartine :

"Puisque tu sais chanter, ami, tu sais pleurer ! "

We can pass over his youthful verses and plays, *Don Paez*, *Portia*, *La coupe et les lèvres*, literary *pastiches* where it is a question of the usual Spain, Italy and Alps as invented by English and French romanticism, to which no value can be attached beyond a certain romanticism in the manner of Metastasio, save for here and there a fine moment of tenderness and passion. By this I mean that the verses are so composed as to enter immediately the memory of the ear and there to resound like the rhythmical surging of waves. But even when Musset conceives a truly poetic motive, as in *Rolla*, he translates it into a ready-made form, instead of developing and so of penetrating it deeply. Thus we hear of conventional romantic heroes (the man of noble, great, loyal and proud heart, who falls into dissoluteness), of philosophico-historical dissertations, which are intended to explain the fall of angels into the modern world, of oratorical invectives and perorations in profusion as though from a preacher in a pulpit, or rather, a lawyer addressing a jury. I have often found myself imagining what Maupassant would have extracted from the last scene of *Rolla* (which contains all the poem's poetical substance), treating it in the sober prose of his sad and sensual short stories.

Even the so celebrated *Nuits* fail to satisfy me altogether, because their creation does not seem to me to arise from within, but to be cheaply acquired by means of dialogues with allegorical personages (the Muse), and a variety of metres intended to supply missing gradations and minute distinctions in the representations of states of the soul, in the images, in the syntax and in the verse, by means of mechanical changes of metre. He whines like a child showing everyone its finger that hurts :

> " Vous saurez tout, et je vais vous conter
>   Le mal que peut faire une femme ;
> Car c'en est une, ô mes pauvres amis,
>   (Hélas ! vous le saurez peut-être !)
> C'est une femme à qui je fus soumis,
>   Comme le serf l'est à son maître.
> Joug détesté ! " . . .

And when he has finished this lament, he tells of the betrayal in another metre, how he awaited the beloved one night at the window, who did not return until dawn, and then was unable to supply satisfactory explanations in response to his anxious and jealous questionings ; he grows mad with anger :

> " Va-t-en, retire toi, spectre de ma maîtresse !
> Rentre dans ton tombeau, si tu t'en es levé ! " . . .

The Muse tries to calm him, and he again changes the metre, in order to curse the traitress :

> " Honte à toi, qui la première
> M'as appris la trahison." . . .

The Muse administers admonishment and reflections :

> " L'homme est un apprenti, la douleur est son maître." . . .

And the poet, who has listened, recognizes the truth of what she has been telling him, and forms a project, indeed pronounces an oath :

> " Par les yeux bleus de ma maîtresse,
> Et par l'azur du firmament,
> Par cette étincelle brûlante." . . .

(there are many more *par*)

> " Je te bannis de ma mémoire,
> Reste d'un amour insensé." . . .

And this is the *Nuit d'octobre*. The others are like it, such as the *Nuit de décembre*, with its man dressed in black, who resembled him like a brother and appeared to him from time to time, and with their methods of enumeration and refrains; and then there is the narrative of his unlucky loves, given in a different metre : and finally the customary figure appears in them also, revealing herself as Solitude.

I feel much pretentiousness and theatricality in these famous compositions, as though of one who fulfils the duty of weeping and accusing, and tries to show himself in the right and to obtain pity for the evil that has been done to him and to draw down upon the perfidious authoress of his misfortunes reproof and reprobation. But they contain little poetry, and it could not be abundant, because the *Nuits* are the result of a practical need rather than anything else, and the querulous lover occupies too often in them the place of the poet.

De Musset, entirely captivated by his loves and lacking any other moral and mental interest, is without the vigour to raise himself above his soul sufferings, in order to contemplate and fix and represent them with that objectivity which is like poetic justice. Certainly the effusions of the heart and the living memories remain in the non-rhetorical passages, but they are rather elements and details of poetry than poetry in themselves :

s

> " Près du ruisseau, quand nous marchions ensemble,
>   Le soir sur le sable argentin,
>   Quand devant nous le blanc spectre du tremble
>   De loin nous montrait le chemin ;
>   Je vois encore, aux rayons de la lune,
>   Ce beau corps plier sur moi." . ⁄.

Or :

> " Pourquoi ces pleurs, cette gorge oppressée,
>   Ces sanglots, si tu n'aimais pas ? " . . . ⁄

Or, again, the meeting after everything is over long ago :

> " Oui, jeune et belle encor, plus belle, osait-on dire,
>   Je l'ai vue, et ses yeux brillaient comme autrefois.
>   Ses lèvres s'entr'ouvraient, et c'était un sourire,
>   Et c'était une voix :
>   Mais non plus cette voix, non plus ce doux langage,
>   Ces regards adorés dans les miens confondus ;
>   Mon cœur, encor plein d'elle, errait sur son visage
>   Et ne la trouvait plus.
>   . . . il me semblait qu'une femme inconnue
>   Avait pris au hasard cette voix et ces yeux." . . .

The same remark seems to me to apply to the *Confessions d'un enfant du siècle*, which are closely related to these compositions and contain also as many lively expressions and fresh pictures, but at the same time much pretence of revealing the psychological mysteries of the " age," in accordance with the promise of the empty and inflated prologue, and notwithstanding this the Confessions are dragged into the realistic and biographical and do not rise to the level of a true work of art. " J'ai à raconter maintenant " (he says at the beginning of the fourth part) " ce qui advint de mon amour et le changement qui se fit en moi. Quelle raison puis-je en donner ? Aucune, sinon que je raconte et je puis dire : C'est la vérité."

Since Musset was in the habit of treating verse as an instrument to be employed in the service of his

amorous adventures and disadventures, it is not to be
wondered at that he also employed it as an instrument
for joking and jesting. Hence his numerous compositions, or parts of compositions, which are capricious
random epistles and narratives, recalling our own
burlesques and works in the style of Bernis, with
which he may have had some historical contact, at
any rate through Byron, who imitated our old Italian
writers in this kind in his *Don Juan*. This part of his
work also is juvenile and appeals to young men by its
impishness and lack of discipline, and by its boast of
being impish and undisciplined.

Where Musset on the contrary attains to art is in the
poems, or parts of poems, light in tone, amorous or
tender, which are to be found among his earliest
work (*Le lever*, *Madame la marquise*, etc.), and in greater
number in the later poems (*Suzon*, *Mimi Pinson*,
Rondeau, etc.), and among the little poems, *Mardoche*,
Namouna, *Une bonne fortune*. For instance in this
latter :

> " S'il venait à passer, sous les grands marronniers,
> Quelque alerte beauté de l'école flamande,
> Une ronde fillette échappée à Teniers,
> Ou quelque ange pensif de candeur allemande :
> Une vierge en or fin d'un livre de légende,
> Dans un flot de velours trainant ses petits pieds :
> Elle viendrait par là, de cette sombre allée,
> Marchant à pas de biche avec un air boudeur,
> Écoutant murmurer le vent dans la feuillée,
> De paresse amoureuse et de langueur voilée,
> Dans ses doigts inquiets tourmentant une fleur,
> Le printemps sur la joue et le ciel dans le cœur.
> Elle s'arrêterait là-bas, sous la tonnelle.
> Je ne lui dirais rien, j'irais tout simplement
> Me mettre à deux genoux par terre devant elle,
> Regarder dans ses yeux l'azur du firmament,
> Et pour toute faveur la prier seulement
> De se laisser aimer d'une amour éternelle."

Or in *Namouna* :

> " Ah ! l'abîme est si grand ! la pente est si glissante !
> Une maîtresse aimée est si près d'une sœur !
> Elle vient si souvent, plaintive et caressante,
> Poser, en chuchotant, son cœur sur votre cœur !
> L'homme est si faible alors ! la femme est si puissante !
> Le chemin est si doux du plaisir au bonheur ! "

And the apostrophe to Manon Lescaut :

> " Comme je crois en toi ! que je t'aime et te haïs !
> Quelle perversité ! quelle ardeur inouïe
> Pour l'or et le plaisir ! Comme toute la vie
> Est dans tes moindres mots ! Ah ! folle que tu es,
> Comme je t'aimerais demain, si tu vivais ! "

It may be said that in this kind of lyric De Musset unites and tempers his erotic-dolorous with his mirthful poetry, in neither of which he was wholly successful when taken separately ; and that in it he frees himself from the practical preoccupations of the first and the frivolity of the second, assuming a more expressly artistic attitude, looking at himself in his affections and in his defects, his illusions and delusions, his serious and his comical aspects, as though at a spectacle. Not however by any means as a spectacle seen from above, with the sense of the grandiose and vertiginous (he was not capable of that), but as a very much more placid, circumscribed, modest spectacle seen from an arm-chair in the frame-work of a pretty little stage. *Un spectacle dans un fauteuil* was indeed the title of his first collection of little comedies, little thought of when they first saw the light, but justly acquiring in the course of time that reputation which his lyrics and small poetical pieces have been gradually shedding. They are really exquisite works : *Les caprices de Marianne, Le chandelier, Fantasio, On ne badine pas avec l'amour, La nuit vénitienne*, and the others. And this is tantamount to assigning them their true place ! Emphasis, declamatory tone, empty and resonant verses, excesses, lack of proportion, incorrections, blandishments, altogether vanish and these little dramas unfold themselves in their lightness and grace, in their sober, acute, incisive and at the same time spontaneous prose. Some magic wand must have touched the primitive personages of De Musset, who appeared to be above the ordinary stature in their loves, their daring, their vices, their crimes, and miraculously reduced them to the minusculous proportions of little men and women, dwarfs and gnomes. And these minusculous creatures play at the game of love. They are small but well made, gracious, provoking and tender as little women, passionate as manikins, grotesque and ridiculous but well-constructed as odious or ridiculous personages. They engage in their intrigues, give way to their fancies, gratify their desires, often discuss the pros and cons, the mode and the manner of the grave problem which alone makes beat their little hearts—when of a sudden the rapacious breath of passion or the cold breath of death overwhelms these marionettes.

With a little reflection, we become aware that we still have before us the old heart of De Musset, that of the stories of Spain and of Italy, of the Nights, of the Confessions; but converted from subject into object, that is to say, into an object of art, and converted as the result of its own work alone in its genial moments. Celio loves Marianna desperately in the *Caprices*, and is ready and desirous of shedding his blood for her, but she does not care for him. You do not hear him tempestuously tossed in eloquent verse, for he sighs in prose, in a series of brief sentences :

" Ah ! que je fusse né dans le temps des tournois et des batailles ! Qu'il m'eût été permis de porter les couleurs de Marianne et de les teindre de mon sang ! Qu'on m'eût donné un rival à combattre, une armée entière à défier ! Que le sacrifice de ma vie eût pu lui être utile ! Je sais agir, mais je ne puis parler. Ma langue ne sert point mon cœur, et je mourrai sans m'être fait comprendre, comme on meurt dans une prison."

It seems to be the sighing of a boy with his head full of romances; but he is a boy who means what he says and suffers death for Marianna. You thought he was a boy, but he was a man, with a deeper and nobler heart than can ever be found among the living. And his friend the dissolute Octavio laments him— as only man can lament the death of man—before Marianna, who had not even noticed that treasure of the rarest virtues, dissipated in an instant for her.

" Moi seul au monde je l'ai connu. Cette urne d'albâtre, couverte de ce long voile de deuil, est sa parfaite image. C'est ainsi qu'une douce mélancolie voilait les perfections de son âme tendre et délicate. Pour moi seul, cette vie silencieuse n'a point été un mystère. Les longues soirées que nous avons pas- sées ensemble sont comme de fraîches oasis dans un désert aride : elles ont versé sur mon cœur les seules gouttes de rosée qui y soient jamais tombées. Cœlio était la bonne partie de moi-même; elle est remontée au ciel avec lui. C'était un homme d'un autre temps : il connaissait les plaisirs et leur préférait la solitude; il savait combien les illusions sont trompeuses, et il préférait ses illusions à la réalité. Elle eût été heureuse, la femme qui l'eût aimé."

And Marianna who was in love with Octavio and
has allowed Celio to perish; Marianna, who witnesses
the despair of the friend who has lost his friend, and
hears him say farewell to love, and cry out that henceforth he is dead to life, says to him as she gently offers
herself :

" Mais non pas dans mon cœur, Octave.   Pourquoi
dis-tu : adieu l'amour !

" OCTAVE.

" Je ne vous aime pas, Marianne; c'était Cœlio qui
vous aimait."

Le chandelier opens with the scene where Master
Andrea, the jealous husband, who has gone to surprise his wife, finds her merged in profound and of
course simulated slumber :

" Holà ! ma femme ! hé ! Jacqueline ! hé ! holà !
Jacqueline ! ma femme !   La peste soit de l'endormie !
Hé ! hé ! ma femme, éveillez-vous ! Holà ! holà !
levez-vous, Jacqueline. — Comme elle dort !   Holà !
holà ! holà ! hé ! hé ! hé !   Ma femme, ma femme,
ma femme !   C'est moi, André, votre mari, qui ai à
vous parler de choses sérieuses. He ! hé, psst !
hem ! brum ! brum ! psst !   Jacqueline, êtes-vous
morte ?   Si vous ne vous éveillez tout à l'heure, je
vous coiffe du pot à l'eau."

Musset's style in these plays should be appreciated
and understood for that it really is as belonging rather
to the theatre for children than to farce. Master
Andrea's little *clerc* Fortunio is a child, who hears
his companions discourse of Jacqueline's intrigues

and of the lover she pulls into her house at night-time through the window, and feels himself as it were carried away by these amorous adventures : " Que de pareilles choses existent, cela me fait bondir le cœur. Vraiment, Landry, tu as vu cela ? "

Fortunio is adopted by Jacqueline and her captain as " candle-holder," a function which he accepts unconsciously owing to his ardent silent devotion to the attractive little lady; but when he suddenly becomes aware of the part that he has been made to play, he is indignant and rebels :

" Rendre un jeune homme amoureux de soi, unique-ment pour détourner sur lui les soupçons tombés sur un autre. . . . Mentir du fond du cœur; faire de son corps un appât; jouer avec tout ce qu'il a de sacré sous le ciel, comme un voleur avec des dés pipés : voilà ce qui fait sourire une femme ! voilà ce qu'elle fait d'un petit air distrait ! . . ."

But at the same time he does not succeed in shaking off from his imagination her attractive little personality and comes himself to explain matters and seek indulgence :

" Non, quand elle me souriait, elle ne m'aimait pas pour cela, mais elle souriait de voir que je l'aimais. Quand elle me tendait la main, elle ne me donnait pas son cœur, mais elle laissait le mien se donner. Quand elle me disait : ' Je vous aime,' elle voulait dire : ' Aimez-moi.' Non, Jacqueline n'est pas méchante; il n'y a là ni calcul ni froideur. Elle ment, elle trompe, elle est femme; elle est coquette, railleuse, joyeuse, audacieuse, mais non infâme, non insensible. Ah !

insensé, tu l'aimes ! tu l'aimes ! tu pries, tu pleures, et elle se rit de toi ! "

But now passion seizes hold of the merry Jacqueline also :

" JACQUELINE.

" Vous savez que je mens, que je trompe, que je vous raille, et que je vous tue ? Vous savez que j'aime Clavaroche et qu'il me fait faire tout ce qu'il veut ? que je joue une comédie ? que là, hier, je vous ai pris pour dupe ? que je suis lâche et méprisable ? que je vous expose à la mort par plaisir ? Vous saviez tout; vous en étiez sûr ? Eh bien ! eh bien . . . qu'est-ce que vous savez maintenant ?

" FORTUNIO.

" Mais, Jacqueline, je crois . . . je sais. . . .

" JACQUELINE.

" Sais-tu que je t'aime, enfant que tu es ? qu'il faut que tu me pardonnes ou que je meure ; et que je te le demande à genoux ? "

Critics have discovered a Shakespearean afflatus in these little dramas, which must at any rate be meant to refer to Shakespeare's juvenile work; and in like manner and perhaps more convincingly may be noted something in them suggestive of Ariosto, in their amiable lightness of touch. The mention of Ariosto would serve to imply and to praise their perfect fusion of colours and the agility of the digressions, which never break the chain of the general tone, always smiling, even in tragical passages.

And since the minor works are becoming more and more clearly revealed as the true major works of De

Musset, will it not be of advantage that his stories and prose narratives should rise in general esteem? If Alfred de Musset to some extent imposed silence upon the passionate or burlesque—passionate tumult of his lyrics, and grew calm and smilingly moved again in the stories and the narratives, so limpid, simple, calm and free in treatment, we sometimes even hear him uttering (as in *Les deux maîtresses*) words of moral wisdom and noble renunciation.

XIX

BALZAC

LITTLE theoretical certainty is to be found in French literary criticism, because in France, differently from Italy and Germany, the theory of art, understood philosophically, has had little development. Notwithstanding this, I place the French psychological or impressionistic critics before the doctrinaire and systematic critics, Sainte-Beuve and Lemaître before Taine and Brunetière. These latter are certainly theoretical, but dominated by that intellectualistic and dogmatic spirit which forms an obstacle to the comprehension of art. One should read Brunetière's volume on Balzac, lately reprinted in an almost popular edition, in order to see how his theories have obscured even those evident truths which are to be found in popular consciousness, and are again to be found, let us say, in Le Breton's modest and diligent study of the same author. Let us pass over (in order not to repeat a criticism which would henceforth be too obvious in Italy) the premiss of the " literary class," certainly not invented by Brunetière, but treated by him with absurd rigidity and in virtue of which the problem of his criticism appears as that of the class of " romance," and of Balzac as of the writer who confers autonomy upon this form, carries out the " true romance " and observes the boundaries which are not to be crossed. But what has he seen of what is romance, or, to limit ourselves to what is particularly in question, the "historical" and "social" romance? And what has he understood of the spiritual disposition of Balzac, both in regard to "historical romance" and to art?

If Brunetière had not lacked both æsthetic culture and philosophical training, it would not have been difficult for him to discover that the "social novel" can indeed be regarded as a form differing from the other forms of art, as an "autonomous class," not because it is a form of art (in which case and when it is such, the distinction shows itself to be altogether empirical and arbitrary), but because, on the contrary, in its origin and proper quality it is not at all a form of art, but simply a didactic scheme. When in Greece the religious, poetical and mythical impetus came to an end and gave place to the work of research and criticism, comedy also, in the imaginative and brilliantly capricious form given to it by Aristophanes, became converted into the comedy of Menander, upon which (as Vico was perhaps the first to note and Nietzsche the last to bring into the sphere of general knowledge) had blown the breath of the Socratic philosophy. Thereupon playwrights and moralists joined hands, and comedy availed itself of the character-ology of the philosophers, and the philosophers adopted and developed the discussion of types of character which had been formed in the theatre. It is well known that the framework of Menander sufficed writers of comedy for centuries, that is to say, not only the Romans, but also the Italians of the Renaissance and the French of the Classical period. Its characters became fixed and conventionalized as those of the old man, the lover, the young girl, the astute slave, the miser, the boaster, and so forth, and if some variety and some accretions came to be added in course of time, yet it never or hardly ever broadened beyond the study and representation of man in general and of human vices and weaknesses.

But between the seventeenth and eighteenth centuries, social struggles and changes and increased interest in history on the one hand reacted also upon comedy and caused it to represent definite social and historical environments, and on the other took possession of the prose of the novels and turned it in the direction of the " historical " and the " social " novel. Balzac's preface to the *Comédie humaine* is a good instance of this renovation of the programmes of Menander and of Theophrastus : a Menander who has behind him the French Revolution and before him the rule of the middle-class, and is itself revolutionary and middle-class in its own way, or counter-revolutionary and anti-middle-class ; a Theophrastus who has learned something about the new historical philosophy and the new science of nature. Balzac, in fact, rallied to the doctrine of Geoffroy Saint-Hilaire and to the literary model offered by Buffon. He asked himself, seeing that at every period " des espèces sociales, comme il y a des espèces zoologiques," why something similar should not be done for society to what Buffon had achieved in his magnificent work, " en essayant de représenter dans un livre l'ensemble de la zoologie." The work which he desired to write was to possess a triple content : " les hommes, les femmes et les choses, c'est à dire les personnes, et la représentation matérielle qu'ils donnent de leur pensée : enfin, l'homme et la vie." He did not propose to restrict himself to simple observation, but to rise to the sphere of the reason or law of social facts, and from this to proceed yet further to the principles of judgment or of the ideals of the Good, the True and the Beautiful. The reference to Walter Scott is also noteworthy, and the demand that history should be " social," that is to say, no longer human in general, as in the individualism and pragmatism of the preceding century.

Balzac's proposal, like those of others who both with, before and after him pointed to social and historical romance as the successor of the Græco-Roman comedy that had disappeared, is not a directly artistic proposal, but is historical, sociological and philosophical, and in so far as those writers wished to avail themselves of the imagination in order to summarize and to expose their observations and theories, they aimed, as I have said, at nothing other than a didactic scheme. But since science and imagination were placed side by side and the fusion of the two turned out to be impossible, two things happened : either the poetical element affirmed itself to be the true centre of the work and enslaved the scientific elements, reducing them to its tones and colours, and a purely poetical work was the result, ascending to the pinnacle of Manzoni's romance-poem, which has been justly described as the concrete historical form of the same author's *Inni sacri ;* or the scientific interest declared itself to be the centre of the work, and then the poetical elements were in their turn enslaved and turned to account as supplying the popular and imaginative appeal of the theme in question. This second course has been usually adopted by those of mediocre talents, compilers of books of instruction and vulgarity, because anyone possessing truly original capacity as an observer and a philosopher is not satisfied to compose fables and apologies and to cut up his images into little pieces, but quickly grasps the good sword of scientific, historical and polemical prose. Artists unendowed with certain gifts proper to critics and thinkers, or a certain tendency towards observation and meditation, have never gone beyond a certain point in the development of such capacities, and have either found expression for their thought and conceptions in living representations, cancelling their properly scientific side, or they have left them scattered in notes, diaries and little essays, without subjecting them to truly systematic treatment.

It is not astonishing that Brunetière paid no attention to this difference of relation between the didactic scheme of the novel and art and poetry and to the various solutions to which it gives rise, because, as has been observed, he cultivated an intellectualistic conception both of art itself and of poetry. But what seems to me to be a proof of singular blindness, a result of false theory, is his insistence upon considering Balzac as the incarnation of the very idea of the novel (Balzac, c'est le roman même), as creator of the book of objective social observation, which should possess the essential characteristic of " rassemblance avec la vie," and be composed with " l'entière soumission de l'observateur à l'objet de son observation," thus adopting the method " qui a renouvelé la science," and which cannot ever be judged in itself, but only " en le comparant avec la vie." This is tantamount to saying that one set of observations must be controlled by comparing it with new observations and experiments. Now anyone who has examined, I do not say the entire works of Balzac, but has tested some of his novels, has at once seen as obvious that Balzac is by temperament the exact opposite of the scientific observer (the one full of doubts and precautions and a foe to precise affirmations, the other sure of himself and triumphant as Balzac always was in his assertions), and also of the lettered pedagogue, who selects certain concepts and historical points of view for symbolical narrative treatment and compiles instructive works illustrated with examples.   And although every reader admires the profound psychological aphorisms to be met with in those novels of Balzac, he is not less sensible of the aphorist's incapacity to demonstrate and systematize, which is clearly manifest in the above-mentioned preface (his principal attempt at theorizing), where his imperfect and trammelled philosophy hastens to crown itself with religion and monarchy, those " deux vérités éternelles : la religion, la monarchie, deux nécessités que les évènements con-temporains proclament, etc." And although some of his observations as to social history shine with a very bright light, they are vivid flashes, not diffused and well-distributed light : that is to say, they are rather suggestions as to questions to be asked rather than answers made to questions.

Balzac will, for instance, have clear vision of the power of finance in modern society, and he will make the little old Jew Gobseck say : " Je suis assez riche pour acheter les consciences de cent qui font mouvoir les ministres, depuis leurs garçons jusqu'à leurs maîtresses : n'est-ce pas le Pouvoir ? Je puis avoir les plus belles femmes et leurs plus tendres caresses : n'est-ce pas le Plaisir ? Le Pouvoir et le Plaisir ne résument-ils pas tout votre ordre social ? Nous sommes en Paris une dizaine ainsi, tous rois silencieux et inconnus, les artistes de nos destinées. La vie n'est-elle pas une machine à laquelle l'argent imprime le mouvement ? . . . L'or est le spiritualisme de vos sociétés." But this is not science, because science begins when a search is made—I was about to say sceptically—as to whether and to what extent gold dominates society, and by what social ends itself is guided and therefore dominated. The scientific problem has hardly dawned upon Balzac when he already changes it into a feeling of stupefaction and terror. " Je retournai chez moi stupéfait. Ce petit vieillard sec avait grandi. Il s'était changé à mes yeux en une image fantastique où se personnifiait le pouvoir de l'Or. La vie, les hommes me faisaient horreur." . . .

Everyone knows that Balzac as a young man devoured the most extravagant romantic literature both in French and English, adventures, conquests, discoveries of treasure, crimes, ghostly apparitions, hallucinations, and that he himself wrote novels of the same sort, and what he was never able to do without such marvellous tales, introducing them more or less freely and sometimes in profusion into many of the works of his maturity. But Balzac does not do otherwise than give an extraordinary aspect to what is ordinary, middle-class and popular even in those novels and in that series of novels which Brunetière considers to be " objective " and " naturalistic." No portrait of character or surroundings but he exaggerates it to the extent of making it altogether marvellous and fantastic, whether he is telling the story of a former officer of Napoleon like Philippe Brideau, or representing Goriot's paternal affection, or the house of father Grandet or the shop of the *chat qui pelotte*. He takes hold here and there of some bits of reality in

T

order to make of them an object of fascination for himself and to enter by means of them into a dream of the unbridled and immense, through which he progresses, half in admiration, half in terror, as though immersed in an apocalyptic vision. To take this for " a methodical application of natural science " is really somewhat singular, as I observed, excusable only in the non-critical, thoughtless crowd, which takes the history of France to be the same as that told in the novels of the elder Dumas : a writer with whom Balzac has no small resemblance of method, so much so that it might be said, not without truth, that he transports the *Trois mousquetaires* into the world of politics, of speculation, of invention, of banking, creating Artagnan business men, Athos manufacturers, Aramis ministers and Porthos acquiring riches by means of violence and crime.

Acute writers had already warned people of this vulgar confusion, as, for example, Baudelaire in one of his essays collected in the *Art romantique* : " J'ai maint fois été étonné que la gloire de Balzac fût de passer pour un observateur : il m'avait toujours semblé que son principal mérite était d'être visionnaire et visionnaire passionné. Tous ses personnages sont doués de l'ardeur vitale dont il était animé lui-même. Toutes ses fictions sont aussi profondément colorées que les rêves. Depuis le sommet de l'aristocratie jusqu'aux bas fonds de la plèbe, tous les acteurs de la Comédie sont plus âpres à la vie, plus actifs et rusés dans la lutte, plus patients dans le malheur, plus goulus dans la jouissance, plus angéliques dans le dévouement, que la comédie du vrai monde ne nous montre. Bref, chacun, chez Balzac, même les portières, a du génie. Toutes les âmes sont des armes chargées de volonté jusqu'à la gueule. C'est Balzac lui-même." . . .

Balzac's ardent imagination not only forbade to him scientific observation, for which Brunetière praised him, but was so violent and voracious as to disturb his very work as an artist, and this point must be made clear, as it supplies guidance in the critical reading of his fiction.) Here too Brunetière comes off badly : " C'est la représentation de la vie que l'intéresse, et non pas du tout la réalisation de la beauté, comme s'il se rendait compte un peu con- fusément, qu'en art la réalisation de la beauté ne s'obtient guère qu'aux dépens, au détriment de la fidélité de l'imitation de la vie." These æsthetic per- versions, which would put an end both to art and criticism, show that Brunetière remained calmly reposing upon two of the worst old rhetorical common- places, the idea of the imitation of reality and of beauty as transcending reality, and did not even suspect that the representation of reality and beauty is the same thing in art, and that where we find beauty wanting, there too is wanting nothing else but the perfection of representation.

How, then, can it be said that the ardour of Balzac's imagination, which seems to be so favourable to artistic production, yet acted injuriously upon that art ? The reason is that in the delicate process of artistic creation, the imagination which embodies and dominates the impressions and the passions of reality must be kept clearly distinct from the fancy which avails itself of the intuitions of the imagination for its own enjoyment, entertainment or bitter alleviation. Balzac's case was precisely so, for with him what is described as his imaginative ardour really contained two diverse activities acting in two different ways under one name, in the one case inspiring him to artistic creation, in the other deforming the art produced or begun to be produced. One feels that Balzac was a poet in the best sense of the word, from the vigour with which he represents characters, situations and surroundings, from the perfection of the forms that burst forth from his stirred imagination. He has nothing in common with Victor Hugo, even as regards defects, for the latter does not start from poetic motives but from intellectual considerations in his plays and novels, and for this reason always preserves clearness of design in the midst of the revel of images which he groups around the aforesaid considerations, although he possesses very little poetical afflatus and genuine imagination.

Balzac, on the contrary, generally proceeds with energetic genius, like a true artist, but gradually in the course of the work, instead of leaving his creations free to follow the law of their true being and so create the companionship, the surroundings, the kind of action, beginning, middle and end that are implied in their fundamental notion, and consequently to moderate attemper and take on their proper tone, he compels them to follow the law of his own rapacious temperament, of Honoré de Balzac, whose taste lies in the direction of passions pushed to the extreme, of violent and intransigent conflicts, of colossal undertakings, of astonishing clevernesses and infernal complications, of astounding successes, all of which he enjoys immensely and intensifies, in order to extract from them yet more enjoyment.

It has been said and repeated (and I think Sainte-Beuve is responsible for the statement), that in Balzac

the characters are excellent, the action less good and
the style vicious.   This further empirical utterance of
criticism must be corrected by means of the exact
theory, namely, that the three things are one, and that
one of them cannot be exempt from the defects of the
others, and the defects of all must be brought home
to a common origin. This common origin is to be found
in Balzac's psychological disposition already described,
owing to which he capriciously applies movement to his
creations, thus making the characters of his personages
revolve rapidly and grow vertiginously upon themselves, becoming ever more and more mad about
themselves, and then, having attained the summit of
this process of expansion, they turn into the opposite
of what they were, or reveal other qualities in an
unexpected way, which are contradictory or out of
harmony with their former qualities.   Their actions,
owing to this same vertiginous rapidity, either lose all
logical consistency, and, in their efforts to develop the
characters, assume the customary form of the serial
novel, or else they too all of a sudden also collapse
and languish, and the style, which is all one with those
actions and characters, falls from simple and robust
plasticity into feebleness and languishment, or assumes
the tone of explanation and comment.   The characters
do not attain to the harmony of discordant concord,
and therefore the action does not unfold itself naturally
and the style is not rhythmical.

Any one of Balzac's novels selected from among the
best offers ready proofs of such inequalities and dis-
harmonies; but I shall limit myself to *Eugènie Grandet*,
which is reputed to be the most perfect of all, or one of
the most perfect.   After the wonderful picture of the
country house and of the family surroundings in

which flourish the gentle affections of the youthful Eugenia, who is there that does not feel that father and mother Grandet and Eugenia herself are being turned into fixed rhetorical types ? Father Grandet is no longer a miser in his humanity, but a madman, and he behaves like a madman in the scene where he finds in his daughter's hands the bag left in her charge by her betrothed :

" Au regard que jeta son mari sur l'or madame Grandet cria : — Mon Dieu, ayez pitié de nous !

Le bonhomme sauta sur le nécessaire comme un tigre fond sur un enfant endormi.

— Qu'est-ce que c'est que cela ? dit-il en emportant le trésor et allant se placer à la fenêtre. — Du bon or ! de l'or ! s'écria-t-il. Beaucoup d'or ! Ça pèse deux livres." . . .

With a maniac of this sort for father and a character without character such as the betrothed cousin, the story of Eugenia, which promised to turn out moving and poetical, loses itself in the insignificant. It seems that the author, who has spent his best strength in forcing characters and oppositions to an extreme, lacks the breadth to represent the drama which he had been preparing. So the story rushes along and what should have been represented is announced as having already happened : " Cinq ans se passèrent "; . . . or : " Pendant que ces choses se passaient à Saumur, Charles faisait fortune aux Indes," etc. Worse still, the style becomes impoverished, and here and there assumes the appearance of a school exercise :

" A trente ans Eugénie ne connaissait encore aucune des félicités de la vie. Sa pâle et triste enfance s'était écoulée auprès d'une mère dont le cœur méconnu, froissé, avait toujours souffert. En quittant avec joie l'existence, cette mère plaignit sa fille d'avoir à vivre, et lui laissa dans l'âme des légers remords et d'éternels regrets. Le premier, le seul amour d'Eugénie était, pour elle, un principe de mélancolie. Après avoir entrevu son amant pendant quelques jours, elle lui avait donné son cœur entre deux baisers furtivement acceptés et rendus; puis il était parti, mettant tout un monde entre elle et lui." . . .

Too often, before Balzac's novels, we experience a feeling of pain as though we had been present at the diminishing of a masterpiece, and our thoughts turn to that story of the same Balzac entitled *Un chef-d'œuvre inconnu*, where it is a question of a picture that is a confused mass of colours, beneath which some fragment magnificently painted is here and there visible.

What more do you want? we shall be asked :— Balzac was built that way. Certainly, and he was a great man in that way also. Because, notwithstanding deformation, inflation and the abandonment of the end of art, which is very common in him, his art was most vigorous, and is strewn throughout with acute thoughts and observations, which vary its attractiveness. But Balzac never or only on rare occasions attained to æsthetic serenity. I admit that I remained astonished at an Italian comparison between him and Alexander Manzoni (and, in this connection, why should Balzac's unfavourable judgment of the *Promessi Sposi* in a conversation at Milan not be remembered? I read it many years ago in a book of Tullo Dandolo's), between him and Manzoni, as I was saying, where Balzac is held to be audacious and fruitful, Manzoni timid and sterile, astonished above all that anyone could have thought of making such a comparison, but worse than astonished at seeing that not even Manzoni's divine equality of level had been sufficient to throw into a clear light the artistic vice with which was afflicted Honoré de Balzac.

XX

BAUDELAIRE

CHARLES BAUDELAIRE was among those who was keenly conscious of what there is of fatuous in the doctrine of natural goodness and human perfectibility, otherwise called progress, as imagined in the eighteenth century and invested with romantic colours by the liberal thought of the nineteenth. He laughed at the free-thinkers and humanitarians who proposed to abolish the death penalty and hell out of friendship for humanity; or war by means of a popular subscription at a halfpenny a head; at the fanatics who imagined that " the devil would one day be gobbled up " by manufactories and machines; and finally at everything that he described as modern *sottise*. Against this he upheld the doctrine of " original sin," stressing the evident truth of the daily observation that " man is always in the savage state." " Progress " seemed to him to be a gospel of sloth and the easy life, well suited to the individual who counts upon his neighbours for doing his work, a " Belgian belief "; and he had prepared a book upon Belgium, of which notes and fragments remain, that would have turned out to be a most savoury satire. Belgium then possessed a representative painter in Wirtz, and Victor Hugo had there pitched his tent. Both these men had formed the design of " saving humanity," and had founded the " great party " of the happiness of the human race, to be attained by means of " international education."

And although Baudelaire admired Victor Hugo in several respects as an artist, he nourished a different sort of admiration for him as affording an example of the mixture of " genius " and " stupidity." Hence he mocked at his poses as " Prometheus " and as a " socialistic Shakespeare," and when the bard moved to Brussels and left the island of his exile and his customary colloquies with the Ocean, he wrote to a friend : " It seems that he and the Ocean have had a difference : either he has not found it possible to stand the Ocean any longer, or the Ocean has got bored with him." He cannot also have even had much reverence for Victor Hugo's " God," because he protested that " the God of Messieurs Rogeard, Michelet, Benjamin Gastineau, Mario Portal, Garibaldi and the Abbé Chatel " was not his. One of his amusements consisted in collecting from the newspapers and speeches those utterances of the democrats which were the most delicious for their idiocy, in the style of a Monsieur Flée, who, talking of bees, defined them in a sugary manner as " those dear little republicans." On the other hand, he had at heart Joseph de Maistre, " the great genius of our time," " a seer "; the scepticism and crudities of our Ferrari pleased him, and he was his friend.[1] Politics in his opinion, was and should be a " science without a heart," and the true politician should always unite in himself the qualities of the " revolutionary " and the " Jesuit."

But Baudelaire covered with sarcasm and contempt yet another ethical conception of more recent origin, foreign to the libertine eighteenth century (clearsighted as to this question), and proper to the nine-

[1] For Ferrari see *l'Art romantique*, p. 27; *Lettres*, pp. 245, 289.

teenth century and romanticism : the religion of love, of love as the expression of what there is of most lofty and noble and gentle in man, love-passion as a heroic form, and erotic adoration, which consecrates its object. Fixing his eye upon the depths of eroticism, he discovered that " the one supreme delight of love lies in the certainty of doing wrong, and man and woman know from birth that in evil all pleasure is found." He used jestingly to remark that love is a crime, " the most tiresome part of which is the necessity of always having an accomplice." All attempts at moralizing it are vain, by introducing " honesty " into the things of love, which would be like wishing " to unite shade and heat in mystic union, night and day." And woman, who is all love, has the right and in a certain way the duty of seeking to " seem magical and supernatural," en-circling herself with fascination and mystery. She performs this work of seduction to evil even as mother, as nurse, as sister, surrounding man in swaddling-clothes, not only by her cares for him, but with " her caresses and sensual pleasure." Thus the infant already loves woman in that aspect, for " the pleasant sensations of her silks and her furs, for the perfume of her bosom and her hair, for the tinkling of her jewels, for her fluttering ribbons, and for all the various *mundus muliebris.*" The Marquis de Sade told hard truths courageously, of the sort from which people hide their faces and thus almost succeed in destroying them, and to such a philosopher as he we must turn, for instance, if we wish to understand, for example, " the horror and the intoxicating love of a woman spy, a thief, and the like." One can imagine Baudelaire's opinion of Sand, of the *femme-Sand,* in the light of such convictions as these.   In matters of love Sand assumed the same appearance as Victor Hugo in those of politics, society and metaphysics.   He held her to be a " Prudhomme of immorality," far inferior to the Marquis de Sade, because he represented " evil which knows itself," and she, on the contrary, " the evil which does not know itself," and " ingenuous evil," which is worse than " Satanism."

In consequence of this, Baudelaire turned against the cult of nature, both of " nature " as it was understood in the eighteenth century and of nature as the romantics understood it.   The whole of nature seemed to him to share in " original sin," and he often fancied that " maleficent and horrible animals are nothing but the vivification, corporification and disclosing in material existence of the evil thoughts of man." Woman is certainly a " natural " being and thus " abominable."   Trees, verdure, insects, and all other natural forms which have given rise to a kind of religion inspired him not at all, nor could he conceive it possible that God could inhabit them, refusing his obedience to " sanctified vegetables."   He had a certain feeling that an evil power existed outside man, since he failed to conceive how, save by means of such intervention, certain sudden acts and thoughts can be explained.   Everywhere he saw mystery, and to him as to others dreams seemed to be " a hieroglyphic language, of which he did not possess the key."   But he had and had not a glimpse of God—of God as different from that of the gentlemen above-mentioned. In a letter of 1864 he says that when he has finished expressing all the reasons for his complete disgust of the human race, when he is " absolutely alone," then he would " search for a religion."   But there is something of jest in this passage. He invokes God here and there in his poems, but here he is certainly a poetical figure. In a note of his diary he proposed to himself to " pray to God every morning, as the source of all strength and justice, his father, to Marietta and to Poe, as intercessors, and to pray them to endow him with force to accomplish all his duties and to give to his mother a life sufficiently long to be able to enjoy his transformation." But it is nothing more than a mode of self-suggestion, or at most a hint of a need he experienced : the need of prayer and confession.

His criticism, then, is altogether negative, on the one hand taking from him the possibility of relying upon ordinary, vulgar or middle-class beliefs, as they are called, that faith of the laity in human brotherhood and progress with the duties which it implies, and on the other tearing every veil from the illusions which irradiate sensual and erotic desire, but substituting nothing for the faith destroyed and opposing nothing to the inrush of turbulent sensuality. Indeed, this remained nevertheless his only rule of life, with the sole difference that it was no longer for him as for others evil unconscious of itself. In him it was conscious of itself and despised itself and was thus less base and more virile, " nearer " (as he not altogether wrongly remarked) to healing. This nearness, however, was very relative, because meanwhile such consciousness bore in itself a methodical cultivation of evil, the art of intensifying it, of complicating it (even with the profanation of the sacred, which he reproved) and of dilating it. And this self-consciousness, linked with complete simplicity, consciousness and firmness, is the originality of his " Satanism," because, as regards the rest, Baudelaire himself records his predecessors, beginning with " the old dandy " Chateaubriand, who left on record the following : " I was always virtuous without pleasure and would have been criminal without remorse " ; and Sainte-Beuve recalled in his turn as he read *Les fleurs du mal,* his *Joseph Delorme,* and referred to it in conversing with his young friend, who argued that the book could be considered as " *Les fleurs du mal* in their vigil."

It would present little attraction (because verse is one thing and prose formulas are another), and in any case it is not necessary, to describe the throng of desires which Baudelaire lets loose within himself, exciting them and sharpening their edge : strange exotic loves, impure and criminal, served up to himself with conscious deception, lying and cynicism, an attraction for things cruel or painful or sad or terrifying, for the process of dissolution and conception, artificial intoxication with wines, with perfumes and with opium. Love and Death were gentle brothers and they dominated the world of Leopardi; but the world of Baudelaire was dominated by two sisters, two amiable girls, Dissoluteness and Death (" *La Débauche et la Mort sont deux aimables filles* . . ."). He believed one day that he had found a definition of the Beautiful as something that should be at once " ardent and sad," and " a little vague," and such as " opens the way to the imagination." He symbolized beauty as a female figure, mingling " voluptuousness and sadness, melancholy, weariness, satiety, with ardour, avidity for life, and the bitterness which results from deprivation, desperation and complaint. Joy could not be associated with it save in an accidental way, as " a vulgar ornament."

Barbey d'Aurevilly concluded his well-known criticism of Baudelaire's poetry by saying that after writing *Les fleurs du mal* there remained but two things for the poet to do : " either to blow out his brains or become a Christian." This dilemma, which is admirably deduced from the premisses that we have supplied, should be considered entirely appropriate if the torments in which Baudelaire was plunged had been a problem of affective, practical life. But perhaps this was not so, or only to a very slight extent. For Baudelaire, as for other artists, it is very difficult to draw the line between real life and the life of the imagination, and for him, as for them, the latter was certain to gain the upper hand. We must also not forget his observation as regards Poe, that " the audacity of certain men in working in the horrible is frequently the result of a great moral energy lacking occupation, sometimes of obstinate chastity and sometimes also of a profound sensibility repressed." The documents relating to his life and the researches of the critics have, however, cleared his biography of many legends, introduced by himself with intent to terrify and make mock of simple folk. He used to smile when people tried to make a " monster " of him, and one of his finest efforts in irony is his candidature for the seat in the French Academy that had become vacant by the death of the Dominican Père Lacordaire. Reading his posthumous works and letters, one receives the impression that although he had not been able to arrange his life practically, yet he was in reality honourable, loyal, dignified, and above all gentle and affectionate of heart. In any case, however, and admitting that he actually did pass through a great part of those forms and vicissitudes of dissoluteness and disgust described in his poems, Barbey d'Aurevilly's dilemma was nevertheless wrong to this extent, that he did not take count of Baudelaire as an artist, and, consequently, of the fact that he had a third course open to him, namely, of dealing with the problem insoluble in life as one that could be solved in art.

Few, not only among French men of letters, but also among philosophers by profession, have spoken of art with more profundity than he; and in this respect he finds a place beside another artist, who was also very profound in his study of the things of art, namely Flaubert. As Flaubert opposed " personality," that is to say, writing to prove a theory, in the field of fiction, which was more properly his, so Baudelaire opposed philosophic poetry, which was then the fashion in France, and from which he must have the more keenly desired to discriminate his lyrical production, for the reason that it occupied a neighbouring field. From his lips, as from those of Flaubert, fell the same words : " great poetry is essentially *bête :* believe that there lies its strength and its glory." [1] Philosophical poetry, on the contrary, returned to *imagerie,* usual in the infancy of a people, at a period when it could not compete in power of bringing conviction with an article of the *Encyclopædia.* For this reason it was useless. Not only was it useless, but harmful, since it artificially introduces philosophy into art, whereas art has its own implicit and spontaneous philosophy, because the poet is " supremely intelligent " and the imagination is " the most scientific of the faculties, being alone in understanding *universal analogy* and what mystical religion terms *correspondence.*"

[1] *Œuvres posthumes,* p. 167.

Like Flaubert, Baudelaire felt how inartistic was passion when it tyrannizes over art, for " the principle of poetry is strictly and simply this, human aspiration to a superior beauty, and it manifests itself by means of an enthusiasm, a transport of soul, altogether independent of passion, which is an intoxication of the heart, and of truth, which is the food of reason. Passion is something natural, too natural, for it introduces a tone that displeases and makes discord in the domain of pure beauty. Passion is too violent and too familiar, so that it shocks those pure longings, those gracious Melancholies and those noble Despairs, which dwell in the supernatural regions of poetry." Hence his disapproval for the styles of Lamartine and of De Musset, " artists lacking in will power and not sufficiently masters of themselves." He was particularly severe as regards De Musset, who " invokes heaven and hell in his adventures of *table d'hôte* and pours out a muddy torrent of grammatical and prosodical errors, and is altogether incapable of performing the work whereby a passing fancy is transmuted into a work of art." When he was in good-natured vein, or rather when he was writing for public consumption, he used to call the poet of the *Nuits* " a lazy-body with graceful moments "; but in private he gave rein to his contempt, asserting that De Musset's works had got what they deserved in finding themselves on the footstools of ladies of easy virtue, side by side with the lapdog in its coral collar.

Hence his literary anti-feminism, which he shared with Poe, and a further reason for his aversion to Sand, who popped her novels into the post as if they were letters, writing them on note paper and giving

U

proof of that *coulant* style so dear to the hearts of the worthy middle class. Women's style, he likewise remarked, changes and fluctuates like their garments and few women writers have failed to be " a desolation, not only for their families, but even for their lovers, since even the least modest men yet love modesty in the object of their love."

But his mind was so clear and exact that he was never led by his constant polemic against formless art into the assertion and exaltation of the abstract form; indeed, he utters a warning against " the monstrous disorders due to an immoderate taste for form, and against " the frantic passion for art," which is " a cancer that devours all the rest " and leads to nothing, " as does every excessive specialization of faculty." Acute observations throng his pages, such as those upon the true draughtsmen " who always draw according to the image written on their brains and never according to nature." He also speaks of the necessity to enlarge the history of art so as to include all the infinite forms of universal beauty excluded by Winckelmann; and of restricting ourselves to *l'impeccable naïveté* in lack of a satisfactory system; or of the history of fashion and dress; or of that good sort of artistic barbarism, which we find even in perfect art, and which is due to the need of " seeing things in the large and of considering them above all in their total effect." He too noticed the slight disposition of the French spirit for pure poetry, " because France has been created by providence for the search of the true rather than of the beautiful," and in modern times the French mind has assumed " a utopian, communistic, alchemistic character, which exclusively delights in social formulas." The only

French writers of his own time whom he liked were Chateaubriand, Balzac, Stendhal, Mérimée, De Vigny, Flaubert, and the friends whose ideals he shared, Gautier, Banville, Leconte de Lisle.

Such was Baudelaire in theory and judgment, and so he tried to be in the practice of art; and it would be to misunderstand him if, letting ourselves be deceived by certain appearances in his work, we were to attribute to him something of that frivolous spirit which plays with its own object and which is one of the forms of caprice and arbitrary choice, which he abhorred in art. His inspiration drawn from lubricious, sad and bestial sources, remains lofty and serious; bound to a sensual world which he cannot overcome, he succeeds in rendering it colossal, tragical, sublime, and here too he appears as a " rebel angel " : a heroic poet compressed and yet unable to abandon his heroics, which he creates upside down, by means of the lustful and the horrible. What there is in his creations that flashes out in irony, or rather in satire, is nothing but the consciousness of evil, inseparable from his mode of embracing the evil. Satan sometimes laughs, because, if he did not, he would be a maniac or a madman, and no one has yet insulted him with such a name. But Satan is also sometimes seized with nausea and disgust of himself, because he is not altogether able to suffocate the memory of the nobility that once was his. At other times, too, he feels himself opening his soul to that image " of holy youth, of simple air, of gentle brow, of eye as limpid and clear as running water," or he envies him " who rises above life with a vigorous stroke of the wing and frees himself from it, and understands without effort the language of flowers and of things mute."

Or he melts altogether in tenderness for the poor dead servant girl, " the great-hearted servant," beneath whose eyes he grew up, and of whom his mother was " jealous," and who now sleeps beneath the humble grass of the little field. His Satan, in fact, is not the traditional Satan, but a man-Satan.

In making these remarks, we do not lay any claim to having done justice to the poetry of Baudelaire. As a poet, he has been torn this way and that by the opposed ranks of those who vituperated him from the moment of his first appearance and found a leader in Brunetière and those who praise him with little discernment, and thus his work as sheer poetry has perhaps received little true critical appreciation. Indeed, the one party opposes him and will have none of him on account of moral or academical prejudice, and the other, for opposite reasons, is taken captive by certain aspects of his poetical content and also by certain of his formal attitudes, which are not among the most beautiful. The observations set forth above have had precisely the intention of placing the reader face to face with the sole problem of Baudelaire's poetry, namely, the *poetical*, and have thus gradually deduced its genesis and the quality of its inspiration, and by means of this deduction have demonstrated its purity and its incontestable right to be regarded as poetry.

A judgment of Baudelaire's poetry could not be obtained without investigating his intimate genius and its attendant dangers without any prejudice and studying it in its various and particular forms, in order to show in which of them the poetical ideal of the author was truly realized and in which others it has failed to reach or gone beyond the mark. I shall merely say that not infrequently Baudelaire's poetry seems to lack that purity of form towards which he nevertheless was striving with all his force. The reason of this failure is that he has within him other loves extraneous to the love of perfect form, which he does not always succeed in conquering. These were, on the one hand, intellectuality or reflection, which insinuate themselves here and there in his composition, owing to which he insisted so strongly upon having given a general design, a beginning, middle and end to his book; and on the other, the sensualism of images and lines, which greatly attracts him, inducing him to coin lines more vigorous and resonant than clear in their imagery, or to unite discordant images, or hyperboles which stand out from the original motive and seem to be sought for themselves. For this reason, the composition is somewhat confused in some of his lyrics, in others too symmetrical, at others glosses are attached or intercalated, at others again it allows us to discover lacunas and leaps beneath the severity of the form. These defects are noticeable even in his greatest creations. I believe that all this can be demonstrated in a clear and convincing manner, but since the preceding explicatives led through the psychology of the author to the problem proper to his art, so this further analysis should in its turn have no other object than to make the power of Baudelaire's art better felt there where it is really powerful. And such it is in reality, whether in certain pictures, such as *Don Juan aux Enfers*, *Les petites vieilles*, *Le vin des chiffonniers*, *Les sept vieillards*, *Les phares*, or in the lyrical effusions of the *Madrigal triste*, the *Examen de la nuit*, the *L' Amour du mensonge*, the *Hymne à la Beauté*, the *Servante au grand cœur*, or the sonnets of the *Parfum exotique*, the *Idéal*, the *Rêve d'un curieux*, and in many others. It is possible that the two last strophes of the *Vin des chiffonniers* containing considerations and conclusions may fail to please others as they fail to please me, for they are useless and empty beside the liveliness of the representations that precede them, and say all that is needed. But what a representation is that of the old rag-picker, rolling drunken along the streets as he dreams and expresses in gesture the heroic and generous dream of humanity; how completely it seems to express at the same time that the sublime is in man, but that he does not discover it save at the bottom of his folly! Yes, enthusiasm and sarcasm, perfectly fused: irrationality: poetry.

> " On voit un chiffonnier qui vient, hochant la tête,
> Buttant, et se cognant aux murs comme un poète,
> Et, sans prendre souci des mouchards, ses sujets,
> Epanche tout son cœur en glorieux projets.
>
> Il prête des serments, dicte des lois sublimes,
> Terrasse les méchants, relève les victimes,
> Et sous le firmament comme un dais suspendu
> S'enivre des splendeurs de sa propre vertu.
>
> .   .   .   .
>
> Suivis de compagnons, blanchis dans les batailles,
> Dont la moustache pend comme les vieux drapeaux;
> —Les bannières, les fleurs et les arcs triomphaux
>
> Se dressent devant eux, solennelle magie !
> Et dans l'étourdissante et lumineuse orgie
> Des clairons, du soleil, des cris et du tambour,
> Ils apportent la gloire au peuple ivre d'amour ! "

In like manner, the same defect will be observed in the other picture, *Les petites vieilles*, in the last part, where the poet meditates upon what has been already expressed and meditated, and re-expresses the already expressed, and also falls into the empty and rhetorical:

" (Ruines ! ma famille ! ô cerveaux congénères !
Je vous fais chaque soir un solennel adieu !
Où serez-vous demain, Èves octogénaires,
Sur qui pèse la griffe effroyable de Dieu ?) "

and even in the body of the composition, after having
depicted those little old women with touches of the
grotesque and pitiful that are truly stupendous, how
they have fallen from various heights of splendour
and now disclose within themselves the most intense
experiences of suffering :

" (Sous des jupons troués et sous de froids tissus

Ils rampent, flagellés par les bises iniques,
Frémissant au fracas roulant des omnibus,
Et serrant, sur leur flanc, ainsi que des reliques,
Un petit sac brodé de fleurs ou de rébus ;

Ils trottent, tout pareils à des marionnettes ;
Se traînent, comme font les animaux blessés,
Ou dansent, sans vouloir danser, pauvres sonnettes
Où se pend un Démon sans pitié ! Tout cassés

Qu'ils sont, ils ont des yeux perçants comme une vrille,
Luisants comme les trous où l'eau dort dans la nuit ;
Ils ont les yeux divins de la petite fille
Qui s'étonne et qui rit à tout ce qui reluit.

— Avez-vous observé que maints cercueils de vieilles
Sont presque aussi petits que celui d'un enfant ? . . .) "

he is not able to refrain from trampling upon and
deforming this last most delicate and most tender of
touches by interweaving around it astonishing eccen-
tricities. But how wonderfully he recovers himself,
particularly where the collective picture contracts
into an episode, and the poet selects and considers
one of many in the crowd of figures presented.

" Ah ! que j'en ai suivi de ces petites vieilles !
Une, entre autres, à l'heure où le soleil tombant
Ensanglante le ciel de blessures vermeilles,
Pensive, s'asseyait à l'écart sur un banc,

> Pour entendre un de ces concerts, riches de cuivre,
> Dont les soldats parfois inondent nos jardins,
> Et qui, dans ces soirs d'or où l'on se sent revivre,
> Versent quelque héroïsme au cœur des citadins.
>
> Celle-là, droite encor, fière et sentant la règle,
> Humait avidement ce chant vif et guerrier ;
> Son œil parfois s'ouvrait comme l'œil d'un vieil aigle ;
> Son front de marbre avait l'air fait pour de laurier ! "

Here, too, one can enjoy the perfect fusion of the sarcastic and the sublime, in which the latter predominates, as was always the case with Baudelaire, whatever subject he was treating, and as it is reflected in the tone and the very technique of his verse.

Examples could be multiplied; but readers will, like me, be pleased to make the last three beautiful strophes quoted resound in their ears and pass before their imaginations and they will seek Baudelaire's book for themselves in order to re-read it with understanding and discernment.

I don't understand Baudelaire
L'Homme Incompréhensible

XXI

FLAUBERT

For Flaubert, as for Balzac, we must set aside distracting considerations as to the " psychological and social novel " and " objective art," and regard the artist in himself, comparing him only with one or two really kindred souls, because observations of affinity aid in making clear certain aspects not easily discovered at a first glance. The depths of Flaubert's soul are no longer enveloped in mystery since the publication of his juvenile manuscripts in addition to his correspondence. (His was one of those sick souls of the romantic period which had lost religious faith but not the aspiration for the infinite, and furthermore had not been successful in adapting themselves to the conditions of modern life, but tortured themselves with dreams of the impossible and fell back exhausted after their vain effort. Such, in certain respects, was Baudelaire, one of the kindred souls of whom we have spoken, and perhaps the most akin to Flaubert.)

" Quelquefois "—is said in a juvenile fragment of Flaubert—" n'en pouvant plus, dévoré de passions sans bornes, plein de la lave ardente qui coulait de mon âme, aimant d'un amour furieux des choses sans nom, regrettant des rêves magnifiques, tenté par toutes les voluptés de la pensée, aspirant à moi toutes les poésies, toutes les harmonies, et écrasé sous le poids de mon cœur et de mon orgueil, je tombais anéanti dans un abîme de douleurs. . . . N'usant point de l'existence, l'existence m'usait. Mes rêves me fatiguaient plus que de grands travaux : une création entiére, immobile, irrévelée à elle-même, vivait sourdement sous ma vie." . . .

The *Récit de Marie* belongs to these years, that cry of desperation of one who has never attained the dreamed-of pleasure :

" Ni les pauvres, ni les riches, ni les beaux, ni les laids n'ont pu assouvir l'amour que je leur démandais à remplir. Tous, faibles, languissants comme dans l'ennui, avortons conçus par des paralytiques, que la vie énerve, que la femme tue, craignant de mourir dans des draps comme on meurt à la guerre, il n'en est pas un que je n'ai vu lassé dès la première heure ! — Il n'y a donc plus sur la terre de ces jeunesses divines d'autrefois ! Plus de Bacchus, plus d'Apollons ! Plus de ces héros qui marchaient couronnés de pampres et de lauriers ! " . . .

He remarks once in a letter to his woman friend Colet, alluding to his youth : " Tu m'as connu quand cette période venait de se clore et arrivé à l'âge d'homme, mais, autrefois, j'ai cru à la réalité de la poésie dans la vie, à la beauté plastique des passions " ; and in another letter he shows himself possessed of a clear consciousness of the relation that exists between this inextinguishable search for pleasure and mystical solutions, observing that if he had not given himself to art, " sans l'amour de la forme," he would perhaps have been " un grand mystique."

The way out that he found, then, was the same as Baudelaire found, since the illness from which he suffered was very similar : art, not art-confession, art-effusion, perverted, passionate art, but art which dominates passionate disturbance with purity of form. Hence his æsthetic theory of " impersonality," which, like many theories of artists, had many senses. Moral elements mingled in it with æsthetic elements such as the just conception of the universal character of art and anxious preoccupation with formal perfection. Among the moral elements may be mentioned a sort of manly shame at exhibiting his own miseries ("à quoi bon se mettre en scène ? un homme n'est pas plus qu'une puce . . ."), and with these and the æsthetic were also mingled psychological elements, such as repugnance for the interests of real life, family, country, humanity, for everything that is practical and as such limited and prosaic in the healthy sense of the term.

Through this freedom from every interest, which was impotence for every interest, he sometimes seemed to reach the romantic concept of art as irony, which he extended so as to embrace even history : " Quand donc consentira-t-on à faire de l'histoire comme on fait du roman, c'est à dire sans amour et sans haine pour les personnages en jeu, au point de vue d'une blague supérieure, exactement comme le bon Dieu voit les choses d'en haut ? " But the conception never left the domain of theory, prevented, whatever he may have thought about it, from realizing itself in his actual work by the dolorous depth of his spirit, for which, when every other interest was lacking, yet the torment of the immense desert of his desires, dreams which were in a way impossible both of being dreamed and satisfied, for that would have been to limit and determine them. Baudelaire contrived to make his lascivious, ghastly and evil dreams present to him, and to represent them in their complete reality. Flaubert, having tried something of the same sort, or prior to returning to something of the same sort, having attained to the maturity of his spirit, resolved to depict, on the contrary, his own dissatisfaction, his own bitterness, his own sarcasm. This resulted in his masterpiece, *Madame Bovary*.

As though to render yet more bitter the sarcasm, Flaubert places that infinity of desires and dreams in the head of a woman, indeed of a little woman, a little provincial, daughter of a half-peasant, educated, or rather " diseducated," in a feminine institution of the county town, a reader of little novels, quickly disillusioned of marriage, overcome with unspeakable emotion on the first and last occasion that she comes in contact with elegant society people, whose principal occupation is love. This personage lends herself to ridicule, which Flaubert not only does not conceal, but, on the contrary, marks with incisive strokes. Yet she does not on this account seem comical, for the author is too well aware from his own experience how irresistible is the seduction of the amorous folly which possesses her, and describes its genesis in so natural and persuasive a way that he compels to seriousness and sadness. Sadness is already present in the prolegomena of the story, in the history of young Charles Bovary, of his family, his studies, of his first marriage, also ridiculous, with his old wife, who is thirsting for love, tormentor and tormented, and quickly carried off by an illness.

" Quand tout fut fini au cimetière, Charles rentra chez lui. Il ne trouva personne en bas ; il monta au

premier dans la chambre, vit sa robe encore accrochée
au pied de l'alcôve; alors, s'appuyant contre le secré-
taire, il resta jusqu'au soir perdu dans une rêverie
douloureuse.   Elle l'avait aimé, après tout."

The tragedy which is to follow is, as it were, pre-
announced at the point where, the lengthy marriage
festivities terminated, Emma's father follows the
married couple some distance along the road that leads
to their house, and as he separates from them returns
to look at them again, feeling his heart melted.   There
is also nothing laughable in the spiritual restlessness
of Emma, beside the beatitude of the enamoured
and satisfied husband, and in his anticipations of the
unknown and the extraordinary. And when Emma,
after her first act of adultery, keeps repeating to herself
in the intoxication of her childish joy : " J'ai un amant !
J'ai un amant ! ", all her reading of trashy novels
rises to the surface of her mind, and the author raises
his tone with ironical solemnity, in order to describe
her emotion :

" — Alors elle se rappela les héroïnes des livres
qu'elle avait lus, et la légion lyrique de ces femmes
adultères se mit à chanter dans sa mémoire avec
des voix de sœurs qui la charmaient. . . . —"

Nor yet do we laugh or smile here, because the
game that Emma has begun is a game of perdition.
She has a feeling of this herself on receiving a letter
from her father, in which he recalls to her memory
pictures of her childhood :

" Quel bonheur dans ce temps-là ! quelle liberté !
quelle abondance d'illusions ! Il n'en restait plus,

maintenant! Elle en avait dépensé à toutes les
aventures de son âme, par toutes les conditions suc-
cessives, dans la virginité, dans le mariage et dans
l'amour;—les perdant ainsi le long de sa vie, comme
un voyageur qui laisse quelque chose de sa richesses
à toutes les auberges de la route."

But if comicality or mockery is excluded from this
representation, it would be impossible to find there
sympathy, tenderness or pity; on the contrary, we
are rather sensible of a certain ferocity in laying bare
every fold of Emma's soul, in refusing to her a single
flash of moral goodness and in degustating the torments that assail her, when she is hunted down and
overcome by the deceptions in which she has become
involved, like a rat caught in a trap. Yet it is impossible
to deny to her a sort of greatness, as of one obsessed
by a demoniac force, which at times becomes heroic.
Emma is not base. With what ardour and resolution
does she give all for all; how superior she feels herself
to every law, which is not that of her dream, her
longing, her passion; how, when she is hemmed in
on every side, does she contrive to shake herself
free of the chains, and then goes deliberately and without a word of complaint to meet her death! Listen
to her outburst of contempt for the lover from whom
she has asked assistance and who shuts himself up
in his egoism and leaves her to struggle alone in the
whirlpool which will suck her under:

". . . Mais, moi, je t'aurais donné tout, j'aurais
tout vendu, j'aurais travaillé de mes mains, j'aurais
mendié sur les routes, pour un sourire, pour un regard,
pour t'entendre dire merci!" . . .

She dies superbly, without repentance, without conversion, without any sort of redemption, obeying the necessity of that death which was bound to follow that life. She says to the poor husband weeping at her side after she has taken the poison :

" — Ne pleure pas ! — lui dit-elle. — Bientôt je ne te tourmenterai plus !
— Pourquoi ? Qui t'a forcée ?
Elle répliqua :
— Il le fallait, mon ami.
— N'étais-tu pas heureuse ? Est-ce ma faute ? J'ai fait tout ce que j'ai pu, pourtant !
— Oui . . . c'est vrai . . . tu es bon, toi !
Et elle lui passait la main dans les cheveux, lentement; mais la douceur de cette sensation surchargeait sur sa tristesse. . . ."

She dies without hatred, without self-pity, with a sense of relief :

" Elle en avait fini — songeait-elle — avec toutes les trahisons, les bassesses et les innombrables convoitises qui la tourmentaient. Elle ne haïssait personne maintenant; une confusion de crépuscule s'abattait sur sa pensée, et de tous les bruits de la terre Emme n'entendait plus que l'intermittente lamentation de ce pauvre cœur, douce et indistincte comme le dernier écho d'une symphonie qui s'éloigne."

Charles Bovary is treated in the same way, without the idealization of sympathy or pity, without the relief of a smile, and he too is finally presented as plunged in the desperation of his dreaming, after the death of Emma—of that Emma who, as the author says, continued to corrupt him from beyond the tomb :

" Il en conçut un désir permanent, furieux, qui enflammait son désespoir et qui n'avait pas de limites parce qu'il était maintenant irréalisable."

He continues, gradually consuming himself miserably, without even obtaining the peace of hebetude, in this incessant torture, in this breaking up of his life, alone with his ailing daughter. Meanwhile :

" en face de lui s'étalait florissante et hilare la famille du pharmacien, que tout au monde contribuait à satisfaire. Napoléon l'aidait au laboratoire, Athalie lui brodait un bonnet grec, Irma découpait des rondelles de papier pour couvrir les confitures, et Franklin récitait tout d'une haleine la table de Pythagore. Il était les plus heureux des pères, le plus fortuné des hommes."

Homais the chemist was the happiest of fathers and the most fortunate of men, impersonating all that Flaubert hates, together with his own self and his vain desires : life according to the laws, accommodating the laws to oneself and oneself to the laws, intent upon satisfying one's own mean needs of individual well-being and social respectability. Flaubert vibrates between these two hatreds of different colours, too refined to adopt the ethical ideals of Monsieur Homais, but not strong enough to cross the fiery furnace of his own morbid passions and attain to a new and loftier ethical ideal. For this reason, few books are so desolately pessimistic as *Madame Bovary*.

Notwithstanding this, Emma Bovary, towards whom her creator is inexorable, becomes dear to readers (I refer to every ingenuous and healthy reader, not to those who have founded the cult of Madame Bovary in France and make pilgrimages to the places where she loved, and have conceived a philosophy of " bovarism ") : dear to readers as the Francesca whom Dante does not redeem, does not make repentant and throws as a prey to the infernal whirlwind which never stays to blow, and those " sweet thoughts " and the " desire " which led her to the dolorous pass he nevertheless hears and is moved by them. Pity is born of things themselves, of the artistic representation itself, which, being true and complete, is also and altogether tremendous and pitiful.

With *Madame Bovary* Flaubert had reached the greatest or rather the only dominion over himself of which he was capable. In the second of his novels, *l'Éducation sentimentale*, holding still the reins of this dominion, he merely repeats the same solution or lack of solution, at which he had stopped : the painful renunciation of dreams without anything more worthy taking their place. But although the idea is the same in substance, the tone of the new story is altogether different. Its protagonist, who dreams of a great love, has not the quickly beating pulse of Emma Bovary, but is a pleasant young man rather disposed to allow circumstances to carry him along than to bend or break them up by running against them. In consequence of this, the narrative contains " nothing that happens," so that the protagonist, when youth is passed, recapitulating the first years of their life, recognizes that both " l'avaient manquée, celui qui avait rêvé l'amour, celui qui avait ambitionné le pouvoir ";—and he does this with an all involving feeling, which is no longer sarcasm, but melancholy; no longer bitterness, but lassitude. The author seems to have been well aware that cupidity, egoism and stupidity are not the

x

only things in the world, but that there are also goodness and self-sacrifice, and a going astray which is
not wickedness, filling his narrative with these things :
yet this does not change his pessimistic vision, but
rather renders it more bitter and pungent. The
Éducation sentimentale is almost a purgatory beside
the inferno of *Madame Bovary*, not because it is crowned
with hope, but on account of the more delicate tints
which the same suffering there assumes. This explains
how it is that some like the one and some the other
story better, the majority the former, the few the
latter. These preferences are due to individual
dispositions, as to which discussion is as unprofitable
as it is unprofitable to discuss the preference displayed
by some for midday by others for the evening.

In these two stories is therefore to be found perpetual contemplation of the self in two tonalities, seen
by the author as he would not wish to see it and yet
cannot help seeing it : that is to say, in the person
of a sensual little woman, excited by reading novels,
who wrecks her own life, and of a vacillating sentimen-
talist who wrecks his time.

But there exists another series of works by
Flaubert, which the critics find it difficult to connect
with these two, with which they are interwoven
in time by precedence or sequence, and in respect
of which they sometimes appear to be internally
connected and sometimes disconnected. These works
are held to be inferior to the two stories by the
verdict pronounced more or less consciously by all
readers, with the exception of a few ultra-refined
people who are consequently of doubtful taste. Let
us call these two stories middle-class stories in order
to distinguish them from those others, whose subject

matter is always the dream of the extraordinary, the impossible, the unknown. Owing to this they are certain to appear sometimes connected and sometimes disconnected with the former, the difference being that this subject-matter, instead of being considered in them with the eye of the doctor, and made an object of sarcastic and melancholy renunciation, is allowed freedom to move about at pleasure and thunders within like an impetuous torrent full of whirlpools. Flaubert felt ashamed to exhibit his morbid longings in the middle-class stories, but in the others not only does he throw shame aside, but approximates to that act of lewdness and lack of restraint which he theoretically condemned and despised.

In order that this should take place, it was necessary that he should set an ambush for himself and create an apparent justification of his action. The ambush and the justification were art as pure form, which is also a phrase of many meanings, sometimes, as we have said, affirming the universal character of art, which attains to the perfection of form in the perfection of content, but sometimes again is understood as in a way a separation of the form from the content. By thus rendering the form a beauty in itself, which has its own virtue " dans la précision des assemblages, la rareté des éléments, le poli de la surface et l'harmonie de l'ensemble," not only does it permit of the contents remaining material and following the desires of the individual, but makes of form itself a sort of lustfulness. Flaubert, who, by means of the limpidity of the art which shines in *Madame Bovary*, had saved himself from the " mysticism " to which his *immensa cupido* was leading him, falls back into a new mysticism by means of this æsthetic doctrine " Soyons religieux ! "

—he wrote in a letter describing his literary fever,— " Moi, tout ce qui m'arrive de fâcheux en grand ou en petit fait que je me resserre de plus en plus à mon éternel souci. Je m'y cramponne à deux mains et je ferme les deux yeux. À force d'appeler la grâce, elle vient ! . . . Je tourne à une espéce de mysticisme esthétique. . . ." Whoever has read in the biographies or directly in his correspondence the way in which Flaubert worked, especially in his later years, comes away with the impression, not so much of an artist creating beauty, as of an erotomaniac in delirium, or, if you like, of a mystic passing from flagellation to ecstasy, and from ecstasy to flagellation.

Salammbo is the blind spasm towards the barbaric-mysterious-luxurious-sanguinary, towards the voluptuously sacrilegious, and the true country of his heroine is certainly not Carthage, but that castle in Brittany where Chateaubriand conceived the first germ of his Atala and Velleda. Flaubert has seized with readiness the opportunity that offered itself of unchaining for a while, under the semblance of an archæological reconstruction perfectly elaborated in style, the demon that he bore within himself, and had only allowed to come out of himself at first shut up and chastised in the body of the faithless wife of a country doctor. In a monograph on Flaubert it has been stated that if he did not satisfy his readers in *Salammbo*, he certainly satisfied himself. That is quite true. But the statement that followed filled me with astonishment : that in so doing he acted " comme tous le grands artistes," who only write " pour se satisfaire." That is to say, what seemed to be and should have been a cause of blame is turned into a motive for praise, namely, the voluptuous satisfaction that Flaubert sought and found in his work. Sainte-Beuve, who was quick at detecting such things, uttered the word " sadism " in connection with that troubling volume. Flaubert protested amicably, alarmed at the effect which the word might have upon the public and at its possible use as a weapon against him by his enemies   But he himself when he composed the celebrated chapters of the serpent and the tent, making a confidant of his friend Feydeau, wrote to him : " Je prépare actuellement un coup, le *coup* du livre ! Il faut que cela soit à la fois cochon, chaste, mystique et réaliste " : so that we know what we are to think of the tentative defence with which he met Sainte-Beuve.   " La curiosité, l'amour qui m'a poussé vers des religions et des peuples disparus, a quelque chose de moral en soi et de sympathique, il me semble." The truth is that although Flaubert has given to *Salammbo* decent artistic form, he has not dominated his material, but covered it up, and although the style and the unified archæological researches certainly cool its sensuality here and there, yet they do not conquer and dominate it.   In this book he lacked the " internal form," in which art really consists, and which he had realized in the *Bovary* and the *Éducation*. In like manner, the *Tentations de Saint-Antoine*, notwithstanding the perfection of their prose versicles, are a chaos, oscillating between the coldness of the learned literary exercise on the one hand, and, on the other, a spasmodic nostalgia towards something inexpressible.   In the *Trois Contes* he continues the same inspiration as in the Carthaginian book, evoking the Judæa of Herodiade, and again in the gusto with which are described the slaughters of the hunter,

St. Julian the hospitable. The third story, on the contrary, rather resumes the manner of the *Éducation*, narrating the existence of a humble creature, all instinct, docile and affectionate, but her virtues are linked with a certain narrowness and weakness of mind which ends in a mild dotage.

That Flaubert tended always more and more as he grew older towards an art that has a dualism of imagination or, not to put too fine a point on it, of ill-humour to be poured out and of formalism in style, is confirmed by his last book at which he was working when he died, *Bouvard et Pécuchet*. Here, not satisfied with the extremely marked portrait that he had already given of Monsieur Homais, he set himself deliberately to utter his aversion for politics and for science in their every form, and in addition for anything else that rightly or wrongly had shocked his nerves, either because it really was something reprehensible or because he did not well understand and consequently did not like it. It is a work to which it is impossible to assign any critical value and of which the artistic value is slight. There are, however, a few felicitous touches, particularly at the beginning, when the two clerks meet and begin to enjoy their mutual discussions and recognize that they are kindred souls :

" Leurs paroles coulaient intarissablemente, les remarques succédant aux anecdotes, les aperçus philosophiques aux considérations individuelles. Ils dénigrèrent le corps des ponts et chaussées, la régie des tabacs, le commerce, les théâtres, notre marine et tout le genre humain, comme des gens qui ont subi de grands déboires : chacun en écoutant l'autre retrouvait des parties de lui-même oubliées." . . .

But on the whole (and the same applies to the comedy *Le Candidat*) the satire of this critical work has lost its form, in the same way as the lyrical element had lost it in the archæological books. These works are therefore to be considered as composed of the same elements as we find fused in the two principal books, save that in the former case they assume the asynthetical form, which they had prior to fusion in *Bovary* and the *Éducation*, or which they have assumed later, owing to the undermining influences of passion.

XXII

ZOLA AND DAUDET

THE " social novel," which, fortunately, did not altogether succeed with Balzac, owing to his passionate temperament and the poetical impetus which he allowed to carry him away, was far more successful in the case of Émile Zola, who possessed a far calmer and more balanced disposition and was not betrayed by poetic inspiration.

This judgment is at variance with that generally accepted, because there hardly exists a history of modern French literature which does not take exception to Zola's attempt at " experimental fiction," directed towards the establishment or verification of " scientific laws," especially that of " heredity." But since other artists are pardoned for attempting an art which shall be, for instance, philosophy or morality, and Balzac himself is pardoned for laying down " social laws " in a cycle of novels, it does not seem fair to make Zola's theoretic illusion weigh upon him too heavily. It will be said that those other artists went wrong rather as critics than as artists, and that they applied morality, philosophy or social laws to their works from without; but Zola also went wrong in this respect as critic rather than as artist, and he too was only able to apply his " law of heredity " and the genealogical table of the Rougon Macquart to his work from without; because it was

also not permitted to him to tear in pieces the nature
of things and to make experiments where experiments
were impossible. Perhaps the reason why people
are severe with Zola and indulgent with others is
that all are able to see at a glance the absurdity of
experiments instituted upon facts that have been
imagined, but all have not sufficient acumen to discern
the equal absurdity of poetry turned into morality
or philosophy. But it is not only equity that demands
an equal indulgence towards him as towards the
others; for we must almost be grateful to him for
having left to history a most significant document
as to the extent to which heads were turned in the
second half of the nineteenth century by the amorous
intoxication and dizziness inspired by physiology,
pathology, zoology and the other natural sciences.
He formulated all this with the utmost simplicity of
spirit in his experimental fiction.

Zola is further blamed for mental narrowness and
limitation and for his simple faith in those same sciences,
or in what was called Science, redemptress of society.
I do not wish to maintain that there was not some
trace of truth in all this, nor that Zola's intelligence
was fine or profound. But here too I fail to compre-
hend why Balzac should be thanked for his theory of
social salvation by means of religion and monarchy
(a reactionary theory, applicable, in any case, only
to particular countries and historical moments), and
Zola treated with severity for having admired in the
crude form of what is called Science a really and
perpetually redeeming force, namely, criticism or
thought.

Finally—and this is the capital accusation—it is
remarked that Zola has limited himself to representing

the base, the animal, the instinctive, and has not rendered the more spiritual and more highly evolved aspects of men, or when he has attempted to do so, has been most infelicitous, false and insipid.   And this too is perfectly true, for it does not take long to see that Zola lacked both the natural breadth of mind and the culture necessary for the comprehension of the highest forms of reality and life.   He did not even possess the sort of philosophy that artists are wont to acquire by means of the poetical and literary works of various times, of which he seems to have been both ignorant and incurious.   But what does it all amount to ?   *Non omnia possumus omnes*, and if Zola courageously carried out his typical representation of modern society in certain of its aspects, vulgar and material as they were, he fulfilled his share in the sort of collaboration which also regulates the life of science and of art.

And could it ever be contested that he rendered admirably peasants and populace, big and little citizens, politicians and men connected with banks and speculation, proletarians and industrials, courtesans and honest working women, soldiers and officials, priests and devotees ?   Could greater energy be displayed in describing environments, markets, drinking-booths, mines, shops, fields of battle, railways, pilgrimages and great cities like Paris at all hours of the day and in all their principal moments ? He accomplished an enormous labour, for which he conscientiously prepared himself, visiting the places and conversing with men of various classes, examining monographs, reports and journals.   For twenty years the world read his representations and descriptions and there learned, or believed that it learned, the

various aspects of modern life and the way the great
social machine worked.

Zola possessed uncommon aptitude for the formation of those representations, since he knew how to
note the characteristic signs by which types are recognized, so that the figures he draws, the gestures and
utterances fixed by him, lend themselves to being recalled
to memory and employed proverbially in daily conversation. He placed his personages in conditions
suitable to them with equal ability and determined
the actions and reactions that they must necessarily
accomplish. Let us mention, as one instance in a
thousand, that of the bad workman, exploiter of women
and dabbler in politics, Lantier, of the *Assommoir*,
and in the same novel the old workman *le père Bru*,
worn out with labour and struggles, resigned and
indifferent. At the banquet in Gervaise's shop
the guests count one another and find that they are
thirteen :

" Attendez ! — reprit Gervaise. — Ça va s'arranger.
Et, sortant sur le trottoir, elle appela le père Bru,
qui traversait justement la chaussée. Le vieil ouvrier,
entra, courbé, roidi, la face muette.
— Asseyez-vous là, mon brave homme, — dit la
blanchisseuse. — Vous voulez bien manger avec nous,
n'est-ce pas ?
Il hocha simplement la tête. Il voulait bien,
ça lui était égal."

The most varied figures pass across the stage of his
novels, from the horrible to the comic, expressed in
a style that is disdainful of refinements, softness and
vagueness, made all of things.

His manifold representations do not, however, follow one another without connection and intention, because we feel everywhere there the soul of Zola, which was not moved, as his adversaries and calumniators maintained, by a sort of satyriasis of the base and ignoble, or by the commercial advantage to be gained by speculating upon the evil tendencies and the unhealthy curiosity of readers, but was serious and thoughtful, feeling deeply the surrounding misery and corruption, observing and revealing them all, tearing aside every veil, like a doctor who wishes to ascertain the extent of an illness and measure its gravity, in order to prepare the remedy. And what a doctor he was, what hopes shone before him, what remedies he set to work to compose, were afterwards seen in his later volumes. He was something of a country practitioner, if you will, not troubled with the critical doubts of the truly scientific man nor weakened by the elegant scepticism of subtle intellects : he was too much of a doctor, that is to say, he relied too much on remedies derived from external things, yet he was worthy of respect for his steady faith in the profession that he exercised. His followers, like all followers, pushing the spirit of the master to the point of exaggeration, arrived finally at—what shall we say ?—at *Charlot s'amuse*.

Zola's fame, most brilliant between 1875 and 1895, is now obscured, and his books are far less read, especially by the cultured, so that nowadays it is almost a sign of bad taste to admit an inclination for him. And this decline was to be expected, because, both the matter of his representations and yet more the ideology that guided him have in great part become historical. The corruption of French politics

under the Second Empire no longer nearly affects us,
nor is Science, that is to say natural science, any longer
the idol of the day, nor does the law of heredity seem
to us to be so unconquerable and fatal as it seemed to
be to him, nor are social evils so dark, nor are all
those things that he held to be evils all of them evil,
nor are the remedies that he proposed so efficacious,
nor their results that he hoped for always quite
desirable.

The conversion of general opinion towards him
would further not have taken place in the way it did,
had he not been the logical executor that he was of
the idea of the " novel of manners," and if he
had sacrificed the clearness of his intention to instruct
and the realism of his sociological representation
and had allowed the balance to lean over in the
direction of poetry, as Balzac had done. But honest
Doctor Zola, the Docteur Tissot of modern society,
was only a poet to a very slight degree, and we must
not confound the moral solicitude, which we have
affirmed to vibrate continuously in his work, with the
feeling that prepares for the poet the material of
imaginative creation. His exaggeration of descriptions has been pointed to as a sign of his great poetical
faculty and his way of personifying the things that
strike him, making living monsters of them, has been
called " hallucinatory symbolism." But on close
inspection we perceive that this hallucination is cold,
that this hyperbolism and personification are not in
him the procedure of a poet, but of an orator and a
pedagogue, intent upon painting the devil as fierce
and as black as he can. One should re-read the
hypotyposis of the great jar from which flows the
brandy in the *Assommoir* :

" L'appareil . . . l'énorme cornue d'où tombait un filet limpide d'alcool : l'alambic, avec ses récipients de forme étrange, ses enroulements sans fin de tuyaux, gardait une mine sombre ; pas une fumée ne s'échappait : à peine entendait-on un souffle intérieur, un ronflement souterrain : c'était comme une besogne de nuit faite en plein jour, par un travailleur morne, puissant et muet. . . . L'alambic sourdement, sans une flamme, sans une gaieté dans les reflets éteints de ses cuivres, continuait, laissait couler sa sueur d'alcool, pareil à une source lente et entêtée, qui à la longue devait envahir la salle, se répandre sur les boulevards extérieurs, inonder le trou immense de Paris. Alors, Gervaise, prise d'un frisson, recula ; et elle tâchait de sourire en murmurant : C'est bête, ça me fait froid, cette machine . . . la boisson me fait froid." . . .

It is the exaggeration of a doctor who wishes to frighten his patients, so that they may not fall into the bad habits which cause their illnesses, and it is so little poetry that Zola repeats the same process with uniform exactitude on every occasion that he finds it useful to have recourse to it for his oratorical purpose. He always employs analogous processes in order to enlarge the characteristic traits of his chosen types, and although French Academicians accustomed to write histories of literature generally ill-treat Zola, yet they praise him for what they call " epic breadth ! " in his representation of crowds ; the real truth is that they do indeed admire the accustomed skill and accustomed style of Zola in those descriptive passages, but that they adopt there their usual procedure of exaggeration and epic quality (as for the rest is natural) has nothing

e matter. And does the close comparison
between Zola's and Victor Hugo's
haracters really furnish any greatly
of of Zola's poetical spirit ? It would
ecessary to prove that those representa-
are poetry, which would be difficult.

n repeated statement of critics lacking
to the incubus which would weigh
personages, dominated, invaded and
d by things external, such as streets, houses
e objects round them, which constantly vibrate
hin them and almost reduce men to material
things, is nothing but an invention. In reality this
linking of things with actions also serves to satisfy
a perpetual desire to teach and to edify.

" Gervaise, tout en répondant avec complaisance,
regardait par les vitres, entre les bocaux de fruits
à l'eau de vie, le mouvement de la rue. . . ."

It is not Gervaise who is unable to take her eyes off
the movement of the street and is obliged to follow
it, but the author is desirous of describing that going
and coming, conformably with his original design.
And so indeed he does describe it.

" Gervaise voulut l'attendre dans la rue. Cepen-
dant, elle ne put s'empêcher de s'enfoncer sous le
porche jusqu'à la loge du concierge, qui était à droite.
Et là, au seuil, elle leva de nouveau les yeux."

The description of the big house follows :

" Et Gervaise lentement promenait son regard,
l'abaissait du sixième étage au pavé, remontait, surprise de cette énormité, se sentant au milieu d'un

organe vivant, au cœur même d'une ville,
par la maison, comme si elle avait eu d
une personne géante."

Here too Gervaise is not gaze charmed and sur
but it is the author who wishes to make her
charmed and surprised :

" Puis dans la cour, pendant que Coupeau dema
dait le cordon d'une voix chantante, Gervaise s
retourna, regarda une dernière fois la maison. . . ."

And it is not Gervaise that turns round, but the author
who does not wish to leave his description uncom-
pleted.—Such a mechanical process is present in all
Zola's novels, and is most evident in the last ones,
when he had attained to that melancholy period, in
which the artist is exhausted and puts forth all his
defects, accomplishing a sort of self-dissolution or
self-analysis, which seems even to render the intervention of the critic with his scalpel superfluous.

Coming from the particular to the general, Gervaise,
the true protagonist of the *Assommoir*, after some
years of healthy and energetic life, abandons herself
to idleness and enjoyment, descending gradually to
extreme moral and physical abjection. This process
is described with great clearness and exactitude.
But Gervaise remains a prosaic creature in art, because
she does not realise, like truly poetical creatures, a
dialectic aspect of the soul that has created her, but
remains an example of vicious hereditary disposition,
which always leads irresistibly to alcoholism, and of
the conditions of popular life favourable to such a
vicious disposition. And such are all the characters,
all the actions and all the scenes of Zola's novels :

they are coloured designs in which the drawing is supplied by the scientific or pseudo-scientific conception, and the colour by the powerful imagination. Sometimes, the events and situations of Zola approach the sublime, as in *Germinal*, when the mine where the workmen are occupied is inundated owing to the damage done by an anarchist to the pumps, and the chief engineer, inexorable and very severe towards the men and hated by them, especially by Étienne, who is his enemy and knows him to be his enemy, sets to work to rescue the victims, going in before all the others, with complete contempt of the risk to his own life, like an honourable official, who, whatever his political opinion, sees nothing but his duty and military responsibility. He finally reaches the entombed miners and Étienne, who was among them, advances to meet the liberators :

" Ce fut seulement dans la galerie de Réquillart qu'il reconnut quelqu'un, l'ingénieur Negrel, debout devant lui ; et ces deux hommes qui se méprisaient, l'ouvrier révolté, le chef sceptique, se jetèrent au cou l'un de l'autre, sanglotèrent à gros sanglots, dans le bouleversement profond de toute l'humanité qui était en eux. C'était une tristesse immense, la misère des générations, l'excès de douleur où peut tomber la vie."

Does not a sob rise in your throat also when you reach this point ? But it is the theme itself that effects this, because Zola has not been able to attain to poetical sublimity. He merely states these things in the abstract or general terms of the critic and strives to swell them out with emphasis : *le bouleversement profond de toute l'humanité qui était en eux ; la misère*

Y

des générations, l'excès de la douleur où peut tomber la vie, une tristesse immense. . . . It was not necessary for him to amplify those few lines; he could even have made them shorter; but had he been a poet, he would have discovered one of those words which poets discover.

The critics and historians of the day regard Zola frowningly and treat him even with rudeness, yet he had a powerful character both as a man and a writer, even if he were destitute of poetical gifts, but towards Alphonse Daudet, on the contrary, they show themselves full of tenderness and obsequiousness. His books, says one of these historians "nous charment et nous émeuvent toujours avec une singulière intensité," with their tender creatures and even with their evil characters, who never have "un air grossier et répugnant," and sometimes even know how "se faire aimer par leurs victimes mêmes": they are written in a truly artistic style with "une admirable délicatesse et fraicheur d'impression."

Here too I do not propose to deny that Daudet is more pleasing, more sociable, more politely educated in the civic sense than Zola, yet let two things be granted to me at the same time: first, that he is in return far less serious and vigorous, more anecdotal and curious, and secondly, that his artistic method is just the same as Zola's and that the one is at bottom as little a poet as the other.

Daudet also is a moralist who observes and selects types, and his observation is often so material and extrinsic that some of his books are altogether chronicles or key novels, such as the *Rois en exil,* the *Nabab,* the *Immortel.* This is never the case with Zola. His observations either take the form of a moral thesis, as in the *Évangeliste*, in *Sapho*, in *Rose et Ninette*, or it is arranged to show the effect of a given character or of a given situation, as in almost all his novels. But the characters, as, for instance, the Nabab or Numa Roumestan, are static and the novel does not develop them, but serves only to exhibit them and set them in the light of certain special scenes, as though they were lay figures or caricatures. So mechanical is his manner of telling a story that no sooner has the machine started, the machine of that character, but we immediately foresee that it will be inflexible and assist impotently at the ill-treatment, the gradual breaking-up, the destruction of some poor creature, caught in that machinery. Some of his novels, such as *Jack*, have so affected me in this way that I have not been able to continue reading them, my heart not permitting me to be present at an execution. This impression of torment and suffering is not (as is commonly believed) the triumph of the artist, but his condemnation, because it means that he has not succeeded in reducing his rough material to food for contemplation and poetic enjoyment.

But all his stories are like this, even those one reads from cover to cover, even the best, such as *Sapho*, while one is already sensible of the first movement of the machine in the first chapter. Here a young provincial, come as a student to Paris, is going up the stairs with the woman he has met, and, since she is tired, he takes her up in his arms, and the higher he mounts the heavier he feels her : " Toute leur histoire " (says the author) " était dans cette montée de l'escalier dans la grise tristesse du matin."

Certainly Daudet's style is limpid and facile, but it is very flowing, often poor, and abounds in fixed formulas and descriptive and narrative expedients. Certainly, the characters described by Daudet have become popular, especially the comic ones or those that contain something of the comical, such as Tartarin and Numa Roumestan, and they lend themselves also to use in current language as designating, for instance, the imaginative Frenchman of the South or the Southerner of copious and fiery eloquence, whose imagination and ease of expression submerge and abolish all truth and all duty, so that he cannot be called either good or bad, to such an extent have the spoken word and the imagination liquefied in him all serious human character. But Zola too has such characters, less pleasing, but not less well described, and they are, as we said, more complex and vigorous. Certainly Daudet was a good man and pitied others' misfortunes, nor was he false to his moral intention, and he can be believed when he writes in his dedication of *Sapho :* " Pour mes fils, quand ils auront vingt ans." But in other fields of ethical consideration, in the social and political rather than in the moral and personal, such was also Zola, as we have seen.

" Que lui a-t-il manqué " — asks the same historian whose words in praise of Daudet we have quoted above— " à cet artiste si français et si humain, pour compter parmi les tout-à-fait grands créateurs, et pour avoir dans notre littérature la place d'un Dickens dans la littérature anglaise ? Est-ce le travail acharné ? est-ce la suprême pointe du génie ? Ou bien plutôt ne serait-ce pas, qu'ayant tant de cœur et de douloureuse pitié, en ne représentant jamais que de tendres victimes de la vie, il n'a pourtant pas su évoquer pour elles et pour nous cette étoile au ciel que Dickens ne manque jamais à faire briller au-dessus de souffrances imméritées et des morts infortunées ? "

For our part, we must not wander between these various hypotheses, some of which are rather strange. Daudet also possessed, in his own nature, that absence of obstacles little to be envied in an artist, towards the carrying out logically and coherently of the " social novel," or the " psychological novel," or the " moral novel."

XXIII

IBSEN

ALL the heroes and heroines of Ibsen are tense with expectation, devoured with longing for the extraordinary, the intense, the sublime, the unattainable; they are disdainful of idyllic felicity in any form or degree, as of modest virtue resigned to the limits of its own imperfection.

Hedda Gabler despises and scorns her laborious, good-natured and mediocre husband, and those holy women, his old aunts; she cannot endure to hear even a whisper of domestic life, of sons or of any sort of duties; she shrinks from infidelity and adultery, as of things common and vulgar; yet she feels herself immersed in the vulgar and commonplace, and worries herself to death, because, although she has no scruple as to the means to be adopted, she seeks the world vainly for "something free and courageous, something illumined with a ray of absolute beauty."

Ellida's soul, fluctuating as the sea, is always turned towards it, yearning for her country of origin and for the man from the sea, an unknown, possibly a criminal, who one day approached her, spoke with her and bound himself to her, by throwing their betrothal rings into the sea.

Nora has patiently awaited for eight years the "miraculous," which alone would have endowed the monotonous course of ordinary events, such as matrimony, sons, social relations, with sense and savour. To cure her husband's illness, she has secretly committed a small forgery, and her heart beats at the thought that if the forgery be discovered her husband will immediately rush forward to protect her by taking the crime upon himself and will gladly sacrifice for her who has sinned for love of him all that he possesses, well-being, social position, reputation, honour.

Rebecca West has introduced herself into the old-fashioned house of Rosmer, austerely religious and conservative, with the desire of conquering by means of her personal charm and art of fascination, the last scion of the family, and of making him the instrument of her own ambition and fortune in the struggle in which she is engaged against the old ideas and in favour of liberty and progress.

Rita has espoused Allmers in order to possess him, all of him. She is jealous of his sister, of the studies which occupy his time, jealous even of their son, with so furious and rapacious a degree of passion as even sometimes to experience fear of herself.

And the men ? Solness wishes to be himself alone the constructor of churches, houses, towers, suppressing others or placing them beneath him as aids or workmen. He is suspicious of the young men who may come forward to steal the position from him. He attempts the " impossible," to climb himself, conquering himself, for he suffers from giddiness, to the top of the very lofty tower which he has constructed, in order there to hold up the inaugural crown.

Rubek has renounced living in order to create art and he is now killing himself with drunkenness, which has allowed him to escape from the consciousness of failure.

Borkmann has dreamed of getting all the sources of power into his own hands by means of his banking operations, and under his yoke all the treasures of the soil, the mountains, the woods, the seas, in order to render thousands and thousands of men happy. Crushed in his course towards dominion, fallen within reach of penal law, imprisoned, rejected, in solitude, he remains firm in his faith and believes every day that people will come to pray and supplicate him to place himself again at their head.

Gregory Werle has a dream of a different kind : to destroy the lies, the hypocrisies, the illusions, upon which men basely rest their heads as though they were a soft cushion, and to build upon truth, truth courageously unveiled and exhibited, upon a new life of pardon, of reciprocal aid and redemption.

Although these examples are taken from the last period, that is to say, the maturity of Ibsen, it must not be thought that the same inspiration does not reign in the earlier plays, because although there is a great diversity of form between them, there is no substantial diversity. Ibsen had no true and definite development either intellectual or sentimental, nor any profound changes and conversions beyond his artistic development. The historian of Ibsen's spirit has been obliged to remain at the same place, because he has always found the same soul facing him, in Ibsen's youth, maturity and old age, always the same changeless longing for the extraordinary and the sublime. If we go back to Peer Gynt, we find him wandering about in search of " the Gyntian self," that is to say, " the crowd of desires, cupidities, passions, the ocean of fancies, claims and rights," everything, in fact, which " makes his breast swell and life be lived in him." Coming to Brant, obsessed with the idea of duty, of duty for duty's sake, of that ultra-Kantian duty so cruel and pitiless to the man himself who puts it in practice, we find him with the motto " all or nothing " separating Agnes from the side of the man who loved her by means of his powerful energy of character, informing her of his hard faith, on account of which faith he allows her son to die and herself to die, tramples upon all his own personal affections, but never upon his superior self, his inexorable will, which does not see any choice outside all or nothing.

If we leave Brant and go further back, to the historical drama *The Claimants of the Crown*, we find that if King Haco, the central figure, is a *pius Æneas*, re-thought in the terms of Germanic philosophy of history (which had reached Ibsen directly or indirectly), characters of passionate intensity, of mad longing, are to be found among those who surround him, the Duke Skule, and especially the terrible figure of Bishop Nicolas. Observe also, in the *Comedy of Love*, the poet Falke, with his ideal of love which overturns every barrier and *omnia vincit*, with his declaration of war against all lying, all hypocrisy, and in the *Northern Expedition*, a play of an altogether different sort, the pathos of nearly all the characters, but above all that of Hjordis, who is Hedda Gabler in a barbaric form and in barbaric society, that is to say, in her true form and in the society that is proper to her.

This impetus towards the sublime and extraordinary is never realized or satisfied, save as self-destruction, that is, as tragedy. The obstacle to such realization

henceforth no longer able to love, either impurely, because she has been purified, nor purely, because she has sinned in the past. Thus she has shut herself off from the two possible felicities : the troublous, bitter felicity of sense, the sweet felicity of the heart.

Some of these and of the other characters of Ibsen save themselves by renouncing their wild ambitions, such as Ellida, the lady of the sea, who by free choice refuses to follow the mysterious man who has returned to take her with him, and thus she acquires peace and re-enters the circle of ordinary life. The Allmers couple, parents of the little drowned Eyolf, feel themselves guilty and propose to adopt a new mode of life, consecrated to the welfare of the derelict. Nora abandons husband and sons and retires to meditate in solitude upon herself and upon reality, which she had not hitherto understood nor sought to understand. The consul Bernick (in the *Pillars of Society*) publicly confesses his guilt and attains to the sublime of expiation in condemning himself to civil death. Gregory Werle, the disastrous moralist, and Mrs. Alving, who has endured her dissolute husband and contrived to create a decent reputation for him out of respect for the law and for human decency, remain desolate : the one with a family reduced in numbers beneath his eyes and the corpse of a poor girl, who had taken her own life owing to her inability to resist the lack of affection for him she believed to be her father; and the other with the son beside her who has inherited the paternal diseases, and has made her swear to give him poison, in order that he may not survive the imbecility of which he feels the approach. These desolations are forerunners of death, but the majority of Ibsen's personages do not waste time in waiting for death, but go resolutely to meet it face to face. Brant climbs the mountain once again, and while he is there asking light of God for the work that he has attempted, he is overwhelmed by an avalanche. Peer Gynt, come to the end of his adventures and peregrinations, and having failed to realize the Gyntian ego, cannot do otherwise than bow his head upon Solveigh's bosom—Solveigh the eternal feminine, a sort of Margaret, who has always awaited him—and breathe his last. Solness mounts the tower to place the garland, and no sooner has he done so than he is seized with dizziness, falls down and is smashed in pieces on the ground. Hedda Gabler, who has instigated Lowborg to commit suicide, in order to destroy him who alone has given her a feeling of the extraordinary up to that day and expects to obtain from him the emotion of the " beautiful death," becomes aware that her secret machinations have been observed by another man, who is watching her, desires to satisfy his lust upon her and now has her at his mercy—and kills herself; Borkmann and Rubek allow themselves to be gently guided towards death by the women whom they have abandoned—and, hand in hand, Rebecca West and Rosmer, the woman who has purified herself by loving and no longer has the right to love, the man who now loves her, but cannot do otherwise than share death with her and dispose her to meet death, go to throw themselves into the torrent. Thus the expectation of the sublime is always deluded in both its forms, of the satanical sublime and the divine sublime, of sensual and ethical passion : in the former because it goes against the moral consciousness, in the latter because that consciousness sins or has sinned against itself.

Here indeed is poetry of despair if ever there were such, not merely pessimism of pleasure that grows arid and of life that passes, but of a pessimism that is the conscious impossibility for man ever to achieve the end towards which his own nature urges him to attain or renders him desirous of attaining. And as already remarked, Ibsen remains fixed in that attitude of mind. Incidents and personages change, but his life closes with the nostalgia and the delusion with which it had begun. His very moral appearance never comes near or familiar to us as do those of other great poets, because he never descends to our level, loving the simple things that we love, loving imperfectly as we love, suffering and enjoying as we do. Ibsen sees everything through a glass of a peculiar colour, never through the glasses, colourless or of various colours, through which the rest of us that are humanity look. But if his psychological attitude be constant, his art, as we have said, develops and grows and perfects itself.

In his first period, Ibsen adopted forms of which models existed, the historical drama of the romantics, the philosophical and humoristic and ironical drama of the same school, the forms of Schiller, of Goethe and of Byron, and of their Scandinavian imitators, who had formed themselves in the German literary environment. *Peer Gynt* is influenced by the second part of *Faust* and becomes engaged in the difficulties and illegitimate tractations of that style; *Brant* is a perpetual flood of weighty eloquence, but is also verbose and redundant; the technique of other plays, such as the *Comedy of Love* and the *League of Youth*, does not differ widely from that of the French thesis comedy. That is not saying we do not discover everywhere the lion's claw, especially in the *Claimants*, but also in *Peer Gynt*, where the scenes of the trolls and of the mother's death are rightly admired, and the oration pronounced by the priest at the graveside of the man " who had only four fingers on one hand " is most beautiful. In *Brant* too there is a finely austere stimulus in the figure and speech of the hero and the play becomes instinct with pathos in that of his companion, Agnes, who has lost her son and does not dare accuse the man who has allowed him to die in order to keep faithful to duty assigned. In the *League of Youth* are profound moments and one of the secondary personages, Selma, clearly prefigures the Nora of the *Doll's House*.

A close study of Ibsen reveals a number of such hints and references, whence the unity of his inspiration becomes enhanced. But it is certain that he only created his own properly original style after 1875, particularly with the *Doll's House* and *Ghosts*. This style grew yet more perfect, and becomes quite pure after 1883, with the *Wild Duck* and with *Rosmersholm*, which is, in my opinion, the masterpiece. It might be said that he then became altogether despairing and without belief, but that is not so, because such he had always been; but there can be no doubt that he then obtains a greater hold upon his desperation and lack of belief, which is not so much a moral change as a deepening of his art, that is to say, a clearer view of his own feelings. He did not see clear enough and did not sufficiently realize this in *Peer Gynt*, where the representation is developed in the capricious, satirical and comic style of the second

Faust ; nor in *Brant,* where the protagonist is on the contrary conceived seriously and positively as a hero and of which the action, even before it reaches the catastrophe, unconsciously posits the criticism of the idea and character of the hero, discovering the weak point in his armour. Ibsen rarely fell into this error again, perhaps only in the character of Doctor Stockmann, the " enemy of the people," where, as in Brant, we remain in some doubt as to whether the poet wishes to portray a hero or a fanatic, a profound or an obtuse mind, a character who tends towards the sublime or towards the grotesque. The true Ibsen is the Ibsen who is able to represent everything together, fused, the longing for the extraordinary, the sin which gnaws it, and the renouncement, desolation or death which awaits it, and to do this in a mode proper to himself.

This form is generated by a kind of monologue, a passionate monologue, which does not conclude, and to the extent to which it does not conclude and is divided and contrasted in itself, is dramatic. Ibsen never wrote anything but plays, with the exception of a few lyrics, to such an extent was dramatization spontaneous, natural and necessary to him. And his dramatic creations are moments and notes of his own spirit, that is to say, of a spirit such as we have described, all absorbed in anxious longing for the felicity to be attained by attaining to the sublime and the extraordinary, and at the same time most sensible and intransigent in the consciousness of responsibility and of guilt. For this reason it is not to be expected of his dramas that they conquer every obstacle and achieve their ideal of life and mould around them a life in conformity with themselves, or dispose them-

selves in harmonious perspective, bathed in a steady
light, in relief against their background with the
definiteness and completeness of characters turned
towards action, and who only reveal themselves by
acting, or what of themselves they wish to reveal or
are able to reveal. His creations are souls who suffer
until they confess themselves, and even before they
do confess themselves, penetrate and divine and
understand one another, discovering one another as
by the light of the divine, of which they do not yet
feel worthy, but which already shines upon them,
like souls in Purgatory. Hence their dialogue, as
though they were attempting to understand themselves by this means, and the resolute and frequent
tearing, all of a sudden, of the veil which still interposes itself between them.   " Let us talk frankly, let
us give up lying," says Ellida to her husband.
Allmers comes to explain to his wife how he has
decided to abandon his scientific work in order to
consecrate himself altogether to their little deformed
son. And Rita, who has read him better than he
knew or wished, replies : " Not out of love for
the boy ! " " For what reason, then, tell me ? "
" Because you have been consuming yourself with
doubts about yourself, because you began to doubt
about your call to a great task." And the other,
without trying to defend himself, as though he too
had already been aware of it, replies : " So you had
noticed that ? " Both of them have inveighed against
the people that were on the shore of the lake, because
they did not risk their lives in order to save their
little Eyolf when he was drowning; but when calm
has returned to their spirits and judgment of themselves and of others acquires strength, and nevertheless

z

under the mildness and the smile of Goethe grown wise.

And, on the other hand, how can what is constantly stormy and disordered be called problems, mental problems? It is certainly true that here and there Ibsen tends to pose problems to himself; but they are precisely the sort of problems which, as the history of Ethics teaches us, have never been solved, and which Logic shows to be insoluble : problems of moral casuistry. Who is right in the *Doll's House*? The husband? But he is an egoist. The wife? But she lacks moral sense. Who is wrong? The husband? But he respects honour and the law. The wife? But she has tried to save her husband from illness and death. Who is right in *John Gabriel Borkmann*? Borkmann, wko, in order to carry out the mission which he believes has been assigned to him, has rejected the woman he loved? But he has slain a soul. The woman? But she could not rightly claim that for the sake of her happiness thousands and thousands of men should not obtain happiness, and that the social level should not be raised. Who is in the wrong? Borkmann? But he has sacrificed above all himself, his heart, because he too loved. The woman? But she could not sacrifice the immediate urgent desire for happiness and for spiritual salvation for herself and the man she loved on account of the remote and problematic happiness of unborn nameless crowds.

It is not astonishing that these insoluble problems made the plays popular, and that they particularly interested women, whose brains are not well endowed with critical capacity, and especially the least critical among them, the feminists, and they soon succeeded in making them suspicious and hateful with their psychological and moralizing or amoralizing discussions about them, to such an extent that certain Scandinavian families even went so far as to add to their cards of invitation to evening parties the request : " Please do not discuss the *Doll's House* "—the anecdote is well known.

Ibsen himself lightly touched upon certain problems in casuistry, but he never went very deeply into them, restrained as he was by his artistic instinct. To me it seems perfectly right that when an English critic called upon him and mentioned that in his works the conception must have preceded the dramatization, Ibsen should have met this with a negation, and equally right that what the critic quotes as " from his declarations resulted at least this, that in the history of his works there was a phase in which they might have become a critical treatise in the same way as a drama." Certainly : but they never did become critical treatises, and Ibsen has never written a page of prose doctrine, and on the contrary they always did become dramas, because dramas they were from the beginning, in their primordial cell, and the soul of the poet was profoundly and solely dramatic.

For this reason his creations are not cold-blooded animals, they are not " fish " (as one of them remarks), such as always are abstract personifications, but they live and suffer and break into savage cries, into vows trembling with emotion, into solemn utterances. Hedda Gabler destroys the manuscript of the man whom she herself does not know whether she loves or detests, but by whom alone she is interested and attracted. He has written the work under the amorous influence and support of another woman. As Hedda throws it into the fire, she exclaims, with a ferocious laugh : " Now, I am burning your son, Thea, O thou beauty of the curling locks ! the child you have had with Eybert Lowborg ! " . . . Irene meets the sculptor Rubek after many years. She had sat to him for her portrait, which is his masterpiece. As they talk of that time, she reproaches him sadly and gently for his manner of receiving the greatest gift of all which she had really made him : " I gave you my soul, my soul proud of life and youth; . . . and I remained with a void in my breast, without soul. After I had given you that gift, Arnold, I died." Ella Rentheim, when she hears Borkmann, grown old and almost mad, tell how he resolved to abandon her, though he loved her, both judges and condemns him, placing herself above him and above herself, like an independent power, but she is really, on the contrary, the most passionate incarnation of femininity when she does this, of a femininity which rises to being a religion to itself : " You have put out the flame of love in me, do you understand ? The Bible talks of a mysterious sin for which there is no pardon. Till to-day, those words were obscure to me. Now I understand. That capital crime, the crime without pardon, is the putting out of the flame of love in a human being."

The poet gives them faces, gestures, garments, realizing them completely, because for him they belong to reality and not to the categories of thought. Borkmann with his grave appearance and his delicate profile, his penetrating eyes, his gray beard and curling hair, dressed in a black suit out of fashion, lonely, separated from his relations, confined to the upper story of the house, walks up and down all day,

chewing the cud of the past and awaiting the future,
to which he is attracted more than ever tenaciously.
Hedda Gabler has " an aristocratic port and appearance, she is pale and looks calm and cold, her hair is
light brown in colour." She appears to us at home
" in an elegant morning dress, cut rather loosely."
Beside her and contrasting with her is her husband,
George Tessmann, with his " jovial aspect, slightly
inclined to fatness, fair hair and beard, wearing
spectacles and not too well dressed." We saw them
all like this, and nevertheless Ibsen's dramas which
have so plastic a poetical form, are developed with a
simplicity which at times is almost simplicism.
Coming from an artist of such ability, this is not an
indication of poverty or of impotence, but of an
intentional neglect of externals. There is no poverty
or impotence in the symbols that he introduces from
time to time : they perform the duty of lyrical images
and comparisons : the tower from which Solness falls,
Alving's asylum that burns, or the wild duck that
waddles about and grows fat on the floor of Ekdal's
house, forgetful of sky and sea. The truth is that
the style and ingenuous procedure of the primitives
suit well this art of chaste and courageous confession,
this art that is almost religious. Ibsen has recourse
to it, sure of his own strength, and showing proof of
his strength by means of this deliberate simplicity.

XXIV

MAUPASSANT

I<small>F</small> any one of modern poets especially deserve the title of " ingenuous " poet, that one seems to me to be the most Parisian, liberal, malicious, jesting, sarcastic story writer, Guy de Maupassant.

He is ingenuous and innocent in his own way, as one without any suspicion of what is called human spirituality or rationality, faith in the true, in purity of the will, in the austerity of duty, the religious conception of life, of the moral struggles and intellectual conflicts, by means of which those ideals develop and maintain themselves. He is all sense— he suffers and enjoys,—suffering far more than he enjoys,—only as sense.

The feeling of love is tender and often refined in the author of *Fort comme la mort* and *Notre Cœur* ; it is also natural, that is to say, not perverted nor perverse, but tenderness and refinement and naturalness do not alter its essentially sensual character. Love is a very sweet thing, the sweetest that life yields, the flower of youth, and indeed youth itself in its illusion perpetually reborn ; but which is altogether consumed in this sweetness, producing nothing and rising to no heights. He who loves, defends the centre of his own being in his love, his own reason for living, which is pleasure, that pleasure which has no equal. So overwhelming is the power of pleasure, of love-pleasure, as to impose itself upon the soul with absolute necessity and to take the place of every ideal interest and of every other source of comfort and of joy, and to withdraw itself from the action of moral law or to pass beyond it.

A woman, a mother, who has had a lover and feels herself condemned by her legitimate son, bursts out passionately into a confession addressed to the other, the child of love : " Dis-toi bien que si j'ai été la maîtresse de ton père, j'ai été encore plus sa femme, sa vraie femme, que je n'ai pas honte au fond du cœur, que je ne regrette rien, que je l'aime encore tout mort qu'il est, que je l'aimerai toujours, que je n'ai aimé que lui, qu'il a été toute ma vie, toute ma joie, tout mon espoir, toute ma consolation, tout, tout, tout pour moi, pendant si longtemps ! Écoute, mon petit : devant Dieu qui m'entend, je n'aurais jamais eu de bon dans l'existence, si je ne l'avais pas rencontré, jamais rien, pas une tendresse, pas une douceur, pas une de ces heures qui nous font regretter de vieillir, rien ! Je lui dois tout ! " This mode of feeling has its own inflexible logic, its pride in itself, expressed in a resolute and defiant manner, which commands, one knows not exactly what form of respect, like every undivided rectilinear force.

That this love, all sense and passion, although it fill the mind with an unspeakable and incomparable voluptuousness, is nothing but a deception of nature, a spring-time intoxication, " the exchange of two imaginations and the contact of two skins," Maupassant is well aware. Perhaps, like Baudelaire, he also has a glimpse of the taste of evil in its depths; but this does not amount to much, because the criticism of love does not take away its reality, the real existence of the illusion. He is also aware that love, as it is faithless, so it is fragile and destroys itself, ending in abandonment, betrayal, weariness, reciprocal tedium. He does not, however, wish it to be otherwise, because, if that pleasure is a sweet fever, the fever cannot be expected to endure for ever, and if love is not moral purity, the betrayal discovered and suffered, although it torture the heart, yet does not move it to ethical indignation and does not elevate it spiritually by suffering. It is a torture similar to the separation by death of beloved beings, which Maupassant feels with the abandonment to anguish of a most sensitive temperament, tells in words of heartfelt grief and portrays in powerful images, such as that of the man who returns to his empty house and stops before the mirror which had so often reflected the dead woman's face and ought somehow to have preserved her image. He stands gazing into it, the eyes fixed upon the flat surface of the glass, empty and profound, the glass that had entirely possessed her, possessed her as he had possessed her, as his loving look had possessed her. Then, again, the portrait of the youth who cannot persuade himself that the being whom he adored, the unique being, with those bright eyes which had smiled with tenderness, is no more, " is dead," will never again exist in any place, that her voice will never sound again among other human voices, that no one will again pronounce a single word in the way that mouth pronounced it. But although weariness, betrayal, loss of the beloved one are the end of loves, they are not the end of love, which is born perpetually anew, ever youthful, ever fascinating.

The true malediction lies elsewhere, in the ending for the individual of the capacity itself of loving, the end of youth, the falling into habits, the drying up, the coming on of old age, of death which waits inexorably and announces his advent with various signs : the loss of interest in everything, the decline of vital power, of nature, which used to seem to speak, but now is silent and lags behind cold and indifferent.

At thirty, the whole book has been read : there is nothing else to be hoped, nothing else can possibly give pleasure; there is merely the habitual round, so distasteful through its likeness to a machine at work, that to see oneself condemned to it without a chance of escape, one experiences a feeling of despair verging on madness or leading to suicide. Such men as these, already tired of life, appear frequently in his stories : sad if they have enjoyed it, sad too if they have not. " Autrefois, j'étais joyeux " — says one of them : — " tout me charmait : les femmes qui passent, l'aspect des rues, les lieux que j'habite; et je m'inté-ressais même à la forme de mes vêtements. Mais la répétition des mêmes visions a fini par me remplir le cœur de lassitude et d'ennui, comme il arriverait pour un spectateur entrant chaque jour au même théâtre." And he thinks of the time when he loved : " Alors les doux romans de ma vie, dont les héroïnes encore vivantes ont aujourd'hui des cheveux tout blancs, m'ont plongé dans l'amère mélancolie des choses à jamais finies. Oh ! les fronts jeunes où frisent des cheveux dorés, la caresse des mains, le regard qui parle, les cœurs qui battent, le sourire qui promet les lèvres, ces lèvres qui promettent l'étreinte. . . . Et le premier baiser . . . ce baiser sans fin qui fait fermer les yeux, qui anéantit toute pensée dans l'incommensurable bonheur de la possession pro-chaine." . . . He looks over old letters, remounts the course of the years in the contrary sense, meets again forgotten faces, lives again certain little happenings in the home of his boyhood, until he comes upon a letter written by him aged seven to his mother and dictated by the teacher. Then he feels that he can stand it no longer, and kills himself. " C'était fini. J'arrivais à la source et brusquement je me retournai pour envisager le reste de mes jours. Je vis la vieillesse hideuse et solitaire, et les infirmités prochaines, et tout fini, fini, fini!   Et personne autour de moi."

The desert, the solitude display themselves with terrifying effect, at a certain point of the journey, before the eyes of the man who has hitherto been going forward enveloped in the rosy haze of pleasures and of love; but that solitude, which only then he sees clearly, has always accompanied him. He has always been alone, alone in the company of his friends, alone in that of his mistresses, alone when he rested his head on the same pillow as another head, always face to face with his *I*, which has become hateful to him, an infernal companion always hitting against the same insurmountable barrier. He cannot free himself from this spiritual solitude, because his egoism shuts itself up in itself and strikes against other egoisms, but does not penetrate or resolve them in itself. Nor can he issue forth from the other solitude, that of mental limitations, because man's thought is " motionless," and poetry itself and all the arts perpetually repeat the same image of the same world. It may be said of Maupassant that his view of reality is the precise opposite of the religious view, which is consciousness of union with all other beings and with God, of communion with the Whole. God is

absent from his world of pleasure and of pain of
pleasure : true, a form of the extraordinary and por-
tentous does sometimes appear there, but it is altogether a natural phenomenon, consisting of strange
fears and wanderings of mind, of hallucinations, of
incubi, of the portentousness of madness, which
always threatens.

But the contracted heart of Maupassant does frequently become distended and softened in a sort of
dolorous calm or calm dolorousness, a feeling of
pity, of a pity that is without justice or redemption, because justice and redemption are linked with
the moral consciousness, and his pity is due, on the
contrary, to sympathy, to vibration in tune with the
vibration of others, and is also sensuality, but of
the tenderest quality, which weeps over others as
over itself. It is a lament inspired by the infinitude
of human misery, as in the story *Le Port*, where a
sailor, disembarking at a seaside town, goes off at
the head of his companions to enjoy himself in a
brothel and finds his own sister in the woman whom
he is clasping in his arms and who unconsciously
tells him of the death of his parents and the ruin of
the family. Note also the indulgence of the young
wives who have been deceived and injured, but are
overcome with unrestrainable emotion upon witness-
ing the desperate anguish of their husbands at the
death of those they had loved, loved wrongly, but
loved with a love that is suffering. Or beings who
crush the very soul in one, such as the woman and
mother whose life is told in *Une vie*, and the artist of
Fort comme la mort, who is attacked and enslaved as
he is growing old with passion for his mistress's
daughter, in whom the mother reappears as once she

was, and his love of her, as once she was. Then,
again, his old maids, like Miss Harriett, ridiculous in
appearance as in deeds, a religious propagandist, who
shuts up and represses in herself an infinite longing
for affection, and who, when love unexpectedly flashes
out in her old mortified heart and takes her by surprise, realizes that she is sailing to shipwreck in the
impossible and throws herself into a well. His
" Queen Hortense " too, raving of children on her
death-bed. Pitiful too are his fragile beings, who
have fallen gradually into opprobrium owing to a
sin of love and determine to die and purify themselves
by confessing themselves when at the point of death,
like the young wife of the old colonel, in the
Ordonnance (" Alors, moi, je me suis dit : Il faut
mourir. Vivante, je n'aurais pu vous confesser un
pareil crime. Morte, j'ose tout. Je ne pouvais plus
faire autrement que de mourir, rien ne m'aurait lavée,
j'étais trop tachée. Je ne pouvais plus aimer, ni être
aimée : il me semblait que je salissais tout le monde,
rien qu'en donnant la main " . . .). And pitiful again
are girls like Yvette, who, born in the midst of vice,
find it naturally repugnant to them almost physically
owing to their purity of nature, yet are obliged to
bow to the fate which encloses them round and
subdues them. Children, such as Châli, the little
Indian girl all laughter and games, who die in an
unexpected and cruel manner. Such too are his
scenes from the war of 1870, such as that of the two
peaceful citizens, united in their love of fishing with
bait, who leave the circle of the besieged city of
Paris in order to satisfy their taste, and while they
are fishing and chatting, are arrested by Prussians
and asked to give information, and when they refuse,

are shot, and at their feet is the tin pail which contains the little fish they have caught. And Mother Sauvage, who when she receives the letter announcing that her son has been killed in the war, sets fire to her house containing four German soldiers quartered upon her, having previously obtained their names in order to send them to their mothers, just as she received news of her own son's death. Tortures of poor beasts, which suffer and make one suffer as if they were human beings, in the stories of *Mademoiselle Cocotte*, of the *Âne*, of *Coco*. . . . Such are some of the innumerable representations of emotional and painful pity expressed with sober restraint by Maupassant.

The pity is spontaneous and effective : it is not sought or provoked, and the laugh too is spontaneous, another form of reaction momentarily calming. This laughter sometimes alternates with pity, as in *Boule de suif*, sometimes with an ironical feeling for things, as in the *Maison Tellier* or the *Pain maudit ;* at other times it has a tinge of contempt, as in certain parts of *Bel Ami*, and the stories of *L'Héritage* and *En famille*. But in many other cases it is simple, frank hilarity, as in certain stories dealing with Norman customs (*Le lapin, L'aveu*), in some dealing with war (*L'aventure de Walter Schnafs*), in the making fun of masonic stupidity (*Mon oncle Sosthène*) or of the English who infest the hotels (*Nos Anglais*), in certain erotic adventures (*Les Épingles, Décoré, Bombard, Les tombales*, and the like), or bizarre (*En wagon, Boitelle*). Boitelle cannot console himself with having missed his life's happiness by renouncing the negress with whom he was in love. His parents had opposed the marriage, although they had done their best to satisfy him and made every effort to get over their first impression; but when they regarded the betrothed, engarlanded with the admiration and the eulogies of their son, they felt that it was really impossible to accept such a daughter-in-law. " Mon pauvre gars," says his mother to him, " elle est trop noire, vrai, elle est trop noire. Seulement, un p'ti en moins, je ne m'opposerais pas, mais c'est trop. On dirait Satan." One laughs till one holds one's sides, without a trace of bitterness, and Maupassant laughs too with the same abandonment to the mood of the moment as on other occasions to feelings of terror and compassion.

Ingenuous and candid in his hedonism, in his amoralism, in his irreligion, in his tears and in his laughter, he cannot and does not make any claim either before others or before himself to sociological, evangelical or ethical reforms. Indeed, ethical-historical reality remains extraneous to him to such an extent that for him it can hardly be said to exist, so much so that on the rare occasions when he does refer to it, he gives proof of his obtuseness for that aspect of the world, as when he talks of war, which to him seems to be nothing but ferocious human stupidity. To profess an opinion in politics (a friend of his tells us) seemed to him " a painful infirmity, which good education teaches us to conceal." The furthest he went was to let us have a glimpse of a certain aristocratic and oligarchic tendency in him with the implied sympathy for the police, against raisers of barricades and dynamitards, who disturb artists at their quiet work or lovers in their loving. But he made no transcendental ideal of art, in the manner of other artists, his predecessors and contemporaries; nor did he even direct a curious glance at the nature of art or engage in any kind of inquiry or criticism relating to it, having little taste for theorizing, discussions or polemics. His essay on Flaubert, a tribute of affection to his great friend and master, does not rise above the mediocre, and the scattered observations he has left reduce themselves to a few psychological observations (such as that one on the artist, who it appears has two souls and feels the repercussion more acutely than the shock, the resonance more than the original sound); he also refuses to be called a " realist," because " great artists are those who manifest their illusion to men "; and above all he protests against the ambitious " artistic writing," against the tongue that is " rich and rare," because a limited number of words sufficed him to gain his end, but they were well arranged, variously constructed and rhythmically musical. Exquisite in his sense for form, Maupassant was very slightly preoccupied with the technical side of composition, he was " literary " only to a very small extent.

His artistic activity arose from an abundance of feeling and experience, which had been maturing within him between 1870 and 1880, bursting forth in an impetuous torrent during the following decade, now shining in the sun in the silver streamlets of his most limpid stories, now assembling itself in the broad lakes of his novels, or breaking its banks and almost losing itself in the hundreds of brooks and becks of the short tales, the anecdotes, the diversions. Sometimes in this wide and rapid course appears the vice of superabundant power, which is regardless of waste. This may be observed in the over great length of some of his stories in respect of their artistic motive, and its opposite in the excessive brevity and too summary treatment of certain little sketches and

A A

anecdotes, which bear traces of journalistic impro-
visation, or indulge the taste of readers for the
salacious. He usually attains to perfection in the
stories of moderate complexity. But Maupassant
never once falls into the artificial or empty in these
ups and downs of artistic intensity. Hardly anything
of his lacks the imprint of artistic talent, however
slight or trifling it may seem. He never once allows
himself to be oppressed and suffocated by external
observation and by the accumulation of details, or
follows abstract schemes.

He was a poet, far more of a poet in his prose
narrative than in his verse, employed in early youth,
but abandoned later. Everyone who knows admires
the altogether poetical form of such stories as the
already mentioned *Le Port*, where not one word, nor
rhythm, nor inflexion of voice but converges to the
final and total effect. He carries it through to the
close, when the companions, who see the involuntarily incestuous sailor rolling upon the ground in a
paroxysm of rage and torment, weeping and howling,
believe him to be drunk and pick him up to lay him
on the bed of the harlot, his sister (" . . . le hissèrent
par l'étroit escalier jusqu'à la chambre de la femme
qui l'avait reçu tout à l'heure, et qui demeura sur une
chaise, au pied de la couche criminelle en pleurant
autant que lui jusqu'au matin ").

Maupassant's stories are lyrical stories, not because
they are written with emphasis and lyricism (things
of which they show themselves to be altogether free),
but because the lyric is really intrinsic to the form of
the narrative, and shapes each part of it, without
mixtures and without leaving any residue. In like
manner those parts which are pointed to as especially

lyrical, in the rhetorical sense of the word, never separate themselves from the narrative and discursive tone of prose, and speaking thus simply, gradually accelerate the rhythm, and rise spontaneously to poetry.

" Je l'avais aimé éperdument. Pourquoi aime-t-on ? Est-ce bizarre de ne plus avoir dans l'esprit qu'une pensée, dans le cœur qu'un désir, et dans la bouche qu'un nom : un nom qui monte incessament, qui monte comme l'eau d'une source, des profondeurs de l'âme, qui monte aux lèvres et qu'on dit, qu'on redit, qu'on murmure sans cesse, partout, ainsi qu'une prière." . . .

There exists in these words that seeing of obvious things with the astonishment and ravishment of childhood, which is a great virtue of poetry. Maupassant wrote phrases that might be described as commonplace : " Que c'est triste, la vie ! ", but he places them in such a way in his text that they reassume their original vigour and seem as if invented and pronounced for the first time. The young painter, who had felt the hand of Miss Harriett tremble in his, the poor lonely creature who afterwards took her own life, repeats to himself, after many years, the funereal lament that he murmured within himself before the dead body of the suicide.

" Comme il y a des êtres malheureux ! Je sentais peser sur cette créature humaine l'éternelle injustice de l'implacable nature ! C'était fini, pour elle, sans que, peut-être, elle eût jamais eu ce qui soutient les plus déshérités, l'espérance d'être aimée une fois ! Car pourquoi se cachait-elle ainsi, fuyait-elle les

autres ?   Pourquoi aimait-elle d'une tendresse si pas-
sionnée les choses et tous les êtres vivants qui ne sont
point les hommes ?

Et je comprenais qu'elle crût à Dieu, celle-là, et
qu'elle eût espéré ailleurs la compensation de sa
misère.   Elle allait maintenant se décomposer et
devenir plante à son tour.   Elle fleurirait au soleil,
serait broutée par les vaches, emportée en grain par
les oiseaux, et, chair des bêtes, elle redeviendrait de la
chair humaine.   Mais ce qu'on appelle l'âme s'était
éteint au fond du puits noir.   Elle ne souffrait plus.
Elle avait changé sa vie contre d'autres vies qu'elle
ferait naître." . . .

How does it come about that these commonplace
reflections, these poor words, move us to tears ?—

Listen to Maupassant telling us, when under the
spell of a different kind of inspiration, the story that
the friend expatriated in Africa tells one evening to
his friend, whom he had not seen for a long time.
His young wife's unfaithfulness had poisoned his life
for ever.   He had had suspicions as to her fidelity
and spied upon her, believing that he would surprise
her in the company of some admirer who deserved
her favours, but found her instead in the society of
an old corpulent general and marquis, to whom she
had given herself out of vanity.   At the end of the
narrative, the indignation, which had been gradually
growing, extends itself to all women, who always
give themselves to young or old for various equally
miserable reasons, because such is their profession,
their vocation, their function, as eternal, unconscious
and serene prostitutes, who shamelessly offer their
bodies as a prey to the libidinous sovereign or to the

celebrated and repulsive man. His invective has
something of Biblical quality :

" Il vociférait comme un prophète antique, d'une
voix furieuse, sous le ciel étoilé, criant, avec une rage
de désespéré, la honte glorifiée de toutes les maîtresses
des vieux monarques, la honte respectée de toutes les
vierges qui acceptent des vieux époux, la honte tolérée
de toutes le jeunes femmes qui cueillent, souriantes,
des vieux baisers.

Je les voyais, depuis la naissance du monde,
évoquées, appelées par lui, surgissant autour de nous
dans cette nuit d'Orient, les filles, les belles filles à
l'âme vile qui, comme les bêtes ignorant l'âge du
mâle, furent dociles à des désirs séniles. Elles se
levaient, servantes des patriarches chantées par la
Bible ! Agar, Ruth, les filles de Loth, la bonne
Abigaïl, la vierge de Sennaar, qui de ses caresses
ranimait David agonisant, et toutes les autres, jeunes,
grasses, blanches, patriciennes ou plébéiennes, irre-
sponsables femelles d'un maître, chair d'esclave sou-
mise, éblouie ou payée ! "

And Maupassant, because he is a poet, although he
knows nothing but matter and sense, and portrays
nothing but the obscure tremblings of matter and the
spasms of the senses, yet employs so much objective
truth in his portrayal, that he makes present the
ethical ideal, by means of pain, pity and displeasure ;
by means of the comical and laughter, the superiority
of the sagacious intelligence ; by means of desolation
and desperation, the claim of religion. I see quite
clearly why Tolstoi separated him at once from all
the French artists of his time and held him to be
moral in spite of appearances. He is moral in his

results, and his most audacious tales leave behind them an impression of purity, just because, as has been said, he is a poet. He distinguishes himself and emerges from the company of his contemporaries and compatriots, the Zolas, Daudets and their like, themselves endowed with noteworthy qualities and possessors of certain artistic forms, but not fundamentally and essentially poetical like him. Such he truly was born, pouring forth poetry with potent facility and consuming his short life. He entered and left the literary world (as he himself one day remarked when he was already infirm and meditating suicide) " like a meteor."

XXV

CARDUCCI

I SHALL conclude this series of notes with the name of Giosue Carducci. Some years ago I devoted an ample study to the consideration of his works, seeking the genesis, character and the various forms and periods of his poetry and examining his work as a historian and a critic. I have nothing now to change or to add to the portrait which I lovingly drew at that time, and consequently no reason to return to what has already been said. But I take the opportunity offered to me by these essays in European literature of the nineteenth century to reaffirm the place and the rank which belongs to Carducci in the ensemble of this literature, and to protest against common opinion which still looks upon him as little more than a respectable man of letters and an Italian patriot, worthy of the veneration of his fellow-countrymen but not such an one as to arouse interest in wider circles. He is in fact regarded as not really possessing the mind of a genius, as a poet of slender inspiration, a learned imitator of the ancient classics and of certain modern French and German poets. And since I have seen in some foreign reviews, in relation to what I have written about Manzoni and Balzac, the suspicion expressed that I have allowed myself to be carried away (these are the very words) by " the propagandist tendency to magnify the Italian genius," I shall candidly say (and at the risk of being judged too candid) that (when writing about philosophy and history I permit myself to be and to remain always free from political or national feelings.) To conduct myself otherwise would seem to me shocking, because spiritual greatness is neither created nor destroyed by " propaganda " (as people believed to be possible during the war), and one only succeeds in destroying one's own seriousness and in finding oneself at last at variance with oneself. How and to what extent Carducci is known and appreciated outside Italy I shall not stay to expose, nor shall I offer a conclusion as to the obstacles big or little which oppose themselves to a greater diffusion of his work, nor shall I express hopes and anticipations as to their removal. Poetical beauty, like philosophical truth, remains sound, whether it be known to few or to many, and speaking deeply, even where there are many who admire and who praise, there are always few who understand, and these alone have the full right of admiring and of praising. My present remarks are directed to those who know. Greater or lesser success, louder or lighter resonance of praise, vary with the variation of the times and with social conditions. It is an affair which concerns not that poetry or that philosophy, but the virtues and deficiencies, the wants and dispositions of that society and of those times. Even in Italy to-day, Carducci's poetry does not possess the soul of the new generations, which esteem that they give evidence of their exquisitely profound reactions from art by looking down upon the work of the rugged Bolognese professor not without disdain. And this is not the problem of Carducci, but entirely that of the new generations and of the ethical and æsthetic discipline to which they should be submitted, with the view also of forming in them a more serious national and patriotic sentiment, which cannot exist without reverence for tradition and for history, and which thus understood, does not lead to a narrow nationalism, but to the vigilant care of an ideal patrimony to preserve, and links itself with a like care in the case of other nations. Exoticism, which is justly feared, is not so save when it acts capriciously, cutting off tradition; and when this base is widened, it should not be called exoticism, but (as Goethe well said) *Weltliteratur*.

So much by way of preface, but what, it may be asked, do I mean by the words " position and rank to be assigned to Carducci in the European literature of the nineteenth century ? " Something very simple. If we hold firmly to the criterion of what is pure poetry, classical poetry, and by the light of this regard the thousands of authors who arose in Europe in the course of that century, those thousands are thinned out and only a few dozens remain, a few dozen free intelligences, each one with his own physiognomy but all illumined with the common light of poetry. These alone should compose, in their various groupings and attitudes, the picture of that literature. The list is short too in our day of writers who can be described as " great," yet non-poets and feeble poets are usually mingled in it with the real ones short as it is, and the place of the real poets is sometimes filled by those who enjoyed fame and power for other reasons and owing to other qualities. Now in the case of the most rigorous selection (towards the making of which the brief

notes of this volume have striven to be of some
assistance) it is my opinion that the Italian poets of
the beginning of the nineteenth century, Foscolo,
Leopardi, Manzoni, can no longer be passed over, as
has hitherto been the case,[1] and that Carducci must
be added to those of the second half of the century,
to the exclusion of certain great names, which find a
more suitable place elsewhere. In the domain of
poetry, for instance, Manzoni, although and perhaps
because he lived shut up in himself and in his thoughts
and did not make a noise in the world with his
personal adventures and political doings, occupies
that place to which (to select a sounding name as an
example) George Byron cannot pretend. If in saying
this I am accused of being moved by patriotic motives,
I certainly cannot prevent the statement being made;
but the real truth is that I am solely moved by love
of poetry, and at the same time by love for precise
thoughts, or philosophy.

To limit myself to Carducci, I had an unexpected
proof of the superior quality of his art when a winter
or two ago I passed some time in reading the lyrical
poetry, the plays and the novels of the European
literature of the last fifty years. Sick of all that
impressionism, symbolism, sensationalism, verism,
boasted of as superfine art, I was involuntarily led to
evoke within myself by way of contrast the pure and
sober poetry of Carducci, where the fundamental and
essential lines of the composition are always drawn
with a sure hand, and which in contrast with those
forms without substance, those scabs of colour, those

---

[1] See what I have already remarked in connection with Brandes's
book on the *Principal Literary Currents of the Nineteenth Century*, in
my *New Essays in Æsthetic*, pp. 199–200.

pandar's dens, all that mass of things of soft and confused outlines, rose up with monumental simplicity and solidity. How many others of his own time (I thought) can stand on a level with him, in Italy, in France, in Germany? And also at that time I came upon a phase of Maurras's, who, referring to Carducci in one of his books, calls him " *le divin Carducci*," and I like to believe that that so acute discoverer and persecutor of literary decadentism and " feminism," having been led to make the same comparison as I, had experienced an identical or similar feeling to my own.

Naturally, when we speak of the " great " or " divine " Carducci, we are referring to Carducci at his point of perfection, at his moments of full poetic autonomy, to the Carducci of the *Canto di marzo*, of the *San Martino*, of the *Comune rustico* and of the *Faida* and the *Canzone di Legnano*, of the *Rimembranze di scuola*, and of the *Davanti San Guido*, of the *Chiesa lombarda*, of the *Stazione*, of *Mors*, of the *Aurora*, of the *Presso l'urna di Shelley*, and to other lyrics or parts of lyrics in the *Odi barbare* and the *Rime nuove*. There is nothing blameworthy in the fact that a great part of the volume containing his complete poems is filled with literary imitations, because Carducci had to learn his art somehow, and if he did not reject those exercises later, it was because, himself a philologist, he knew that what he might have rejected would be picked up again and reprinted by future publishers. That another part consists of occasional verses, very conventional in form, was almost inevitable in the case of the work of a young poet who was connected with the events of 1859 and 1860. It is also true that he wrote invectives and polemics in verse, in

imitation of Victor Hugo, Barbier and Heine; but
there is no necessity to dwell so long upon the lack
of originality and of intrinsic poetry in those compositions, the marvel is rather in the progress made
by the youthful Tuscan, who had grown up in the
narrow provincial life of Florence with its literary
tricks and who yet, by means of those imitations and
by letting himself go freely in those enthusiasms and
indulging those political feelings, set himself free from
the over-close bonds of classicistic tradition.

Carducci, like others of our great poets, roamed
the literary plain before ascending the heights and
entering the grove of the Muses.   He served long
before winning his freedom; but his roaming and his
servitude were salutary, to so great an extent that one
remarks its absence as something missing in the
works of those who were exempt.   The same can be
said of his erudition, in which he sometimes took too
much pleasure and which sometimes weighed upon
his poetry or occupied its place.   But erudition also
supplied nourishment to his soul and to his imagination.   Like other great Italian poets of the nineteenth
century, Carducci did not profess himself a poet, but
had his daily task as a philologist, a critic, a teacher,
and allowed poetry to visit him when it pleased
poetry to do so.   A different type of poet has since
appeared in Italy, due to foreign (especially Parisian)
example, modelled upon the " poet of the theatre,"
the poet who supplies theatrical impresarios, publishers and editors of newspapers with plays, novels,
stories and lyrics.   Poetry is too rare a flower to lend
itself to this sort of extensive cultivation.

Carducci's form then is not impressionistic, but
what is called essential or classical.   We are sensible

in his verse of the deep breath exhaled from the powerful chest, which rises from the practical world and transports us into the ideal world beyond, whence (as he once wrote in a letter) " we embrace in an instant and feel with the universe." Aurora rises :

> " Tu sali e baci, o dea, co 'l roseo fiato le nubi,
> baci de' marmorëi templi le fosche cime.
> Ti sente e con gelido fremito destasi il bosco,
> spiccasi il falco a volo su con rapace gioia ;
> mentre ne l'umida foglia pispigliano garruli i nidi. . . ." [1]

Death descends :

> " Quando a le nostre case la diva severa discende,
> da lungi il rombo de la volante s'ode,
> e l'ombra de l'ala che gelida gelida avanza
> diffonde intorno lugubre silenzio.
> Sotto la venïente ripiegan gli uomini il capo. . . ." [2]

But his painting of little things is not less broad. The boy plunges the struggling lamb into the waters of the Clitumnus, and behold

> " una poppante volgesi e dal viso
> tondo sorride. . . ." [3]

in his direction from the mother's breast which has just suckled him, while she sits barefoot at her cottage door and sings.

The poet sees his mother in a dream as a young

[1] " Thou risest and kissest with rosy breath the clouds, O goddess, kissest the marble temples and the dusky peaks. The wood feels thee and awakes with a cold shiver, the falcon swoops upward with rapacious joy, while the nests are whispering garrulous in the damp foliage."

[2] " When the severe goddess descends to our homes, we hear the sound of her flight from afar, and the shadow of her wing drawing nearer, so cold, so cold, sheds around a lugubrious sadness. Men bow their heads as she comes towards them."

[3] " A suckling turned and smiled with his round face."

woman, leading him by the hand, a little fellow with golden curls :

"Andava il fanciulletto con piccolo passo di gloria. . . . " [1]

A young woman is praying on her knees in the Lombard church, and while earnestly praying, raised her head a little :

"umido a la piumata ombra del nero
cappello il nero sguardo luccicò. . . ." [2]

The railway station is realistically represented and at the same time transfigured and idealized on a rainy dawn in autumn :

"Van lungo il nero convoglio e vengono
incappucciati di nero i vigili,
com'ombre; una fioca lanterna
hanno, e mazze di ferro; ed i ferrei
freni tentati rendono un lugubre
rintócco lungo. . . ." [3]

These verses and images which flower in the memory and render us vividly aware of Carducci's style must suffice.

We know that in the poets the style may be classical and the abstract material romantic, that is to say, one-sided, partial, exaggerated, sickly, only recovering its universal humanity, its measure and its equilibrium on being raised to the sphere of poetry. Such, for instance, is the case with Leopardi, or, in different conditions of life, with Baudelaire, and with that sort

---

[1] "The child walked with glory in his little steps."
[2] "The dark glance shone liquid in the plumed shadow of the black hair."
[3] "The watchers move like shadows along the black line of carriages hooded in black : they carry a feeble lantern and hammers of iron and the iron brakes utter a long melancholy sound as they are tested."

of Parisian Leopardi who was Maupassant. In Carducci not only is the style essential and integral, but
also the feeling for the world, and for this reason I
had occasion to describe him on another occasion as
a poet-Vates, a heroic poet, " an ultimate pure
descendant from Homer." Battle, glory, song, love,
joy, melancholy, death, all the fundamental chords of
humanity resound and sound together in his poetry,
which truly belongs to what Goethe called " Tyrtaic
poetry," suited to prepare and to comfort man in the
battles of life with its potent, lofty and virile tone.
This complete humanity is perhaps not among the
minor causes that make Carducci but little acceptable
in times when health seems to be something inferior,
simplicity something poor; yet it constitutes the
character of all great spirits. If few among the men
of letters of the nineteenth century possessed that
character, Carducci was among the few. We have
been moved to apply to him on reflecting again upon
his work the words with which he evoked, saluted
and admired the figure of Torquato Tasso arriving
at the epic Ferrara of the Renaissance :

" Here comes the last bard of great and ancient
Italy ! "

INDEX